"There are some who call Yiddish a dead language, but so was Hebrew called for two thousand years.... Yiddish has not yet said its last word. It contains treasures that have not been revealed to the eyes of the world. It was the tongue of martyrs and saints, of dreamers and Cabalists—rich in humor and in memories that mankind may never forget. In a figurative way, Yiddish is the wise and humble language of us all, the idiom of frightened and hopeful Humanity."

—Isaac Bashevis Singer,
Nobel Prize acceptance speech, December 8, 1978

# Meshuggenary

## Celebrating the World of Yiddish

**meshuggenary** <meh-'shoo-geh-nar-ee> *noun.*
**1.** A crazy-quilt guide to Yiddish language, people, culture, and history.
**2.** A Yiddish bestiary. **3.** A reference you need like a **lokh in kop**!

Payson R. Stevens

Charles M. Levine

Sol Steinmetz

Simon & Schuster

New York London Toronto Sydney Singapore

To our **mames** and **tates** who carried the bright light of Yiddish into our lives.

SIMON & SCHUSTER
Rockefeller Center
1230 Avenue of the Americas
New York, NY 10020



For information about special discounts for bulk purchases,
please contact Simon & Schuster Special Sales:
1-800-456-6798 or business@simonandschuster.com.

Line drawings by Leonard Sirota
Designed by Charlotte Staub of CharStaub Graphic Design
Composed by Jennifer Dowling of Seaside Press

The RamahMod Hebrew-Yiddish font used to print this work is available
from Linguist's Software, Inc., P.O. Box 580, Edmonds, WA 98020-0580,
USA, tel.: (425) 775-1130; www.linguistsoftware.com.

Manufactured in the United States of America

1 3 5 7 9 10 8 6 4 2

Library of Congress Cataloging-in-Publication Data
Stevens, Payson R.
Meshuggenary : celebrating the world of Yiddish / Payson R. Stevens,
Charles M. Levine, Sol Steinmetz.
p. cm.
Includes bibliographical references and index.
1. Yiddish literature—United States. 2. Jews—United States—Languages.
I. Levine, Charles M. II. Steinmetz, Sol. III. Title.
PJ5119.U5 S76 2002
439'.1'0973—dc21 2002067003
ISBN 0-7432-2742-5
Available in eBook ISBN 0-7432-3335-2

We gratefully acknowledge permission to reprint the following:
"The Calf" by Mendele Mocher Sforim [Mendele Mokher Seforim], translated by Jacob Sloan, and "The Dead Town" by I. L. Peretz, translated by Irving Howe, from *A Treasury of Yiddish Stories* by Irving Howe and Eliezer Greenberg, editors, copyright 1953, 1954, 1989 by Viking Penguin, renewed © 1981, 1982 by Irving Howe and Eva Greenberg. Used by permission of Viking Penguin, a division of Penguin Putnam Inc.

The Nobel Lecture by Isaac Bashevis Singer,
copyright © The Nobel Foundation 1978.

"Body of Golden Rings: Yiddish Women Poets,"
copyright © 2002 by Kathryn Ann Hellerstein.

"Techinah for Easy Labor" by Geela Rayzel Raphael, from *Voices of the Matriarchs* by Chava Weissler, copyright © 1998 by Chava Weissler.
Reprinted by permission of Beacon Press, Boston.

# Contents

# Acknowledgments

Every book is made possible by the unflagging help and support of people too numerous to mention in full. We are especially grateful to the following individuals:

Leonard Sirota, for early design concepts and illustrations

Roger Parker, for the design and page layouts of the book proposal

Gabriel Levine, who helped with graphic ideas

Dr. Ilya S. Perlingieri, for her recipe contribution

Dr. Kathryn Hellerstein, for her sparkling essay on women Yiddish poets

Erica Blankstein, Project Archivist at YIVO, New York, for her energetic help

Lyn Slome, archivist at the American Jewish Historical Society, New York

Rebecca Pine, Jewish Museum, New York, for illustration research

Eileen Morales and Anne Guernsey, Museum of the City of New York, for illustration research

Christian Mari, for photo research in Paris

Kamla Kapur, for advice and moral support

Naomi Miller Coval-Apel, for introducing Payson to Yiddish

Sydny Weinberg Miner, our editor, whose good advice never failed

Walter Weintz, our deputy publisher and original champion

Connie Baboukis, for her sharp proofreading and advice on pronunciations

Charlotte Staub, the sine qua non reference-book designer

Jennifer Dowling, who became Yiddish, at least while composing these pages

# Preface

## *Nu? A Meshuggenary?*

What motivated us to put this book together, anyway? We have only one answer: We are **meshugga** about Yiddish! (And that's the best explanation we can provide for the book's title.) Our parents spoke it fluently at home and with their friends, partly because Yiddish was the lingua franca that enabled Jews to communicate with one another no matter where they were from, and partly because it served as a secret language to keep us kids from understanding their private **schmooze**. Of course, we could not help picking up much of what they said, and some of our fondest childhood memories are our attempts to decipher the sounds of our parents' patter in Yiddish.

While the three of us love this strangely beautiful language filled with humor and pathos, we are not equally expert in it. Yet we share equally a sense of the poignancy and complexity of Yiddish culture and history, and so we joined together to do homage to this important part of our Eastern European roots.

Although spoken Yiddish has steadily declined in America since the 1930s, the language has not been forgotten. Many Yiddish words and expressions from our childhood have infiltrated our English, and we cannot let them go. How could we? The Yiddish lexicon is so rich that Jews and even non-Jews sprinkle Yiddishisms in their everyday conversations. Read the sections on "Yinglish 101" and "The Heart of Yiddish Vocabulary," and you will know what we mean.

The *Meshuggenary* is our small effort to put together some of the great aspects of the Yiddish world: the words and phrases that are soulful, hilarious, and punchy, and that capture the essence of the human condition, from pain, to put-downs, to passion; the amazing literature, the glorious theater, and the great music that Yiddish has engendered; and some of the major personalities and groups at the center of the Yiddish world, past and present.

When you finish this book we hope you'll know a lot more about Yiddish than you previously thought you did. Still, we have only grazed the surface. We expect you, the readers, to remind us of all the things we should have said but, like the **meshuggenas** we are, we left out.

Be our guest. Enjoy!

# A Note on Yiddish Words

**Typography**. Because the *Meshuggenary* is all about Yiddish, we do not italicize the Yiddish words in order to make them more readable and accessible. In sections such as "Yiddish Proverbs and Sayings," we have even reversed the emphasis—placing the Yiddish in bold with the English translation in italics:

**A kluger veyst vos er zogt, a nar zogt vos er veyst.**
*A smart person knows what he says, [but] a fool says what he knows.*

**A kluger farshteyt fun eyn vort tsvey.**
*From one word, a smart person grasps two.*

Within the text, we emphasize Yiddish and Yiddish-origin words in bold only the first time they appear in that section or sidebar. When an English translation follows the Yiddish word or words, the translation usually appears in parentheses, without using italics or quotation marks, even when translating Yiddish titles:

**shprikhverter** (folk sayings)

*Di Kishefmakhern* (The Sorceress)

the female names Blume (flower), Golde (gold), and Royze (rose)

**Spelling**. We are following what has now become the generally accepted standard transcription guidelines for Yiddish, established by the YIVO Institute for Jewish Research. (For more details see "The YIVO Transcription Scheme" at the back of the book.) This system provides a uniform and simplified way to use the English alphabet to write any Yiddish word in any Yiddish dialect.

The YIVO system has streamlined the transcription of Yiddish. For example, unlike earlier attempts, there are now no double consonants—**ale**, **alemen**, **bobe**, **feder**, **got** (God), **shabes**, **yidish** (*not* alle, allemen, bobbe, fedder, gott, shabbes, yiddish). Silent e's have been dropped—for example, **bisl**, **fargesn**, **gutn**, **lakhn**, **zisn**, **shtetl** (*not* bisel, fargesen, guten, lakhen, zisen, shtetel). However, when words like **chutzpah** or **mensch** become commonly accepted in English, we generally use the current English spelling instead of the Yiddish one. (See "The Heart of Yiddish Vocabulary" for both the Americanized and the transcribed Yiddish spellings of more than 250 common Yiddish-origin words and phrases.)

**Pronunciations**. We provide pronunciations only for the more difficult, less obviously articulated, Yiddish-origin words, following a modified non-dictionary, or "newspaper," style that uses the regular English alphabet. A stress mark appears *before* the main stressed syllable. (Newspaper-style pronunciations often put the stressed syllable in ungainly capital letters, which we eschew.) The pronunciations are easy to find, placed between angle brackets < >. The following handful illustrates the simple and accessible pronunciation style of the *Meshuggenary:*

**chutzpah** <′hoots-peh *or more guttural* ′khoots-peh> *noun.*

**geshmak** <geh-′shmock *or* geh-′shmack> *adjective.*

**haimish** <′hey-mish> *adjective.*

**meshuga** <meh-′shoo-geh> *adjective.*

**paskudnyak** <pahs-kood-′nyahk> *noun.*

**schmatte** <′shmot-eh *or* ′shmah-teh> *noun.*

**schmegegge** <shmeh-′geg-ee> *noun.*

Also see "The YIVO Transcription Scheme" at the back of the book for more information about pronouncing transcribed Yiddish words.

# General Jewish-English Glossary

The following Jewish technical terms appear sporadically in parts of this book, and constitute the platform on which the discussion of Yiddish—and Yiddish itself as a language, a people, and a culture—is made possible.

**Aramaic**. A Semitic language closely related to Hebrew, spoken by most Jews of the Middle East until the beginning of the **Diaspora**.

**Ashkenazim**. Jews whose customs and traditions originated in Germany and spread into Eastern Europe. They are distinguished from **Sephardim**.

**Diaspora**. The exile and dispersion of Jews outside the Land of Israel after the destruction of the First Temple in 586 B.C.E., and of the Second Temple in 70 C.E.

**Gemara**. The Aramaic part of the **Talmud** that explains and comments on the **Mishnah**.

**Hasidim**. Adherents of **Hasidism**, a Jewish religious movement steeped in mysticism that was founded in Poland in the 1700s.

**Haskalah**. An intellectual movement to modernize Jewish life that originated in Germany in the late 1700s. Also called **Jewish Enlightenment**.

**kabbalah**. Jewish mystical teachings, especially as found in the *Zohar* (the main literary source) and in Hasidism; Jewish mysticism.

**Mishnah**. The written text of the Jewish oral law that forms the basis of the **Talmud**.

**Mussar**. Jewish religious ethics, especially as a subject of study.

**Sephardim**. Jews whose customs and traditions originated in Spain and Portugal and spread to other Mediterranean countries. They are distinguished from **Ashkenazim**.

**Talmud**. The body of Jewish law and tradition as expounded by the ancient rabbis, compiled about 30 B.C.E.–500 C.E., and consisting of the **Mishnah** and the **Gemara**.

**Torah**. **1.** The Hebrew Scriptures or Bible. **2.** Jewish learning and tradition, including the written and oral law.

**yeshiva**. A school or academy devoted to religious instruction, especially an academy of higher Jewish learning or a rabbinical seminary.

# Meshuggenary

## Celebrating the World of Yiddish

# Introduction

## *A Language, a People, a Culture*

Yiddish is more than a language. It's a culture that embodies a thousand years of European Jewish history. Yiddish has been a personal communication system between Jews scattered in different countries speaking different local languages. It united them in a self-created voice that articulated more than just a vocabulary, a grammar, a syntax. Like the people themselves, the language adapted to the conditions these wanderers encountered, adopting and modifying some German here, some Russian there. The voice of an oppressed people using all their wits to survive, Yiddish modulations and inflections conveyed deeper levels of meaning; and its strange and singular words and expressions imparted humor, biting sarcasm, or deprecating self-parody—all as a means to survive as a minority surrounded by an often hostile or murderous majority.

Yiddish is rich and heavy; painful and thick with pathos; funny and absurd. It holds up an incisive mirror, reflecting psychological depth that can describe a specific character type with twenty variations. Subversive and memorable, its words and expressions have embedded themselves in the dictionaries of many languages, because Yiddish uniquely captures the flavor of what it describes.

The *Oxford English Dictionary* lists more than one hundred Yiddish words that are now considered part of the English language. American media sprinkles Yiddish in its reporting, and even in the American heartland everyone knows a **nebbish** or a **schlemiel**, and who hasn't encountered a neighbor with **chutzpah**?

This introduction offers the briefest background and history of Yiddish. It's really just a **shtikl** introduction. To **khap** in the whole history of Yiddish, from **zup** to **nislekh**, you have to do your homework. But in the meantime the *Meshuggenary* will hopefully give you a satisfying taste of this enduring language and culture.

## *A Language*

The Yiddish language is almost as old as English. Linguists trace English back to about the year 600 C.E. and Yiddish to about 1000 C.E. Both languages are Germanic, which means that the two are as closely related as first cousins. A comparison of some words in English, German, and Yiddish illustrates the close kinship among these languages:

| **English** | **German** | **Yiddish** |
|---|---|---|
| come | kommen | kumen |
| earth | Erde | erd |
| fire | Feuer | fayer |
| great | gross | groys |
| hand | Hand | hant |
| water | Wasser | vaser |
| young | jung | yung |

The name *Yiddish* originally meant "Jewish," and it derived from the German word *jüdisch*, by which Gentiles in Germany referred to the language of the Jews. The prehistory of Yiddish began about 800–900 C.E., when Jews of northern France and northern Italy began to migrate into the German-speaking region of the Rhine Valley, an area bounded by the cities of Köln (Cologne), Mainz, Worms, and Speyer. The new immigrants spoke dialects of Old French and Old Italian mixed with many Hebrew and Aramaic words. These dialects in turn became mixed with the medieval German spoken in the areas where the immigrants settled. Within a few generations a distinct language began emerging, consisting of a fusion of German, Romance (French and Italian), and Hebrew-Aramaic. The oldest Yiddish words—such as **bentshn** (to bless) formed from a Romance form of Latin *benedicere*, to bless, and the German verb ending *-(e)n*—go back to that early formative period of Yiddish.

Scholars divide the history of Yiddish into several distinct periods: *Early Yiddish* (from about 1000 to 1250 C.E.); *Old Yiddish* (from 1250 to 1500); *Middle Yiddish* (from 1500 to 1700); and *Modern Yiddish* (from 1700 to the present). There were two great watershed periods in the development of the language: (1) the introduction of a Slavic component into the Yiddish language, and (2) the division of Yiddish into several dialects.

During the 1200s and 1300s, as the Crusades swept across Western Europe, killing Jews and destroying their communities, the Jews of Germany were forced to move eastward into Slavic countries, a development of great consequence to their language and culture. Throughout the Middle Yiddish period, German influence on Yiddish was replaced by the influence of Slavic languages, chiefly Polish, Ukrainian, Belorussian, and Russian. Contact with these languages enriched Yiddish with a wealth of new words and expressions—for example, **nudyen** (to bore, pester); **shmate** (rag); **paskudne** (nasty); **nu?** (so?, well?); and the suffixes *-nik*, *-ke*—and greatly affected the word order, stress patterns, and sentence structure in the language.

The migration into Eastern Europe brought about the first major dialectal division in Yiddish, that between Western and Eastern Yiddish. The former was spoken in Germany, the Netherlands, Switzerland, and Alsace, but by the 1800s, due to assimilation with the majority populations, it had started to decline as a viable dialect. Meanwhile, Eastern Yiddish flourished, and with the spread of Yiddish speakers across the vastness of Eastern Europe, the language inevitably split into several new dialects. These were Northeastern (Lithuanian) Yiddish, spoken in Lithuania, Latvia, and Belorussia; Central or Mideastern (Polish) Yiddish, spoken in Poland, western Galicia, and parts of Czechoslovakia and Hungary; and Southeastern (Ukrainian) Yiddish, spoken in the Ukraine, Romania, and eastern Galicia.

Speakers of these different dialects sometimes have difficulty understanding each other. While there are considerable differences in their vocabularies, the main obstacle in understanding lies in the way they pronounce the vowels. For example, a Northeastern Yiddish speaker pronounces the Yiddish words for *come, buy, meat,* and *day* as **kumen**, **keyfn**, **fleysh**, **tog**; while a Central Yiddish speaker pronounces them as **kimen**, **koyfn**, **flaysh**, **tug**; and a Southeastern Yiddish speaker pronounces them as **kumen**, **koyfn**, **fleysh**, **tug**. There are, of course, many more differences, and the cumulative effect is at times an obstacle to communication. (For more on pronunciation, see "YIVO Transcription Scheme" at the end of the book.)

Modern, standard Yiddish—the form of the language taught in secular schools and colleges—attempts to cut across these differences with a compromise: it is closest to Northeastern Yiddish in pronunciation and closest to Central Yiddish in grammar.

After the great immigration of Yiddish speakers from Eastern Europe to America at the end of the 19th century, Eastern Yiddish continued to be widely spoken in the United States, but also started to absorb many American English words. These borrowings consisted of two types: words embodying distinctly American concepts (for example, **beysbol**, **sobvey**, **ayzkrim**, **hayskul**—baseball, subway, ice cream, high school) for which no Yiddish words existed; and words that were used so habitually that they pushed aside their legitimate Yiddish equivalents (for example, **boy**, **biznis**, **tshiken**, **pitsher**—boy, business, chicken, picture). The resulting mélange has long been a matter of controversy among Yiddish scholars. One school believes that "American Yiddish" is a valid form or variety of Yiddish, one that deserves to be recorded, for example, in a dictionary of Yiddish. The opposing school tends to consider unnecessary Americanisms in the same negative light as most Yiddishists regard the so-called *daytshmerish* or Germanized Yiddish words that infested the language during the early part of the 20th century.

Standard Yiddish has a vocabulary that is largely derived (about 65 percent) from Middle High German (the dialect spoken in central and southern Germany during the Middle Ages), with a distinctive component of about 18 percent Hebrew and Aramaic, about 16 percent Slavic (Polish, Russian, etc.), and a substratum of Romance elements from the Jewish correlates of Old French and Old Italian. Yiddish is the only Germanic language written in Hebrew letters. While words of Hebrew and Aramaic origin remain unchanged in their spelling, words of German and Slavic origin are spelled phonetically, as they are pronounced.

Before World War II, the number of Yiddish speakers was estimated to be close to eleven million, with about six and a half million in Eastern and Central Europe, nearly three million in North America, and the balance in Western Europe, Palestine, South and Central America, Africa, Asia (excluding Palestine), and Australia. During World War II, most of the six and a half million Yiddish speakers in Eastern and Central Europe perished in the Holocaust. Since then, there has been a steady decline, in America and elsewhere, in the use of Yiddish. Nevertheless, Yiddish continues to be spoken today by many Jews, especially by the strictly Orthodox and Hasidic Jews in North America and Israel, and it is estimated that there are some two million Jews worldwide for whom Yiddish remains a living language.

## *A People*

The people who speak Yiddish, or whose ancestors spoke Yiddish, belong to a large division of Jewry known as **Ashkenazim**. They are so called because they originally lived in Germany, which in Hebrew was called *Ashkenaz*, after an ancient people mentioned in the Bible (Jeremiah 51:27). In fact, their language was first called **losh ashkenaz**, "language of Ashkenaz," and it was not until the 1500s that the name **yidish** (from German *jüdisch*) began to be used instead. At first, only the German Jews were called Ashkenazim. But as the Crusades forced them to migrate eastward, they carried with them into Eastern Europe the customs and traditions they had developed over the centuries. Thereafter the name *Ashkenazim* became an umbrella term for all the Jews of Europe except those of Spain and Portugal, who are known as **Sephardim** (after the Biblical place name *Sepharad*, traditionally associated with Spain).

From the 10th until the 13th century, traditional Jewish life flourished among the Ashkenazim in the Rhine Valley. Many religious scholars of great authority arose, and their teachings and edicts laid the foundations of Ashkenazi Jewish life. One of the earliest and greatest was Rabbenu Gershom (about 960–1030), whose ordinances regulating Jewish life included a famous ban against having more than one wife. The pinnacle of **Ashkenazi** scholarship was reached with Rabbi Shlomo Yitzchaki (1040–1105), known by the acronym Rashi, whose commentaries on the **Torah** and **Talmud** have never been equaled, much less superseded. Rashi's grandsons and disciples, known as the Tosafists, expanded and elaborated on his teachings. They, in turn, built academies of higher learning that produced generations of illustrious Talmudic scholars.

Then, in the 1300s, the forced migration of German Jews to Eastern Europe caused an upheaval in the Ashkenazi way of life. The Jews arriving in Slavic lands were poor, practically destitute. They did not know Czech, Polish, or Ukrainian and were treated with scorn or hatred by the Gentile inhabitants. They settled in **shtetls**, secluded small villages and towns, where they went on to live for generations in virtual isolation. In this environment, their religious way of life remained unchanged for the next two centuries. Limited by the harsh economic conditions in which they lived, forced to work long days in menial, unrewarding occupations, their only relief from hard work and drudgery came on the Sabbath and holidays. Under these conditions, intellectual growth was stunted and stagnant, and no new ideas or schools of thought were born. (See "Shtetl Life.")

But in time the East European Ashkenazim, especially those living in large concentrations in Poland, became integrated into the general economy, so that by the 1500s some of them found the time and leisure to devote themselves to the serious study and teaching of the Torah, the Talmud, and the codes of Jewish law. This development led to the rise of important centers of learning in cities like Poznan (Posen), Lublin, Cracow, and Lvov (Lemberg), which produced many outstanding rabbis and scholars. Among them were such luminaries as Rabbi Moshe Isserles (about 1525–1572), known by the acronym Ramo, who codified Ashkenazi customs and practices, and Rabbi Shlomo Luria (about 1510–1573), known as the Maharshal, whose commentaries are found in the printed tomes of the Talmud along with those of Rashi and the Tosafists.

Alongside learning and scholarship, however, an almost opposite trend among East European Jewry was the growing popularity of **kabbalah** or Jewish mysticism. During the 1600s the study of kabbalah, and the mystical and supernatural beliefs it engendered among the people, paved the way to the development of **Hasidism**, a major movement of lasting significance in Judaism. (See "Hasidism and Kabbalah—The Yiddish Connection.")

The **Hasidim**, who became established during the late 1700s in Poland and Galicia, were opposed by the **Misnagdim** (literally, opponents) of Lithuania, who condemned Hasidic practices and beliefs, centering on charismatic leaders known as **rebbes** and **tzaddikim**, as heretical, contrary to the letter and spirit of traditional Judaism. The hostility between the two camps lasted into the early 19th century, when they were compelled to join forces in order to fight their common enemy, the **Haskalah** movement.

The destruction of most of European Jewry in World War II did not succeed in destroying the divisions among Ashkenazim. The survivors who made their way after the war to the United States and Israel included **Maskilim** (adherents of the Haskalah), Hasidim, and Misnagdim, and each group went on to build institutions in the image of their European predecessors. The Maskilim built schools and organizations dedicated to modern Yiddish and Hebrew studies; the Misnagdim built many great **yeshivas** to advance the teachings of rabbinic Judaism; and the Hasidim created many sectarian communities, such as Satmar, Gur, Belz, and Lubavitch, where they live in much the same way their European forerunners have, speaking Yiddish as their daily language.

## *A Culture*

The fabric of Yiddish culture is woven from many strands. Paramount in the culture is the unique Yiddish vernacular of Ashkenazic Jews—a lingua franca whose speakers can be found one time or another, speaking one dialect or another, in practically every major country and city in the world.

Another strand is Judaism, without which Yiddish culture would not exist. For example, Ashkenazim who attend religious services on Rosh Hashanah and Yom Kippur go to a **shul** where the prayers are recited or chanted in **nusekh ashkenaz**, the Ashkenazic style—or to a Hasidic **shtibl**, where men wearing fur-trimmed **shtraymlekh** talk only in Yiddish. Even secular-minded Yiddishists pepper their Yiddish with countless allusions to their religious roots, such as **al hatoyre ve-al ho-avoyde**, meaning literally on Torah study and Divine service, and figuratively to be industrious and diligent; or **kedin ukedas**, meaning literally according to the Jewish law and religion, and figuratively in a fair or just manner.

Then there is the **mishpokhe**, or family strand, that runs deep, beginning with one's given name and family name. An Ashkenazi man and woman may be named after a deceased grandparent or great-grandparent, but *never* after a living parent or any living person (as distinguished from Sephardim, who often bear a living father's name as an insigne of honor). One can easily recognize Ashkenazi men or women by their Yiddish first names: (men) Anshl, Berl, Fayvl, Fishl, Hershl, Leybl, Kalmen, Khaskl, Leyzer, Shaye, Shie, Velvl, Yankl, Yidl, Yoshe, Yosi, Yosl, Zalmen, Zelig; (women) Beyle, Blume, Brayne, Dreyzl, Feyge, Frume, Gitl, Golde, Henye, Hindl, Libe, Mashe, Mirl, Perl, Pesl, Toltse, Toybe, Yetta, Zisl. (See "Yiddish First Names: From Alter to Yentl.")

The family names of Yiddish speakers form a motley group. A great many are derived from the names of East European towns, cities, and vil-

## Shtetl Life

The word **shtetl** (a small town or village) summons a place and time that are now gone. The word is associated with poor villages that were predominately or entirely Jewish. These were villages that retained the flavor of the Middle Ages: filled with the bustle of crowded shops and stalls, thatched-roof buildings, markets crammed with people, and the jostling of horses and carts. And everywhere the sound of Yiddish, the language of the shtetl, reverberated through the narrow, dusty streets.

For centuries, shtetls were the locus of Jewish life and community in Eastern Europe. Millions of Jews in countries like Poland, Russia, Romania, Hungary, Ukraine, Bohemia, and Galicia, lived in poverty and forced isolation from their Gentile countrymen. In these countries, Jews were persecuted and numerous laws prevented them from assuming the rights of most citizens. Oppressed, they lived in constant fear and uncertainty. Whenever it was politically or religiously expedient, hostile rulers forced Jews from one town to the next, one country to another, or instigated their destruction.

Jews living in shtetls had few legal rights. In many countries they were prevented from living in cities. They were excluded from secondary schools and universities. Merchants had to register with the police. Civil service, medical, legal, and teaching professions were often closed to Jews. At any moment their homes and lives could be eliminated, their possessions taken. Pogroms, rampages, and killings by thugs or Russian Cossacks were ignored or encouraged by the ruling class. In Russia, the Pale of Settlement (created by Catherine II in 1769) confined Jews to specific provinces in Poland, Lithuania, and Russia. And under Czar Nicholas I (1825–1855), young boys were forced to serve as soldiers for many years.

Yet despite all these crushing burdens, the shtetl was the center of communal life, preserving unique Jewish traits and rituals. Specific regulations for prayer, dress, diet, morality, and charity guided Jews no matter where they lived. These united the Jews living in the shtetls and traditions flourished. Here in this isolated, ethnic enclave, Yiddish was the language of the home and marketplace.

The shtetl's conservative and insular environment resisted the social changes of the 19th and 20th centuries. Men survived as merchants and craftsmen doing business with each other or by trade with non-Jewish peasants. Religious life was the core of the home that was run by the women and guided by custom. Jewish religious identity was key to maintaining one's dignity. Religious continuity and faith, coupled with tradition and culture, enabled Jews to survive. Mystical Hasidism provided spirituality and joy. The Talmud (the body of Jewish law and tradition) was constantly studied and discussed. Boys learned Hebrew and the Torah in the **cheder** (religious elementary school), most becoming literate before the age of six. The **shul** (synagogue) and **shtibl** (small prayer house) were the important social gathering places. Within the community, distinctions between rich and poor, well educated and less educated existed, but everyone belonged.

Many Jews believed that the Messiah would soon arrive, freeing them from their difficult lives. Others, worn from unrelenting persecution, left Eastern Europe and emigrated in huge waves between 1880 and 1920. Many came to America looking for the better life that they or their children ultimately found. But many stayed behind. In Poland, there were over three million Jews at the beginning of World War II. By the end of the war, less than 10 percent of the Polish Jewish population survived. The victims joined the millions of other Jews who were exterminated in Hitler's "Final Solution." The shtetls became vanished worlds, erased by human intolerance and evil. In reality shtetls were a dream and a nightmare: in part evoked by the happy images of Marc Chagall's paintings, but more realistically by countless poor souls who suffered unspeakable oppressions.

Wooden synagogue and school in a shtetl near Vilna, Lithuania, undated. (YIVO Institute for Jewish Research)

lages, for example, Brisker, Kovner, Litvinov, Varshavski, Vilner. Others are based on male or female given names, for example, Adelman, Avramski, Chaneles, Hershman, Isaacson, Jakobovitz, Perlov, Wolfson. Some are occupational names, such as Buchhalter (bookkeeper), Melamed (teacher), Reznik (ritual slaughterer), Schneider (tailor), Schreiber (scribe), Schuster (cobbler), Vinokur (distiller). And countless surnames are ornamental, beginning with Appel, Gold, Rosen, Silver and ending with **baum** (tree), **berg** (mountain), **blat** (leaf), or **blum** (flower).

Among the staples of Yiddish culture are the foods, often connected with Jewish holidays. For example, **homentashn** (literally, Haman-pockets) are three-cornered cookies with a sweet filling eaten on Purim; **kneydlekh** are matzo-meal dumplings cooked for Passover; **latkes** are fried potato pancakes served on Chanukah; **tsimes** is a sweet stew prepared for Rosh Hashanah; **tsholnt** is a slowly simmering dish of meat, potatoes, and beans eaten on the Sabbath; **gefilte fish**, too, is a Sabbath favorite; **boksers**, the pods of the carob tree, are consumed on Tu Bishvat, the Jewish arbor day. (See "Yiddish Food and Cooking.")

A significant part of East European **Yiddishkeit** or Jewish life was the distinctive way men and women dressed. No man or boy ever went

Shtetl girls at a watering well, Eastern Europe, 1938.
(YIVO Institute for Jewish Research)

bareheaded; he either wore a **kapelyush**, a black cap or hat, or a black **yarmulke**, a skullcap. Under or over his shirt he wore an **arbe-kanfes** or four-cornered garment with fringes, also called **tales-kotn** (little prayer shawl), **tsitses** (fringes), or **laybtsudekl** (little body-covering). Women and girls wore long dresses topped by a **fartekh** (apron), and married women covered their heads with a **sheytl** (wig) or a **tikhl** (kerchief).

## Hasidism and Kabbalah—The Yiddish Connection

**Hasidism** (from the Hebrew word *chasid* and Yiddish *khosed*, meaning "pious person") has been defined as "**kabbalah** for the masses." Kabbalah, the Jewish mystical system developed from the 1100s to the 1500s, was essentially an esoteric study engaged in by an elitist circle of mystical scholars until the emergence of Hasidism in the 1700s. This popular pietistic religious movement, founded by Israel Baal Shem Tov (Master of the Good Name) in Poland, popularized the teachings of the kabbalah by making them part of the everyday life of simple **shtetl** Jews. It did that by transferring leadership from traditional, erudite yeshiva rabbis to charismatic spiritual guides thoroughly versed in kabbalah, who were known as **rebbes** or **tzaddikim** (righteous men) and who were thought to possess supernatural powers.

Hasidism emphasized a simple faith in God, deep spirituality, and placed greater value on sincere prayer and the performance of good deeds than on learning and erudition. And, unlike the masters of kabbalah, who spoke and wrote in Hebrew, the Hasidic leaders expressed themselves in the mother tongue of East European Jews, Yiddish, injecting into its vocabulary a wealth of new words and expressions that have become part of mainstream Jewish culture. To mention just a few of the Yiddish terms popularized by Hasidism: **dybbuk**, **golem**, **kamea** (mystically inscribed amulet), **kloyz** (small Hasidic synagogue), **kvitl** (written petition submitted to a rebbe), **lamedvovnik** (any of thirty-six righteous men in whose merit the world exists), **maggid** (itinerant preacher), **niggun** (Hasidic melody or tune), **shtibl** (small Hasidic house of prayer and study), **tish** (a rebbe's table).

Many kabbalistic terms were also introduced into Hasidic lore and transmitted into mainstream Judaism, among them such basic terms as **En-Sof** (Infinite God, literally, Without End), **sefirah** (any of the ten emanations from the En-Sof)), **tzimtzum** (contraction of the En-Sof), **nitzotzos** (divine sparks spilled over from the En-Sof), and **sitra achra** (the realm of evil or demonic powers).

Hasidic clothing, worn to this day, is especially distinctive. On weekdays, Hasidic men wear over their yarmulkes either a large black felt hat or a **biberhit**, a short-crowned, wide-brimmed hat made of beaver fur, while on the Sabbath and holidays they put on a fur-trimmed hat called a **shtrayml** or a high, plush-trimmed fur hat called a **spodek**. Instead of jackets, many Hasidim wear long black cloaks called **kaftans**, **kapotes**, or **bekeshes**, and at home don lightweight robes called **khalats**. Before prayer, they tie around their waist a black sash or girdle called a **gartl**. All their clothes are black, except for white shirts and white **kitl** (linen frock) worn at the Passover seders and other special occasions.

In Yiddish culture, the rites of passage in everyday life are marked by age-old ceremonies and celebrations. To take one example, a traditional wedding is preceded by the **ufrufns** (also spelled **ufruf** or **aufruf**), meaning calling-up, at which the groom is called up on Sabbath morning to the Torah-reading desk in the synagogue and in a custom called **bavarfns** (literally, peltings) is showered with candy and other sweets. That same afternoon or evening the bride is entertained by friends at a **forshpil** (prelude) in anticipation of the wedding. Just before the wedding ceremony, before the **badekns** (covering), at which the groom covers the bride's face with a veil, a **badkhen** (merrymaker) sings improvised rhymes called **gramen** at the **khosn's tish** (the groom's table) and often leads in the singing and dancing. A **klezmer** or **kapelye** (Jewish band or orchestra) may provide the music for the traditional dances. These might include a **kazatske**, a lively dance of Cossack origin, a **freylekhs**, which is a cheerful folk dance, a **flash tants** (literally, bottle dance), in which men dance with bottles balanced on their heads, a **sher**, a square dance with partners, a **broygez tants** (angry dance), a group dance consisting of the groom, his father, and his father-in-law, and the obligatory **mitsve tants** (mitzvah dance), in which men take turns dancing with the bride while she holds one end of a handkerchief or napkin and they hold the other end.

On the opposite end of the spectrum of Yiddish culture are the ethnic secularists, often called Yiddishists, who through their Sholom Aleichem and Workmen's Circle schools, and through organizations such as YIVO, Yugentruf, and the Yiddish League, promote the Yiddish language, literature, theater, and other Yiddish-centered cultural activities. Their books, periodicals, radio, and Web sites all reflect a sincere commitment to maintain and perpetuate the cultural treasures of Yiddish.

## A Yiddish Hall of Fame

**Jacob Adler** (1855–1926), Yiddish actor who founded a distinguished theatrical dynasty.

**Israel Baal Shem Tov** (1700–1760), the founder of Hasidism, a movement steeped in Yiddish that still thrives today.

**Abraham Cahan** (1860–1951), journalist who founded the *Jewish Daily Forward* in 1897 and was its editor for half a century.

**Glikl bas Yehuda Leyb** (1646–1724), author of *Memoirs*, one of the earliest publications in Yiddish by a woman.

**Abraham Goldfaden** (1840–1908), Yiddish playwright and composer, regarded as the father of the Yiddish theater.

**Alexander Harkavy** (1863–1939), first Yiddish lexicographer, author of classic Yiddish-English-Hebrew Dictionary (1928).

**Isa Kremer** (1887–1956), called a diva and a nightingale, brought Yiddish songs to people around the world.

**H. Leivick** (1886–1962), Yiddish poet and playwright whose work covered the range of European Jewish experience.

**Mendele Mokher Seforim** (1836–1917), Yiddish writer, one of the creators of modern literary Yiddish.

**Isaac Leib Peretz** (1852–1915), Yiddish writer, one of the founders of modern Yiddish literature.

**Molly Picon** (1898–1992), Yiddish actress, noted for roles on stage, film, and television.

**Abraham Reisen** (1876–1953), popular Yiddish poet and writer, known for his lyrical poetry.

**Isaac Bashevis Singer** (1904–1991), Yiddish writer, winner in 1978 of the Nobel Prize for literature.

**Sholom Aleichem** (1859–1916), pen name of the most widely read Yiddish writer, known as "the Yiddish Mark Twain."

**Max Weinreich** (1894–1969), and his son, **Uriel Weinreich** (1925–1967), leading Yiddish linguists, authors respectively of *History of the Yiddish Language* (published posthumously in 1973) and *College Yiddish* (1949).

**Yehoash** (1872–1927) pen name of Yehoash Solomon Bloomgarden, translator of the Bible into Yiddish.

# Yinglish 101

## Yiddish-English for Everyone

*allrightnik allrightnitse bagel bagel shift beygl Beugel bialy Bialystok blintze bletl blintz bobkes bubkes borscht schav borscht belt borscht [illegible] boychi[illegible] [illegible]oytshikl boytshikele boy-chick bo[illegible] [illegible] [illegible] [illegible] b[illegible]e bobe bubee bubby chot[illegible] [illegible] [illegible]h chutzpa hutzpa hutzpah dre[illegible] dre[illegible] fancy-[illegible] [illegible]octor-shmoc-ter wealthy-sh[illegible] famous-shmamous fonfe fonfer fonferer fonfe[illegible] fre[illegible] fresn esn fresser futz around arumfartsn a futz farts ganef gefilte fish filn gefilte fish line gelt shekels Chanukah gelt Geld glitch glitsh glitchy glitsh gonnif gonif ganef a metsiye fun a ganef! Fonye Ganef goy goyish Shabbos goy haimish heimish kibitz kib-itzer kibetsn kibbutz kishke derma stuffed derma kishkes klezmer klezmer music klezmorim klutz klutzy klutzier klutziest klutziness knish knock-er knaker kosher kvell kvetch kvetcher kvetsh lokh in kop lox laks macher makher big macher mamzer momzer maven meyvn mavin mazel tov! l'chaim megillah megile whole megillah mishmash*

Yiddish came of age in America over seventy-five years ago, on the wings of Hollywood and the borscht belt. Today, when someone wants to say "he's a good guy," you are apt to hear "he's a **mensch**." The word mensch, of course, comes straight from Yiddish **mentsh**, unchanged except in spelling, which was adopted from German. In both Yiddish and German the literal meaning is "man, human being," but Yiddish added the emphasis of "a true man!," someone whom you could rely on and be proud of. A truly good fellow. Like "my main man" in hip hop.

Where would English be today without such Yiddish-origin words as **chutzpah, gonnif, kibitz, klutz, maven, nebbish, nosh, schlep, schlock, schmatte, schmooze, schmuck,** and **tush**—to name a bit more than a few? Each one of these additions to contemporary English brings with it versatility, depth of feeling, and a touch of humor. String them together and you might be writing the script of a Marx Brothers movie or an episode of Seinfeld: "Scene Summary: The klutz does a pratfall landing on his tush, while his buddies laughingly kibitz as a gonnif runs off with his wallet."

Such words are commonly called Yinglish (a blend of Yiddish and English) because they have become part of spoken and written English. The proof? Just open any standard English desk dictionary and you're bound to find them there.

In this chapter we tell the story of eighty-odd Yinglish words that have firmly joined everyday English.

**allrightnik** *noun, Americanism.* A newly rich or well-to-do upstart, one who boasts that he has "done all right" for himself and flaunts his success by wearing fancy-shmancy clothes and driving a Cadillac. The **allrightnik** and his wife, the **allrightnitse**, are heartily despised by their less fortunate neighbors.

**Allrightnik** was one of the earliest Yiddish-English words ending in *-nik* (another was holdupnik, a thief) and was the forerunner of such English words as Beatnik, peacenik, and refusenik. See also **nudnik**.

**bagel** *noun.* The doughnut-shaped bread-like food that has taken over America and the world. You can find **bagels** in Bali and Bogota. There are even chocolate-flavored **bagels**, and, green ones on Saint Patrick's Day.

The secret to making good bagels lies in first poaching them in steaming vats, before they are baked to a firm, brownish glazed crust. Bagels have been called doughnuts with a college degree; and in their versatility at any meal, they are certainly a cut above their sweeter cousins. But bagels truly shine as a favorite breakfast food, usually topped with a **schmear** of cream cheese—and a paper-thin slice of **lox**, or smoked salmon.

**Bagel shift** refers to an early morning work shift, as on a news or talk show.

The word bagel came from Yiddish **beygl** and is thought to derive ultimately from the German *Beugel*, from the root word *beug-*, meaning ring. Legend has it that the first bagels were baked in Vienna in 1683 to celebrate its victory over the Turks.

**bialy** *noun.* A flat baked roll having a softer texture than a **bagel**, with a depression in the center and topped with toasted-brown onions. Though they remain relatively lesser known than **bagels**, **bialys** are savored and cherished nonetheless for their more pliant taste.

The well-known food critic Mimi Sheraton wrote an entire book about the subject, *The Bialy Eaters: The Story of a Bread and a Lost World* (see "Bialy—the Other Kukhen."). Bialys were invented by Jews in the northeastern Polish town of Bialystok, who generations later brought them to New York's Lower East Side, where they are still a staple at famous bakeries like Kossar's on Grand Street.

**blintze** *noun, Jewish Cookery.* A thin pancake wrapped around a filling of cottage cheese and cream cheese, or fruit, or mashed potatoes, eaten with sour cream or jam. Similar to French crêpes, blintzes were considered a delicacy throughout Eastern European countries—called *bliny* in Polish and *blin* in Russian—whence they became a favorite of Jewish cuisine. Eaten as either an appetizer or a dessert, **blintzes** exude an air of elegance and indulgence. The flour pancake is called a **bletl**, "leaf." Also spelled **blintz**.

**bobkes** </bub-kiss> *noun*. Triflings, chicken feed, zilch (literally, sheep dip). If you are left with **bobkes** after paying the bills, or collecting on

### Instant Yinglish—Google.com's Top Hits

Searching on Google.com gives a good indication of which Yinglish words are most frequently used today. **Glitch** and **kosher** top the charts, way ahead of all the rest; while even such well-known Yinglish words as **nosh**, **knish**, **schnoz**, and **gonnif** seem to have fallen behind in popularity. With the following list of the top dozen in hand, you'll be instantly up and running in Yinglish.

**glitch**. Slip-up; bug in the system. [*232,000 hits*]

**kosher**. Legit, on the up-and-up; ritually clean. [*222,000*]

**bagel**. The doughnut-shaped bread of champions. [*145,000*]

**maven**. Expert; pundit; smart aleck. [*70,800*]

**yid**. Yiddish word for Jew, pronounced <yeed>. But use with care: in U.S. slang, pronounced with a short i (as in *bid*), it is very disparaging. [*62,800*]

**klezmer**. Lively, heart-tugging Yiddish folk music. [*46,800*]

**mensch**. Decent, trustworthy person. [*42,600*]

**tush**. Backside; rear end. [*39,500*]

**schlock**. Cheap or shoddy goods; junk. [*39,300*]

**klutz**. Clumsy, inept person; blockhead. [*39,000*]

**schmooze**. To chat or gossip; by extension, to network. [*38,100*]

**chutzpah**. Impudence; moxie; cojones. [*32,700*]

The above results on Google.com were restricted to English Web pages, searching on word clusters such as [glitch glitsh glitchy], [mensch mensh], and [tush tushy], taking into account alternative spellings and closely related uses.

an investment, you really have less than nothing—you have also suffered the humiliation of getting the short end of the stick. When someone's advice or opinion is **bobkes**, it is useless drivel. The word can be used playfully, as in "He paid me **bobkes** (peanuts)," but it works better when used with a more biting sting, as in "You think you know somehing? You know **bobkes**!" Also spelled **bubkes**.

**borscht** *noun, Jewish cookery*. Beet soup, originally a favorite dish in Russian, Polish, and Ukrainian cooking. It is served either hot or cold, sometimes with a dollop of sour cream, an island of boiled potato, and a garnishing of cucumber slices. The word lent its name to the famous Catskills resort circuit.

Another soup popular in Yiddishdom, called **schav**, is made in a similar fashion from sorrel leaves.

**borscht belt** or **borscht circuit** *noun (sometimes with initial capitals)*. The hotels of the once predominantly Jewish resort area located in the Catskill Mountains of mid-New York State, many of which offered nightclub or cabaret entertainment. The **borscht belt** reached its heyday after World War II, when families from the East Coast flocked there for lots of food washed down with lots of good humor. The term facetiously refers to the quantities of **borscht** sometimes consumed there.

An understanding of **borscht belt** culture is needed to appreciate this review of comedian Gary Shandling's appearance in the film *What Planet Are You From?*:

> "Shandling is very funny, but his canny gift for a quip seems to come from that very human planet, the Catskills. And his face...the sad-dog face of a **Borscht Belt** Humphrey Bogart...is so personable, so **menschy**, that it's rather hard for us to accept Harold as an alien ignorant of emotions."

Source: David Elliot, MSNBC, March 3, 2000

**boychik** *noun, Americanism*. A boy or young man; usually said affectionately. Grandparents and older relatives used to enjoy vigorously pinching the cheeks of a favorite offspring until the **boychick** cried tears. This familiar endearment is somewhat like "kiddo." In Yiddish an endearing word can be doubled and redoubled by adding diminutive suffixes, whence in American Yiddish **boytshikl** and **boytshikele**. The word was formed in a cute moment from "boy" + the Slavic diminutive *-chik*. Also spelled **boychick** or **boytshik**.

Popular singer Eddie Fisher and young friends at Grossinger's hotel in the Catskills, around 1950. (YIVO Institute for Jewish Research)

**bubele** <ˈboob-eh-leh> *noun*. Darling or sweetheart. Sometimes shortened to **bubby** (though beware that the intonation doesn't hide sarcasm). **Bubele** is a completely unisex endearment, used between spouses, lovers, parents, and children. The Yiddish word literally means little grandma, and was originally an endearment for baby girls; but, as all babies can be equally cute, the word got to be used for baby **boychiks** as well, and from there it was only a short step to universality. Also spelled **bubeleh**.

**Bubele** is a diminutive of **bube** <ˈboob-eh>, the Polish and Ukrainian Yiddish word for grandmother. The Lithuanian and standard Yiddish form is **bobe** <ˈboh-beh>: Sometimes the Americanized endearment for grandmother, **bubee** or **bubby** <ˈbub-ee>, derived from **bobe**, is confused with **bubby** <ˈboob-ee> the endearment derived from **bubele** for sweetheart. (You might try diagramming the interrelations.) May all your mix-ups in life be so small!

To squelch an unfounded rumor: **bobe** is *not* the origin of the Southern U.S. nickname Bubba.

**Bubele** has had a run as a popular term in the media, frequently found in newsprint and heard on TV.

**chotchke** *noun*. See the more common spelling **tchotchke**.

**chutzpah** <ˈhoots-peh, *or more guttural* ˈkhoots-peh> *noun*. English has never been the same since the introduction of this Yiddish word for impudence, gall, or effrontery. Some claim that no English word can match its full meaning, and that's partly because Yiddish is a more musical and emotive language: The "hoots" or "khoots" sound at the beginning of **chutzpah** can gurgle deep in the throat to express a full range of disdain or derision. Sometimes spelled **chutzpa**, **hutzpa**, or **hutzpah**.

The ultimate **chutzpah** is said to be that of a man who has done in both his parents and then throws himself at the mercy of the court because he is an orphan.

Or of the man who shoots you and then blames you for getting in the way of the bullet.

**dreck** *noun, vulgar*. A word with about the same meaning and tonality as "crap" or "shit." Be careful, then, before uttering it in polite company. It can mean junk or cheap and worthless things, too. A movie or book that is terrible merits the criticism "It's dreck." The word comes from Yiddish **drek**, meaning filth or excrement, but the English spelling follows the German.

**fancy-shmancy** *adjective, Americanism, Slang*. Fancy or decorative to the point of being overdone or ostentatious. The opposite of casual or unpretentious. The well-heeled may live in a **fancy-shmancy** home, dine in a **fancy-shmancy** restaurant, and throw a **fancy-shmancy** bar or bas mitzvah. Related in spirit only to "fancy-pants" (snobbish or foppish), the term illustrates the Yiddish penchant for word humor, in this case by substituting the prefix **shm-** (or **schm-**) in mockery or derision. Other examples are doctor-shmoctor, wealthy-shmealthy, famous-shmamous.

**fonfe** *verb*. To mumble or speak unclearly. **Fonfe** sounds like words wending their way through a person's nose, instead of directly from

## The Jaws of Yinglish

Leo Rosten, who popularized the term Yinglish, explained it this way: "By 'Yinglish' I mean Yiddish words that are used in colloquial English in both the United States and the United Kingdom: *kibitzer, mish-mash, bagel,* etc."

But language scholars aren't sure what to make of the term Yinglish, since it is a slang term without a formal, scholarly equivalent. Instead of Yinglish, some have preferred the phrase "Yiddishized English." Others have opted for "bastardized Yiddishisms."

In actual usage today, though, the term Yinglish, which is a blend of "*Yi*(ddish)" and "(E)*nglish,*" can describe three different things:

(1) A form of English containing many Yiddish words and expressions. Some examples of this type of speech are: *She **sheps** a lot of **nakhes** from her **kinder** and **eyniklekh*** (translation: She gets a lot of pleasure from her children and grandchildren). *I gave him a **patsh** in **ponem** and he gave me a **klap** in **kop.*** (translation: I slapped his face and he hit me on the head). Scholars have called this kind of speech *Jewish English.*

(2) Yiddish words that have become part of informal English, such as, ***kosher, nudnik, gefilte fish, kibitz, tchotchke.*** These are the type of words Leo Rosten called Yinglish. Others have called such words *Yiddishisms.*

(3) True blends of Yiddish and English, such as, ***fancy-shmancy, borscht circuit, allrightnik, enough already, don't be a crazy.*** These are truly Yinglish. There is no other word for them. There are two kinds of blends. One combines an English word with a Yiddish one (or vice versa), as in *a big **tzimmes*** (a big fuss), *a whole **megillah*** (a long story), ***boychikl*** (little boy), ***Nosheria*** (cafeteria for snacks, a play on Yiddish ***nasheray,*** tidbits, snacks). And another translates a Yiddish expression into English, as *Be well* (Yiddish, ***Zay gezunt***), *not to worry* (Yiddish, ***nit gedayget***), *Again with the...?* (Yiddish, ***Vider mit di...?***), *Better you should...* (Yiddish, ***Beser zolstu...***): Better you should be rich and well than be rich and sick.

the voicebox and out the mouth. A **fonfer** or **fonferer** (*noun*) can mean a double-talker, or one who hems and haws without speaking forthrightly or getting to the point. To give a poor business presentation or to mumble one's bar or bas mitzvah lines is to **fonfe**.

Comedian Jackie Mason illustrated **fonfeing** in his inimitable way: You're riding a bus and you catch a pickpocket red-handed with his paw in your pocket. He **fonfes**, "Hey, I didn't know it was your pocket! There are lots of pockets on this bus. Am I supposed to know which one is mine?"

**fress** *verb*. To eat or snack, often in large quantities; to eat like a pig. It comes from Yiddish **fresn**, the word for eating applied to animals (**esn** is reserved for people), which suggests that eating heartily is considered in Yiddish to be an enjoyment God granted to all creatures. It can also be used to describe eating noisily, slurping soup, or squirting out the insides of an overstuffed sandwich. A **fresser** (*noun*) is either a hearty eater or a glutton. A Jewish mother believes everyone at her kitchen table must **fress**, or she has failed in the first duty of good homemaking.

**futz around** (*often followed by* with) *verb, Slang*. To fool, putter, or mess around (with someone or something). It suggests aimless toying without results. The verb is thought to derive from the Yiddish **arumfartsn**, which has a similar meaning. A **futz** (*noun*) is a fool or simpleton, probably coming from the Yiddish slang **farts**, an insulting term for a jerk (literally, a fart).

**ganef** *noun*. See **gonnif**.

**gefilte fish** *noun, Jewish Cookery*. A traditional appetizer of fish balls or cakes, usually eaten cold with horseradish; served at almost every important meal, for example, the Sabbath-eve dinner. Made from finely minced fish—usually whitefish, pike, or carp—mixed with bread crumbs or matzo meal, eggs, and seasonings, the fish patties are cooked slowly in simmering broth. **Gefilte fish**, along with **matzo**, has become a recognized symbol of traditional Jewish cooking. In Yiddish, **gefilt** is the past participle of **filn**, to fill or stuff—because, originally, the preparation was wrapped and cooked in the fish skin.

Marvin Herzog, the editor-in-chief of the *Language and Culture Atlas of Ashkenazic Jewry* (ongoing since 1992), showed how sweetened and unsweetened variants of **gefilte fish** followed the same boundaries as did the Polish and Lithuanian Yiddish dialects respectively.

**gelt** *noun.* Money or cash. Sometimes used interchangeably with **shekels** (from the Biblical monetary unit): "It feels good to have extra **gelt/shekels** to throw around." It is traditional to give a gift of **Chanukah gelt** to children, during this Festival of Lights. The Yiddish word derives from German *Geld.*

## Y2B: Yiddish to Business

Yiddish has infiltrated the business world and transformed it forever. You can't aspire to success in the corner office without knowing this handful of indispensable Yinglish terms they don't teach at B school.

**bobkes.** Zilch, nada, zip; the bottom line and your bonus for screw-ups.

**chutzpah.** Moxie, gall, big cojones; a must-have that goes with the territory.

**gonnif.** Thief, swindler; someone to steer clear of.

**gelt.** Money, coins; making that sweet kchink sound.

**kosher.** Legit, on the up-and-up; like something out of *Chicken Soup for Wheelers and Dealers*.

**maven.** Expert, smart ass; a designation for those you need to keep on a short leash.

**schlock.** Shoddy goods; sure sign it's time to move uptown.

**schmoozing.** Chitchatting, networking; where you'll do your best work.

**schnook.** A person easily duped in a deal, a dope; someone you should drop like a hot knish.

**tchotchke.** Cheap giveaway; something at least the neighborhood kids will love.

Also see "Yidisher Kop: Goldwynisms and Other Mind-Benders".

**glitch** *noun, Slang.* A defect, malfunction, or bug in a system; a slip or skid. **Glitch** can be used to describe any slip-up, hang-up, or hitch, especially unforeseen, in a plan or scheme. The term has become a favorite of both computer geeks and astronauts—with John Glenn cited as a popularizer of this term to mean sudden, unwelcome spurts in the voltage of an on-board electrical system. It comes from Yiddish **glitsh**, meaning a slip (as on a banana peel), and was probably influenced by English *slip-up*. Something that is **glitchy** is prone to errors and screw-ups. Also spelled **glitsh**.

**gonnif** *noun, Slang.* A thief, swindler, or rascal. From Yiddish **ganef**. A long-time English standby, **gonnif** appears as early as 1852 in Charles Dickens' *Bleak House*. In business, calling an associate a **gonnif** can be a serious accusation, suggesting double dealing and chicanery. Also spelled **gonif, ganef**.

Several English dictionaries have jumped the gun by putting Yiddish **ganef** as the preferred spelling, but evidence supports the use of Anglicized **gonnif** in English.

Yiddish expression: **A metsiye fun a ganef!** It's a steal (sarcastically and literally, a bargain from a thief).

"I loved reading how [her] grandmother would tease her and call her a **ganef**, meaning a thief, for trying to grab matzoh balls from the kitchen and then how, many years later, [she] found an old cookbook that referred to a kind of matzoh ball actually called a **ganef**."

Source: Florence Fabricant, review of *The Gefilte Variations* by Jayne Cohen, *New York Times On the Web*, April 5, 2000.

On a grimmer note, the Russian czar was called **Fonye Ganef**, the Russian Thief, because of the practice of kidnapping Jewish boys as young as eight for forced conscription into the Russian army for as long as twenty-five years.

**goy** *noun* (*can be disparaging and offensive*). A non-Jew or Gentile, of whatever religion or nationality. Depending on the context, **goy** can range in connotation from a neutral term to one of strong condescension and disparagement, and is today considered too offensive to be used indiscriminantly or without care. (The literal meaning of the word, found in the Bible, is actually "nation, people.") The modern usage, born in a time when Yiddish speakers lived mostly in isolated communities, still suggests things foreign, discomforting, or unkosher in the world at large. Plural is **goyim**. —*adjective*, **goyish**.

In Yiddish, **goy** is also applied disparagingly to a Jew who is either irreligious or ignorant of things Jewish.

A **Shabbos goy** is a non-Jew retained by religiously observant Jews to perform tasks forbidden on the Sabbath; for example, turning lights on or off. As a young man, Elvis Presley is said to have been a **Shabbos goy** for a neighboring Jewish family.

**haimish** <'hey-mish> *adjective*. A versatile word for homelike, cozy, or familiar. Things **haimish** can elicit warm, fuzzy feelings that conjure up hearth and home and community. But, when applied to a young man or woman, it can also suggest being a homebody, overly domestic, plain, or dull. Also spelled **heimish**.

**kibitz** *verb*. To act like a **kibitzer**, giving uninvited advice, maybe kiddingly. Comes from the Yiddish **kibetsn** and German *kiebitzen* meaning "to look on at cards." Contrast with **noodge**.

**kibitzer** <*accent on* 'kib-> *noun*. Someone who gives unsolicited, and at times unwanted or irritating, advice; like a hanger-on at a card game, or a big mouth at a ball park who thinks he knows more than the coach or players. A **kibitzer** can also be a person who jokes or wisecracks when others are trying to work or talk earnestly, making himself or herself a nuisance and a hindrance. Thus, while **kibitzers** can at times be entertaining, they seldom make a useful or welcome contribution. Contrast with **noodge**, **nudnik**.

If a **kibitzer** really knew something, he or she would be called a **maven** and could qualify for remuneration instead of ridicule.

Sound bite: Edward G. Robinson first gained fame acting in the 1929 play *The Kibitzer*, written by Jo Swerling.

The misspellings *kibbitz* and *kibbitzer* are probably influenced by the spelling of the Hebraism **kibbutz**, the Israeli term for a community settlement (usually agricultural).

**kishke** *noun, Jewish Cookery*. Sausage casing stuffed with meat and spices. Also called **derma** or **stuffed derma**. Used in the plural, **kishkes** can mean intestines or guts, as in "My **kishkes** are killing me," meaning that I am suffering from severe indigestion. To hit someone in the **kishkes** means to punch them in the stomach; or figuratively, to deliver a low blow to their reputation or plans. To speak, feel, or think something from your **kishkes** is to speak from your heart or guts. Also spelled **kishka**.

The versatile, figurative uses of **kishkes** illustrate a "psycho-gastronomic" aspect of Yiddish: other examples might be the use of **fress/fresser** for human eating; expressions like "What am I, chopped liver?" (figuratively meaning, Am I insignificant? Invisible? A side dish?); and the elevation of a young **nosher** to the status of a semi-hero.

**klezmer** *noun (usually used attributively)*. Also, **klezmer music**. The lively, heart-tugging folk music of the East European **shtetl**. In recent years, this traditional Yiddish music has enjoyed a resurgence the world over. The music is similar to jazz in its use of improvisation and interplay between soloists and instrumental chorus. The lilting, raucously joyous melodies—a vaudevillean combination of notes and rhythms—can have a nearly intoxicating effect on players and audiences alike.

**Klezmer** also refers to the musicians or bands that play such music, usually using string instruments, especially violins, and wind instruments like the flute and clarinet. In Yiddish, the word means simply a musician or band, and is often used in the plural **klezmorim**. American and other modern **klezmer** bands or groups often call themselves by variations of the word, as in The Klezmatics, Klezical (a wordplay on classical), and The Klez or The New Klez. Traditional **klezmorim** were often itinerant musicians wandering from **shtetl** to **shtetl**, playing at weddings, bar mitzvahs, and other celebrations, as when a new Torah scroll was introduced in the synagogue. Today's **klezmer** bands perform on radio and television and are regarded as folk artists.

Interestingly, the Yiddish word **klezmer** is a contraction of the Hebrew term *kley-zemer*, a plural phrase meaning musical instruments or, informally, a band of popular musicians (of any kind). Also see "Yiddish Music—Klezmer and Beyond."

**klutz** *noun, Slang*. A clumsy, inept person; a blockhead. A **klutz** is generally a bungler by nature, not by fault: so the designation often carries one part pity, one part exasperation. *—adjective*, **klutzy**, **klutzier**, **klutziest**. *—noun*, **klutziness**.

Appropriately, an innovative, small publisher, Klutz Press of Palo Alto, California, got its start publishing a book on how to juggle, entitled *Juggling for the Complete Klutz*, sold with three bean bags.

**knish** <keh-ˈnish> *noun, Jewish Cookery*. A baked, dumpling-like hearty traditional snack food or appetizer, filled with potatoes, meat, or cheese. **Knishes** can be garnished with poppy, caraway, or sesame seeds, and are best served hot, fresh from the oven. They come both large and small, though the ones that have gained most fame are the hefty size of a large bagel and each a filling meal by itself.

Recalled at a recent conference on Catskills culture: "Ruby the **Knish** Man...drove up to the colony to sell his goods and announced his presence in a gravelly Yiddish-inflected voice: 'Ladies and gentlemen, this is Ruby the **Knish** Man. I'm now on the premises with my homogenized, pasteurized and recently circumcised potato **knishes**. Please folks come. I need the money.'"

Source: Arthur J. Tanney, quoted in *The New York Times*, August 31, 2000

"Eat! Eat! Eat, so from hunger you won't starve."

Source: *Love and Knishes: An Irrepressible Guide to Jewish Cooking*, by Sara Kasdan

**knocker** <keh-ʹnock-er> *noun*. A big shot or know-it-all; wise guy. From Yiddish **knaker**. It's common to load up on the effect by adding "big," as in **big knocker**. Also spelled **knaker**.

"My father used it to refer to people who boasted of their triumphs or drove showy cars or displayed signs of having absorbed the teaching of the Talmud on the blessedness of charity without going on to read the section that says that the most blessed charity is the kind given anonymously. These were the big k'nockers."

Source: *Messages from My Father* by Calvin Trillin (New York: Farrar, Strauss and Giroux, 1996)

**kosher** *adjective*. Fit or permissible to eat, according to Jewish dietary laws. By extension, a popular slang term meaning fit, satisfactory, or legitimate. Kosher foods in recent years have diversified widely, with **kosher** sushi, egg rolls, and pizza available for those following traditional eating strictures.

In a similar way, the slang uses of **kosher** have diversified into broad versatility in English. "Is it **kosher?**" questions whether a deal, offer, or proposed undertaking is "for real," legal, or reliable. A person who is **kosher** is on the up-and-up, genuine, believable. "That's not **kosher**" means just the opposite—ranging from not nice to unfair, unsavory, or illegal.

**kvell** *verb, Slang*. To be delighted with; to revel in; to burst with pride.

The word has a songlike ring, suggesting the oohing and aahing of proud parents or grandparents delighting in the accomplishments of children or other family. It is also used less frequently to mean gloating over someone's defeat or humiliation.

Variant of an old standby: One Jewish mother to another, "Oh what beautiful children you have. How old are they?" Reply kvelling, "The doctor is two years old and the lawyer nine months."

**kvetch** *verb, noun, Slang.* To complain or gripe. The word suggests a cranky, hard-to-please disposition. Like so much Yiddish, the word's musical ring helps convey the meaning, in this case annoyance and irritation. A **kvetch** (*noun*, also **kvetcher**) is a continual complainer, who can and will find fault with almost everyone and everything. The personality, nearly archetypal, is closely related to that of the **noodge**.

"The Beatles...came along in the middle of a wave of **kvetching** songs constantly stressing the negative."

*Holiday*, July 1965 (OED On-line)

Andy Rooney is "the resident **kvetch** of *60 Minutes*...[and] an unabashed fogy."

Sue Halpern, *The New York Times*, October 7, 1984; in *Simpson's Contemporary Quotations*

Derived from the Yiddish **kvetshn**, to squeeze or complain, it conveys the sense of squeezing the joy out of life.

**lokh in kop** *phrase.* A hole in the head, usually used in the expression "I need it like a **lokh in kop**." Because of its expressiveness, it is one of the few Yiddish phrases to show up in English conversation in toto. Why? Don't ask; it's a conversation stopper. (Instead see "Yidisher Kop: Goldwynisms and Other Mind-Benders.")

**lox** *noun.* Smoked salmon that has been first cured with sugar or salt. It is the classic topping of a bagel first **schmeared** with cream cheese. From Yiddish **laks**.

**macher** <ˈmah-kher> *noun.* A mover and shaker; big shot; person of importance. It can also be used sarcastically to describe a blowhard or braggart. A **macher** can be a fixer or operator, able to finagle hard-to-come-by tickets or invitations to an exclusive event. Though the current English use came from Yiddish **makher**, the spelling follows German *Macher* for maker. It's common to load up on the effect by adding "big" as in **big macher**. Also see **knocker**.

## Jewbilations: Yidishe Nakhes from Things Jewish

**Jewbilate** is a made-up word meaning to take pride and joy in discovering that (1) a favorite celebrity, star, or big shot in the news is Jewish—even though cosmetic or family-name surgery may have camouflaged his or her roots (like Howard Cosell, Mike Nichols, Kirk Douglas, and Curly of the Three Stooges); (2) a favorite celebrity or star has a Jewish name, even though he or she is *not* Jewish (like Whoopi Goldberg and Lenny Kravitz); and (3) interest in Yiddish has spawned many freshly minted pseudo-Yiddish neologisms, a few of which are actually funny.

The following is a short list of pseudo-Yiddish terms disseminated by **Jewbilants** over the Internet and provided with suitable daffynitions:

**chutz-spa** *noun*. An expensive, pretentious spa, catering to Jewish American Princesses.

**deja nu** *noun*. The recurring sinking feeling which you first experienced when you forgot your bar or bas mitzvah lines and your relatives kept saying "nu? nu?" to get you back on track.

**drektions** *noun plural*. Misleading or lousy directions, usually several different ones with one more confusing than the other, given to you by the host of a wedding or bar/bas mitzvah, to which you really don't want to go.

**goyfer** *noun*. 1. A non-Jewish gofer at the office. 2. A **Shabbos goy**, who turns lights on or off and does other chores for observant Jews on the Sabbath. Elvis Presley was a famous **goyfer**.

**jewdo** *noun*. The Jewish art of verbal self-defense using age-old Yiddish stand-bys like **oy! nu? feh! shoyn! sha! gevald!** and the like. It invariably causes your opponent to retreat in disgust.

**meshuggenut** *noun*. A nutty person who can drive you crazy.

**reshtetle** *verb*. To move from Brooklyn to Boca, only to find that the people in your co-op or condo are the same ones you thought you'd left behind.

**yidentification** *noun*. The ability to spot a fellow **yid** in a large group.

**mamzer** *noun*. The main meaning in Yiddish-English is rascal or scoundrel, and is used mostly in this playful, figurative sense. Its traditional meaning in Yiddish and Biblical Hebrew is a child born from incest or adultery—a mortal sin—which makes the word *not* exactly the equivalent of the English word bastard, which can be applied with equal opprobrium to all births out of wedlock (see the "Heart of Yiddish Vocabulary"). Also spelled **momzer**.

**maven** *noun*. An expert or connoisseur. From the Yiddish **meyvn**, literally, one who understands. The word is now completely integrated into English—newsstories and ads regularly feature legal, money, music, computer, or you-name-it **mavens**. As with almost everything of Yiddish origin, however, the word can convey deep sarcasm, depending on the context and intonation.

The humorist Jeff MacGregor published in the *New York Times* (December 10, 1995) a rhymed satirical piece—called "The **Maven** (with Apologies to Edgar Allan Poe)"—about pundits on TV who are always at the ready to "pontificate, educate, elaborate...illuminate, corroborate, and ruminate...."

Source: Zellig Bach, *Mendele* On-line, 5.195

The *New York Times* columnist William Safire calls himself a language **maven**. Two of his books are titled *Language Maven Strikes Again* (1990) and *Quoth the Maven* (1993).

Also spelled **mavin**.

**mazel tov!** *interjection*. Congratulations (literally, good luck). This has become the indispensable felicitation appropriate for every joyous occasion, from a birth to a **bar** or **bas mitzvah**, graduation, promotion, groundbreaking, wedding. The Yiddish **mazl-tov** derives from Hebrew words meaning a good constellation of stars and destiny.

Even though the literal meaning is "good luck," it is not considered good form to wish a person **mazel tov!** before any dangerous undertaking, such as entering a hospital for treatment, or embarking on a perilous journey. Beforehand, one can wish them well (or use the English "good luck"), reserving a hearty **mazel tov!** for afterward, upon their success, triumph, or safe and sound return.

Commonly heard at celebrations along with **mazel tov!** is the toast **l'chaim**, meaning "to life!" With these two in hand, you are equipped to participate in all Jewish rejoicings.

The **schlimazel** is the poor fellow constantly prone to bad luck (see "S-Words of Yiddish").

**megillah** <meh-ˈgil-eh> *noun, Slang*. A long, sometimes drawn-out or long-winded story. It comes from the Yiddish **megile**, meaning long letter or document (from the Biblical story of Esther). English has eagerly and playfully adopted the word: The **whole megillah** means the whole thing or affair, with about the same connotation as the "whole enchilada." A **big megillah** can mean a big shot who is full of hot air, and of himself. Also spelled **megilla**.

Some English thesauruses give synonyms for the **whole megillah** as the "whole ball of wax" and the "kitchen sink."

**mensch** *noun*. A good person; a decent or trustworthy human being. The word comes directly from Yiddish **mentsh**, which in turn derives from German *Mensch*, with the literal meaning in both these languages of "man or human being." But, Yiddish added feeling and depth to the word, so that it epitomizes good behavior and the best in us. How to raise a **mensch** has preoccupied generations of conscientious parents; while how to find and marry one, generations of singles. Also spelled **mentsh**, *plural* **mentshn**.

"...[a **mensch** is] a person who always does the right thing in matters large or small, a person who would not only put himself at serious risk for a friend but also leave a borrowed apartment in better shape than he found it. My father clearly meant for me to be a **mensch**. It has always interested me, though, that he did not say, 'You must always be a **mensch**' or 'The honor of this family demands that you be a **mensch**' but [instead] 'You might as well be a **mensch**,' as if he had given some consideration to the alternatives."

Source: *Messages from My Father*, by Calvin Trillin (New York: Farrar, Strauss and Giroux, 1996)

Any beast can cry over the misfortunes of its own child. It takes a **mensch** to weep for others' children.

Source: The comedian Sam Levenson

**meshuga** <meh-ˈshoo-geh> *adjective, Slang*. Crazy; insane. Something far-out, off-the-wall, zany. "His ideas were just **meshuga** and won't get anywhere." (Also spelled **meshugga**.) The noun **meshugas** (pronounced with a strong emphasis on the last syllable <meh-sheh-ˈgahs>) means madness, a craze, or mania: "She always gets caught up in other people's **meshugas**." Also spelled **meshugaas**, **mishegas**.

**meshugana** <meh-ˈshoo-geh-neh> *noun, Slang.* A crazy person; lunatic. It can also be used playfully for someone who does zany or off-the-wall things. Also spelled **meshuggana**, **meshuggena**, **meshuggener**.

We chose the spelling **meshuggena** to create the title of this book.

**mishmash** <ˈmish-mosh *or* ˈmish-mahsh> *noun.* A mixture; hodgepodge; mess. A **mishmash** of ideas is an illogical jumble or an ill-conceived creation or plan.

> The word doubling here has an interesting history, coming from the Yiddish **mishmash** (a redoubling of **mishn**, "to mix"), while the same wordplay has been found in English as early as 1585; as well as in German *Mischmasch*, which Lewis Carroll adopted as the title of one of his books in 1855. The Yiddish and English words have all but blended together in recent years.
>
> Source: *Yiddish and English* by Sol Steinmetz

> Leo Rosten considers **mishmash** "a triumph of onomatopeia—and a word unlike any I know to suggest flagrant disorder." (*The Joys of Yiddish*)

Also spelled **mishmosh** (and sometimes hyphenated as **mish-mash** or **mish-mosh**).

**nebbish** *noun, adjective, Slang.* An ineffectual person; sadsack. Probably closest to a **schmo** in character, a **nebbish** is a pitiable nonentity who gets lost in the crowd. Living life just below the radar screen, he or she is the opposite of the life of the party. Marrying a **nebbish** means settling for leftovers. The word can also be used as an adjective: "She has a **nebbish** job," "He comes from a **nebbish** family." Also **nebbishy** *adjective*. Less common spelling, **nebish**.

Running the gamut: "The **nebbish**, the cynic, the sophisticate."

Source: *Commentary,* June 1960 (OED On-line)

"The central character is so **nebbish** he has not even a name."

Source: *Times* (of London), April 6, 1968 (OED On-line)

**noodge** *verb, noun.* To nag or pester. As a noun, it is close in meaning to **nudnik**, who is usually less pushy, but possibly noisier, than a **noodge**—but it can be a toss-up which one you will be able to tolerate longer. A **noodge** starts out under one's skin and only digs deeper. (A **kibitzer**, in further contrast, often tries to be entertaining.) **Noodge** also suggests a physical push or prod (a surreptitious kick under the table?) to drive the "**noodgee**" onward. Also spelled **nudge** (but still pronounced <nooj>), which is easily confused with the English verb *nudge* <nuj>, meaning to push or prod lightly.

**nosh** *verb, noun*. To nibble or snack between meals. A **nosh** (*noun*) is a snack or quick bite to eat. A **nosher** usually has a weakness for food or a sweet tooth, and can be an inveterate snacker. Most cultures admire children with healthy appetites, but rarely is it a compliment to say "God bless, he or she is a real **nosher**."

**Nosh** is one of the few Yiddish words to become thoroughly entrenched in British English, where it often means an entire meal or food in general, in addition to a snack, as well as an eating establishment. Similarly, the verb **to nosh** in British English more often means to eat a full meal, in addition to eating a snack. In both British and American English, however, the word seems to have retained the Yiddish sense of breezy or light eating.

**nosherei** <nosh-eh-ʹrye> *noun, Slang*. Food for snacking or nibbling; finger food; junk food; sometimes applied to appetizers or hors d'oeuvres. A **noshery** is an establishment that serves light food or snacks: Playing on this form, we have **knishery**.

**nu?** *interjection*. Well? So? What's up? It can be used to convey the rhetorical question "Is this ever going to happen?" to prod someone into action, like "come on" or "get on with it." Used in response to a comment or criticism, **nu?** is a foil that can mean "so what?", "who cares," or "big deal!"—"I saw you peeking at the answers." "Nu?"

The Yiddish word came from Russian *nu* meaning "well" or "well now."

**nudnik** *noun, Slang*. A pest or bore. As a child, a **nudnik** may be tolerated as showing signs of an active intelligence; but, when the trait continues into adulthood, everyone's patience frays.

The word derives from the same root as **noodge**, with the addition of the Slavic suffix *-nik*, meaning follower or practitioner. Similar word formation has resulted in Yinglish **no-goodnik** (no gooder, rogue), Hebrew-English **kibbutznik** (resident of a kibbutz), and English **Beatnik** (member of the Beat Generation) and **peacenik** (peace supporter, pacifist). Also see **allrightnik**.

**oy!** *interjection*. Oh! Oh my! It can apply to a wide spectrum of human emotions, from surprise and elation, to dismay, distress, outrage, and horror. Go figure. It is used in so many contexts, one would think it is a natural sound babies make at birth.

"**Oy!** is not a word; it is a vocabulary."

Source: Leo Rosten (*The Joys of Yiddish*)

The late Rastafarian singer Bob Marley used **oy!** in several of his songs, including "Buffalo Soldiers" and "We and Dem."

**Oy vey!** Similar in meaning to "oh my goodness," used in circumstances where "God help me/us" might follow. **Oy vey!** is **oy!** squared and literally means "oh pain!" or "ouch!"—often a soul-wrenching or cosmic ouch. It lies on the opposite side of the coin from **mazel tov!**

**Vey** comes from the German *Weh* (woe) and in Yiddish one commonly hears the fuller lament **oy vey iz mir!** "woe is me!"

**plotz** *verb, Slang*. To lose one's composure or become unnerved, due to emotional upset, anger, fear, or exhaustion. It comes from the Yiddish **platsn** "to burst," and suggests a sudden loss of self-control in an emotional outburst. "She nearly **plotzed** (broke down, fainted) when she heard the sad news." "He **plotzed** (exploded in anger) when he got the bill." "She laughed till she nearly **plotzed** (collapsed)."

**putz** *noun, Slang*. A jerk or prick. Derived from Yiddish **pots**, it is a vulgar term for "penis," but its offensiveness has been mostly lost among English speakers. "He's a real **putz**" suggests foolish behavior that is well out of place or inappropriate.

Yiddish **pots** (*plural* **pets**) is apparently of Slavic origin. It did not come from the German *Putz*, meaning "decoration or ornament." A common Yiddish euphemism for it is **pey-tsadek**, from the first and last letters of the word.

"'You,' she said, enunciating clearly, 'are a **putz**, a **schmekel**, a **schmuck**, a **schlong**, and a **shvantz**. And a WASP **putz**, at that.'"

Source: Judith Krantz, *Scruples* (OED On-line)

—**putz around** *verb*, to mess or screw around. When you **putz around**, someone usually has to clean up afterwards, undoing the damage, literal or figurative. Compare **futz around**.

**schlemiel** *noun, Slang*. A clumsy person; bungler; fool. While **klutz** suggests a physically awkward person who is "all thumbs" or has "two left feet," **schlemiel** is more suggestive of mental clumsiness as the root of the problem—a person who "cannot connect the dots" or

### Do You Schlep or Shlep—Schmooze or Shmooze?

Many words starting with **sh-** in modern Yiddish transcription have taken **sch-** in English as the preferred spelling; for example, **schlep, schlock, schmooze,** and **schmuck** (while **shlep,** etc., are still acceptable as alternate spellings). English seems more comfortable using **sch-,** which it associates with Germanic words (think of schnauzer, schnitzel, and Schubert), even though many of the Yiddish-origin **sch-** words in Yinglish have non-German roots.

Some Yiddish-origin words less integrated into English—like **shiksa,** and **shul**—still wear more Yiddish clothing. (*Schiksa* is a misspelling probably influenced by the Germanized words above.)

Also see the "S-Words of Yiddish" for more about these flavorful and colorful recent additions to mainstream English.

get it straight. Also spelled **shlemiel, schlemihl**. (See "S-Words of Yiddish" and the "Heart of Yiddish Vocabulary.")

**schlep** *verb, Slang*; **schlepped**, **schlepping**. To drag or lug. As a noun, it means either a slowpoke, a drag, or a tiresome trip. Also, **schlepper** *noun*. Also spelled **shlep; shlepper**. (See "S-Words of Yiddish.")

**schlock** *noun, adjective, Slang*. Cheap or inferior goods; junk; trashy items. Can refer to people as well as to things whenever they display or embody poor taste. (See "S-Words of Yiddish.") *—adjective* **schlocky**, **schlockier**, **schlockiest**. Also spelled **shlock**; **shlocky**.

**schlockmeister** *noun, Slang*. Someone who sells cheap or inferior goods. The addition of the suffix *-meister* (from the German word for expert or master) is all tongue-in-cheek, suggesting that **schlockmeisters** are so unabashed and shameless in their promotion of shoddy things, they have turned hustling into an art: "Have I got a deal for you!" From American Yiddish **shlakmayster**.

It appears that Yinglish started the trend of adding the suffix *-meister* in derision or disparagement. English now boasts several others, such as, spinmeister and opinionmeister. (This formation was also probably influenced by earlier, more earnest journalistic compounds like quizmaster and spymaster.)

**schlub** *noun*. See **zhlob**.

**schmaltzy** *adjective, Informal*; **schmaltzier, schmaltziest**. Overly sentimental; mawkish. The word comes from Yiddish **shmalts** (and German *Schmaltz*) for fat drippings melted and purified for eating like butter (still popular in parts of Europe). Hence the sense of dripping or oozing with emotion. To **schmaltz it up** means to ham it up, act corny. **Schmaltz** (*noun*), as in "That's pure **schmaltz**," applies to something said or acted out that is overly sentimental or corny, and can suggest a more definitive put-down.

**schmatte** <ˈshmot-eh *or* ˈshmah-teh> *noun, Slang*. Literally, a rag; figuratively, an ill-fitting or poorly designed dress or suit. If you call a person a **schmatte**, you mean he or she is worthless, a doormat everyone steps on. Also spelled **shmatte, shmate**.

**schmear** *verb, noun, Slang*. To spread, as butter or paint, usually thickly or unevenly. It can also mean to trounce an opponent, like "wipe (up) the mat or floor (with someone)." Also spelled **shmeer**.

**schmo** *noun, Slang*; *plural* **schmoes**. A foolish and boring person. A **schmo** takes the **nebbish** a rung or two down the intelligence ladder (see "S-Words of Yiddish"). Also spelled **schmoe, shmo**.

**schmooze** *verb, noun, Slang*; **schmoozed, schmoozing**. To chat idly or gossip. In today's offices you can **schmooze** by the water cooler in real or virtual space. A **schmooze** (*noun*) is a friendly chat or conversation. By extension, **schmoozing** now sometimes means networking or politicking, possibly by ingratiating onself; and someone who's "a real **schmoozer**" may be adept at getting his or her way through networking and arm twisting. Also spelled **schmoose, schmoos**.

**schmuck** *noun, Slang*. A vulgar term for a jerk or prick, a degree less offensive than **putz**. In American slang (but not in Yiddish), there is now an extended sense meaning a contemptible or disgusting fool (as in "He's a lying **schmuck**!") which is more-or-less synonymous with "son of a bitch, bastard." Also spelled **shmuck**.

**schnook** *noun*. A stupid or gullible person, one who is mostly weak-minded, pitiable, and harmless. Derived from Yiddish **shnuk**, literally, (elephant) trunk, snout. Also spelled **shnook**.

**schnoz** *noun, Slang*. Nose, especially a large or ungainly one. Also spelled **schnozz, shnoz**. Variants, **schnozzle, schnozzola**.

**schtick** *noun, Slang*. An entertainment routine; an interlude or aside to get laughs. By extension, a person's special talent or penchant.

*"Trust me Mort—no electronic-communications superhighway, no matter how vast and sophisticated, will ever replace the art of the schmooze."*

Someone's **schtick** can also mean his or her idiosyncratic routines, likes and dislikes. Also spelled **schtik, shtick.**

**schtup** *verb, noun, vulgar.* Literally, to push; vulgar term for sexual intercourse. Also spelled **shtup**. (See "S-Words of Yiddish.")

Contrary to the impression conjured up by the media and stand-up comedy, Yiddish is actually a prudish language, much like Hebrew. Most Yiddish speakers would use euphemisms or circumlocutions to discuss sexual matters, the form of which would be universally clear: for example, **dos shlofn mit** (sleeping with), **dos lebn mit** (living with). Or more straightforwardly, **der seks** (sex), **seksuele batsiungen** (sexual intercourse).

**shamus** *noun, Slang; plural* **shamuses**. A detective or policeman. Derived from Yiddish **shames**, meaning a synagogue caretaker, a sexton.

**shiksa** *noun.* A Gentile woman, usually a young, attractive one—and the archetypal temptress who can cause a former **mensch** to stray from marrying within the faith.

**shtetl** *noun; plural* **shtetls, shtetlach.** An East European village or town populated with Yiddish speakers, which existed prior to World War II. (See "Shtetl Life.")

**shul** *noun*. A synagogue or house of worship. Wherever there are at least ten to form a congregation, and a place in which to house a Torah, there can be a **shul**.

The classic **shul** joke involves two Jewish castaways marooned on an island. Each builds a **shul**, since neither would attend the other's. After a time they agree to build a third **shul**, one that both of them would never set foot in.

**tchotchke** <ˈchoch-kee> *noun, Slang*. A trinket, bauble, or knicknack. Now a widespread term used in marketing for inexpensive free give-aways, to promote a brand name or entice prospective buyers. Also spelled **chotchke**.

**toches** <ˈtook-ehs> *noun, Slang*. The behind, buttocks, backside. Also spelled **tochis**, **tuches**, **tuchis**.

**tsuris** *noun, Slang*. Headaches; troubles; woes. Also spelled **tsouris**, **tsores**.

**tush** *noun, Slang*. Backside. A baby-talk diminutive formed from dialectal Yiddish **tukhes**, variant of **tokhes** (in Yinglish **toches**). Also, **tushy**.

**yarmulke** *noun*. A skullcap worn in conformance with religious stricture. Traditionally it was considered an affront to an omnipresent God to go bareheaded (see "Heart of Yiddish Vocabulary"). Also spelled **yarmulka**.

**yenta** *noun, Slang*. A busybody or gossip, originally applied to a woman. From Yiddish **yente**.

**yid** *noun, Slang (often disparaging)*. In English, a highly demeaning name for a Jew—although in Yiddish it is neutral and the only such designation. In Yiddish it is pronounced <yeed>, with a long i (as in *weed, seed*); while in American slang the word is pronounced more harshly with a shortened i (as in *pin* or *bid*), often used derisively as an ethnic slur. Note well: it is *not* a shortened form of the word Yiddish.

**zaftig** *adjective, Slang*. Juicy; plump; shapely; voluptuous. A word from a pre-Weight Watchers era, **zaftig** is generally used for a woman with a full, healthy, buxom figure: Just what a young unmarried man's meddling relatives might order. Also spelled **zoftig**.

**zhlob** *noun, Slang*. A gross or boring person; slob. Also spelled **zhlub**, **schlub**.

## Yiddishkeit and Yiddishism: What's the Difference?

In recent years the term **Yiddishkeit** has become a catchword for all things Jewish. Hundreds of Web sites claim to represent, teach, discuss, define, walk you through, and test you on Yiddishkeit. What do they mean?

For starters, the term Yiddishkeit comes from Yiddish **yidishkeyt**, which for centuries has meant one thing only: Judaism, or the Jewish religion. But the meaning of Judaism has itself changed over the past few hundred years, and the term is usually modified to specify a variety of the religion, such as Conservative, Orthodox, or Reform Judaism. For that reason, many of today's Orthodox Jews, especially those of Ashkenazic (chiefly East European) descent, avoid the term Judaism and prefer instead the term Yiddishkeit, which not only means traditional, rabbinic Judaism but also suggests a strong emotional attachment to the ancestral faith.

A change in usage came about when non-Orthodox Jews began using the term Yiddishkeit to mean not Judaism but *Jewishness*, meaning the state or condition of being Jewish, regardless of religious affiliation. Thus, the experience of spending summers in the Jewish resorts and bungalow colonies in the Catskills got to be called "The Yiddishkeit Experience." Thus, a gay Jew, in an article titled "Queer Yiddishkeit?" writes that "by being gay, I have more access to Yiddishkeit." And thus, the Jews for Jesus Newsletter (issue of March 1998), lists among its articles a feature titled "Test Your Yiddishkeit," which purports to be a quiz on such "Jewish" facts as "For whom is the Jewish women's organization *Hadassah* named?"

The term **Yiddishism** is used by Yiddishists, secular Jews devoted to the Yiddish language and culture. As to what exactly Yiddishism is and encompasses, the music critic Evan Variano, writing about the Klezmer revival (see "Yiddish Music—Klezmer and Beyond"), has this to say: "Yiddishism is cultural Judaism—the idea that one can be Jewish by appropriating elements of secular Jewish culture.... Whether this is a valid form of Judaism is open to debate, and has been a major question in contemporary Jewish thought. Much of the debate over the Jewishness of the [Klezmer] revival is just a reformulation of this larger debate about the nature of Judaism."

# S-Words of Yiddish

## Put-downs Without Peer

*schlemazel schlemiel "Der shlemiel falt afn tokhes un brekhts zikh di noz." schlep schlepped schlepper schlimazel schlock schlocky schlub zhlob zhlub schlump schlumpy schlumperdik doctor-shmoc[illegible] [illegible]er-shmancer Oedipus-schm[illegible]edipus schmaltz schmaltzy schmatte [illegible]eiche[illegible] sc[illegible] [illegible] shmegege di velt iz zer ayn[illegible]nem." [illegible]chmendrick schmo schmuck schmutz schmutzik schnook shnuk schnorrer shnorer shnorrer schnoz schtunk farschtunkener [illegible] [illegible] schtupper schvartz schvartze schvitzer sheygets shikker shiker shiksa shiksa goddess shlong shlang shmays shmaysn shpilkes shver shvindl Se shtinkt! Es zol dir grizhen in boykh! Sha, sha! Shihi-pihi. "Shlog zikh di kop in vant." "Shlog zikh mit Got arum!" Shoyn genug! Shtik drek. Shtik goy. "Strashe mikh nit!" "Shtup es in tokhes!" alter kaker beheyme farbisener mentsh farshtunkener mentsh ganef grober yung khaim yankl khazer kholerye klots klutz kvetsh kvetch*

**Schnooks** and **schmegegges**, **schlubs** and **schleppers**. As with every language, Yiddish has a lexicon of cutting and vulgar words. They're sharp arrows, finely honed to insult just about anybody and everybody in any situation. In Yiddish, colorful S-words are reserved for the big put-downs, and they have the bite to express it all: frustration to outrage; sarcasm to contempt; disgust to lust.

We have all met **schmutzik schlubs** and **schlumperdik schleppers** wearing **schmattes**. And how about that noisy **schlump** of a **shikker**? Yep, Yiddish S-words fill the mouth, pucker the lips, and push the tongue against the hard palate. They're meant to hiss or shush with that acid *s* or noisy *sh* flowing off the first syllable. They sound funny and immediately evoke the image of whom they're describing.

S-words make you laugh if they're not directed at you, but can make you feel like a **schmendrick** or **schmegegge** if they are. Their saving grace is that they generally leave the speaker feeling quite satisfied and the recipient feeling pretty insignificant.

Even the most forlorn inhabitant of a 19th-century **shtetl** in Eastern Europe had the power, in the privacy of his fellow Yiddish speakers, to flay an oppressor with an S-word or two. They're part of the humor through which Yiddish has enabled countless generations to laugh at themselves, their oppressors, and the travails of life.

Some of these Yiddish S-words are so effective that they've become an integral part of the English vocabulary. You read them in books and magazines, you hear them on television and in the movies: only a **schnook** wouldn't know them. Go ahead already, use an S-word right now—didn't some **schmuck** drive you nuts today?!

**schlemazel** *noun*. See **schlimazel** below, the more common spelling.

**schlemiel** *noun*. A professional bungler who's always making a mess of things. Life seems stacked against him and he hasn't a clue. He's a good buddy of a **schlimazel**.

**Der shlemil falt afn tokhes un brekhts zikh di noz.**
*The schlemiel lands on his behind and breaks his nose.*

**schlep** *verb, noun*. To drag or pull something or someone (even oneself). Here's one word fully integrated into English. We've all **schlepped** our baggage (and ourselves) around the airport, or were **schlepped** by our mothers when we were small. It can also serve well as a derogatory noun, as in, "You know that **schlep** hasn't worn an ironed shirt in years."

**schlepper** *noun*. Also **schlep**. A sloppy jerk. In the underworld, a petty thief. In Orchard Street, on New York's Lower East Side, a hustler who **schleps** in reluctant customers.

**schlimazel** *noun*. A real jerk, plagued by bad luck; a pathetic nebbish always screwing up. He's a good buddy of a **schlemiel**. You can distinguish them by remembering that a **schlimazel** gets soup spilled on him by a **schlemiel**. The *schlim* comes from the German for bad; the *mazel* from the Hebrew for luck. Put them together and you get a person not blessed with any luck. Everything goes wrong for the **schlimazel**. He's the one whose new car is a lemon, or who goes into the hospital for an appendectomy but instead gets open-heart surgery. As the proverb says, "Only a **schlimazel** believes in **mazel**." Also spelled **schlemazel**.

**schlock** *adjective, noun*. Describing really cheap and shoddy goods. Low class, no matter what it costs. Works equally well for stuff and people. You can call someone who is disagreeable and even shrewish a schlock. When referring to a woman, a **schlock** is a real **yenta** and a whining harpy. Your pretentious friends live in a **schlocky** apartment filled with schlock things. Cheapskate friends have **schlock** mentalities. Variant, **schlocky**.

**schlub** *noun*. A crude individual lacking in social skills and blessed with insensitivity, clumsiness, and no manners. Also spelled **zhlob**, **zhlub**.

A **schlub** put an ad in the personals which read: Sweet Jewish guy, 40. No skeletons, no heavy baggage. No personality either.

And then came the **schnorrer's** ad: Jewish male, 35. Smart, independent, self-made. Looking for nice Jewish girl with rich father.

**schlump** *noun*. A pathetic character often disheveled in appearance, with a real hang-dog look. **Schlumps** often wear **schmattes**. The adjective is **schlumpy**.

**schlumperdik** *adjective*. Unkempt, sloppy.

**schm-**, **shm-**. A wonderful Yinglish prefix which when added to the beginning of a word adds an element of mockery, sarcasm, or dismissal. As in, "Doctor-**shm**octor, he thinks he knows more about my condition than I do?" Or, "Cancer-**shm**ancer, as long as you're healthy." Or, "Oedipus-**schm**oedipus, the main thing is that **boychik** loves his mother."

**schmaltz** *noun, verb*. **Schmaltz**, the noun, is delicious rendered chicken fat that your **bobele schmeared** on a piece of bread or mixed into chopped liver to give it that delightful smoothness. Or it can also mean something that's maudlin or mawkish, dripping with sentimentality. As in, "**Oy**, was that movie pure **schmaltz**." And as a verb, when you **schmaltz up** something (like a song), you make it mawkish. **Schmaltzy**, the adjective, on the other hand, is pure corn, dripping with treacle.

### Insulting Expressions

**Gey in drerd!**
*Go to hell!*

**Ikh hob dikh in drerd!**
*To hell with you!*

**Kush mir in tokhes.**
*Kiss my ass.*

**A sheynem dank dir im pupik.**
*Many thanks in your bellybutton.*

**Shenere mentshn hot men geleygt in drerd.**
*They've buried nicer looking people than that.*

**Ver derharget!**
*Drop dead!*

**Zi iz geven a kurve in di mames boykh.**
*She was a whore in her mother's stomach.*

**schmatte** <ˈshmot-eh *or* ˈshmah-teh> *noun*. When referring to stuff, it's rags and shoddy merchandise, no matter what the price tag. Referring to people, it can mean someone not worthy of respect or someone who is a brown-nosing sycophant. A woman who is a **schmatte** is weak-willed. Your friend wearing that flashy thousand-dollar suit you covet is dressed in a **schmatte**, something eye-catching and expensive, but probably too flashy and in poor taste.

**schmeichel** *verb*. To butter up (literally, to smile). Also to flatter, con, or fast talk.

**schmegegge** <shmeh-ˈgeg-ee> *noun*. A real put-down to describe an incompetent nincompoop, who is also a servile flatterer and hanger-on, and a sniveler and bootlicker to boot.

**Tsu a shmegege di velt iz zer ayngenem.**
*To a schmegegge the world is very pleasant.*

**schmendrick** *noun*. Another one of those weak, S-word characters most related to the **schlemiel**. Usually a small and inconsequential individual with very few prospects. **Schmendricks** can harbor delusions of grandeur, thinking their determination will bear fruit. Can also be used to refer with derision to a small penis.

**A kranker vert gezunt, a shiker vert nikhter, ober a shmendrik blaybt alemol a shmendrik.**
*A sick person gets well, a drunk can sober up, but a schmendrick always remains a schmendrick.*

**schmo** *noun*. Al Capp named his white bowling-pin-like creatures **shmos** since they liked to be kicked. But according to Leo Rosten, a **schmo** is the polite Yinglish neologism for a **schmuck**. So this nebbish-kind of individual is more than just a **schlemiel** and hapless fool: He's a jerk and a boob to top it off.

**schmuck** *noun*. A self-made fool. Also obscene for penis. Used very derisively when putting down a man, when it can also mean a contemptible son-of-a-bitch.

**A tsig geyt men tsu fun hintn, a ferd fun fornt, un tsu a shmok geyt men in gantsn nisht.**
*A goat you approach from the back, a horse from the front, and a schmuck you don't go near at all.*

**schmutz** *noun*. Dirt, filth, gunk.

**schmutzik** *adjective.* Dirty, soiled.

**schnook** *noun.* Comes from Yiddish **shnuk**, literally, a snout or elephant's trunk. This guy is a pitiful **schlemiel**, a pathetic misfit who is pitied more than despised.

**schnorrer** *noun.* Somebody who sponges off friends, this beggar's a real moocher. S/he can be clever in figuring out all the ways to get into your pockets, the deeper the better. A **schnorrer** can also be a inveterate bargain hunter, never paying more than s/he absolutely

### Insulting Names of People You'd Rather Avoid

| | |
|---|---|
| **alter kaker** | old fogey (literally, old shitter). Abbreviated A.K. |
| **beheyme** | animal, ignorant drudge |
| **farbisener mentsh** | a sour, stubborn person |
| **farshtunkener mentsh** | a rotten person |
| **ganef** | thief |
| **grober yung** | a crude fellow, an ignoramus |
| **khaim yankl** | a half-wit |
| **khazer** | selfish person; also, glutton (literally, pig) |
| **kholerye** | a good-for-nothing |
| **klots** (Yinglish, **klutz**) | a clumsy person |
| **kvetsh** (Yinglish, **kvetch**) | whiner, complainer |
| **mamzer** | bastard |
| **mieskayt** | unattractive person |
| **moyshe pupik** | a jerk |
| **nebekhl** (Yinglish, **nebbish**) | a loser |
| **nokhshleper** | a hanger on |
| **nudzh** (Yinglish, **noodge**); **nudnik** | a bore, a pest |
| **paskudnyak** | horrible person |
| **pisher** | one who is wet behind the ears |
| **shoyte** | a complete fool |
| **tokhes leker** | an ass kisser, brown-noser. Abbreviated T.L. |
| **tsatskele** | a bimbo |
| **vilder khaye** | a wild animal, a savage |
| **yente** (Yinglish, **yenta**) | a busybody, a gossip |

has to. And when a **schnorrer** takes your last dollar, s/he usually insults you to boot: "What, only a hundred dollars you can give me?—such a cheapskate!" Also spelled **shnorer**, **shnorrer**.

A wealthy patron supports Mendel, a **schnorrer**, with a monthly stipend. One day Mendel's check comes and it's half the usual amount. Upset, he immediately goes to his patron's home to request the other half.

"Look, Mendel," says the patron. "My son recently married an actress with expensive tastes, so I have to pay her bills."

"That's all very fine," replies Mendel, "just don't expect me to pay them too."

A street merchant selling geese in Baluty, a suburb of Lodz, Poland, 1933. (YIVO Institute for Jewish Research)

**schnoz** *noun.* A way too big nose.

**schtunk** *noun.* A stinker of a person, nasty and ungrateful. Take a **schlemiel** and add a dash of bitters and you get a **schtunk**. A no good **farschtunkener** is someone you want to cross the street to avoid. Can also mean a real disturbance, reeking of disgrace and slander.

**schtup** *verb, noun, considered vulgar.* This word has a double-edged meaning. It's derived from Yiddish **shtupn**, "to push," or **shtup**, "a push," and as a verb can mean to be aggressive in a pushy way. The act of fornicating or the fornicatee is another use of this word, as in "That was some **schtup** he had last night." A **schtupper** is someone who likes to do the nasty.

**schvartz** *adjective,* **schvartze** *noun; often disparaging.* Black or dark, usually referring to something difficult, unhappy, or ominous. Can also mean inept as well as refer to illegal or contraband goods. When it's used as a noun it refers to an African-American or black person and usually has a pejorative undercurrent. Not a nice word to describe a person.

**schvitzer** *noun.* A loudmouth, bullshitter, and usually a show-off, too.

**sheygets** *noun.* A non-Jewish male (the corresponding female is a **shiksa**). Other meanings can include: a quick-witted, clever, rogue; a boor without any education or interest in study.

**shikker** *noun.* A drinker who's over the limit; a drunkard. For our parents' generation, a **shikker** was a terrible embarrassment, as few Jews drank to the gills. But Jews are not teetotalers, and wine is often a part of many religious services and celebrations. Thus for Jews alcohol was meant to be taken with moderation and even reverence. This word comes from Yiddish **shiker**, and originally from Hebrew.

**shiksa** *noun.* A non-Jewish woman, usually young, pretty, and of marriageable age. She's the bane of every Jewish mother who dreads her son will date a **shiksa** and worse yet, **oy gevalt**, want to marry her. **Shiksas** are usually idealized as minxes, hence the expression, **a shiksa goddess**. A non-Jewish household maid is another type of **shiksa**; and sometimes a Jewish girl who doesn't act like one is dubbed "a regular **shiksa**." The corresponding male is called a **sheygets**.

**shlong** *noun.* A snake. Can also refer to a man's third leg, usually a long one. Obscene term for penis. Also spelled **shlang**, as in Yiddish.

**shmays** *verb*. To thrash, whip, or lash. From Yiddish **shmaysn**.

**shpilkes** *noun*. Pins. To sit on **shpilkes** is to be on pins and needles, to have ants in ones pants.

**shver** *noun*. Father-in-law. —*adjective*. Heavy, hard, difficult (as a father-in-law).

**shvindl** *noun*. Fraud, deception, swindle. —*verb*. To swindle.

### Yiddish Curses

**A curse is much worse than an insult. While an insult is intended only to hurt another's feelings or self-respect, a curse invokes God and asks to send down misfortune or injury on the cursed. When Moses asked Pharaoh to free the Jewish slaves, the paskudnyak was unresponsive. So, God sent down ten curses, one worse than the next, and the Jews got to leave. But as an oppressed people, without a homeland for 2,000 years, words became their most potent weapons. And who knows, God forbid, maybe He heard some of these Yiddish oaths hurled from some shtetl!**

**Beser zol er lebn—un mutshn zikh.**
*Better he should live—and suffer.*

**Du zolst nor fartsn in drerd.**
*You should only fart in the earth (i.e., you should be dead in your grave).*

**A brokh tsu dayn lebn.**
*Your life should be a disaster.*

**A kholerye im in beyner, a make im in boykh, a ruekh in zayn tatns tate arayn!**
*A cholera in his bones, a plague in his belly, a devil into his father's father!*

**A kholeyre af dir! A make af dir!**
*A cholera on you! A plague on you!*

**Zol di markh oprinen fun dayne beyner!**
*May your bones be drained of marrow!*

**Zol er lebn—ober nit lang.**
*May he live—but not long.*

**Zol er lebn biz hundert un tsvantsik yor—on a kop.**
*May he live to be a hundred-and-twenty—without a head.*

**Zol er vern geharget! Zol er vern dershtikt! Zol er brenen in gehenem!**
*May he be murdered! May he be strangled! May he burn in hell!*

**Zolst hobn a ziser toyt—a vagon mit tsuker zol dir iberforn!**
*May you have a sweet death—a truck full of sugar should run you over!*

**A mise meshune af dir!**
*May an unnatural death be your fate!*

**Zolst farlirn ale dayne tseyn akhuts eyner, un in dem zolst hobn a shreklikher tseynveytik.**
*You should lose all your teeth except one, and in it you should have a roaring toothache.*

**Zolst lebn vi a tsibele, mit dayn kop in drerd un dayn fis in di luft.**
*You should live like an onion, with your head in the ground and your feet in the air.*

**Zolst tsebrekhn ale dayne beyner az oft mol vi di brekhts di aseres hadibres.**
*You should break all your bones as often as you break the Ten Commandments.*

**Zolst hobn a zun vos men ruft nokh dir...un in gikhn.**
*You should have a son named after you...and soon.*

(It is the Ashkenazic Jewish custom to name children only in honor of the deceased.)

But Yiddish also allows the curse to be softened, which adds its own signature irony:

**Beyde oygn dayne zoln faln fun dayn kop, khas vesholem!**
*Both your eyes should fall out of your head, God forbid!*

**A brokh tsu dayn lebn, nisht far dir gedakht!**
*Your life should be a disaster, may it never happen to you!*

**A shvarts yor af dir, ikh zol nit visn derfun!**
*May it be a black year for you, may I know nothing of it!*

## When the Mob Spoke Yiddish

Pious, Torah-studying Jews have always been highly critical of criminal behavior. But despite the prevalence of the non-combative, peaceful Jew, immigration to America threw some into a melting pot where anything could happen. Out of that cauldron, Yiddish-speaking criminals emerged, some of whom allegedly helped invent organized crime in America.

The most sensational aspect of modern Jewish crime came out of America's slums in the first half of the 20th century. New York's Lower East Side, Los Angeles' Boyle Heights, and Chicago's Maxwell Street were homes to Jewish gangsters who were as tough as their counterparts from the other organized syndicates, such as the Italian Mafia. Most came from desperately poor families who arrived from Eastern Europe in the waves of immigration in the 1890s and early 1900s. As the offspring of East European Jewish immigrants, they spoke Yiddish, and had few opportunities to pursue conventional professions. Prohibition, gambling, narcotics and vice all offered astounding profits for those criminally inclined and strong enough to fight for their turf.

Three men stand out as Yiddish-speaking criminal masterminds from the 1920s to 1950s. Arnold Rothstein could probably be considered one of the kingpins of American crime. He was born in New York City in 1883 and started in professional gambling while still very young. He was a high roller and ran a gambling empire and related "legitimate" businesses that included real estate, bail bonds, and horse stables. Rothstein was implicated in the 1919 World Series "Black Sox" gambling fix, in which several Chicago White Sox ballplayers were bribed to throw the series (depicted in the 1988 movie *Eight Men Out*). Murdered in 1928, he's often referred to as the father of modern crime for his early efforts to organize criminal activities and use legitimate businesses to launder money.

Benjamin "Bugsy" Siegel was an imposing gangster who charmed the ladies and brutally eliminated his enemies. Many considered him a sociopath who feared no one but was feared by most. He was born in 1906 and grew up in the slums of Brooklyn. With his friend, Meyer Lansky, they formed Murder, Inc., a gang of assassins who were aligned with "Lucky" Luciano and the Italian mob in the 1930s. He looked after the Mafia's interests in Hollywood and became a celebrity gangster who organized gambling, narcotic trafficking, and prostitution. Siegel is considered the "father of Las

Vegas," and built its first multi-million dollar casino-hotel in 1946. He allegedly skimmed gambling profits from his partners Lansky and Luciano and was killed in 1947. Warren Beatty portrayed Siegel in the film *Bugsy* (1991).

Meyer Lansky was born Maier Suchowljansky in 1902. He grew up in New York City after his parents emigrated from Grodno, Russia, in 1911. At the age of 16 he teamed up with Bugsy Siegel and by the early 1920s they formed Murder, Inc. Lansky helped Lucky Luciano take over the New York mob. He was considered a brilliant moneyman who was in charge of Luciano's finances and money laundering. Lansky's criminal activities were wide-ranging and included labor racketeering and extortion. He built hotels and casinos in the Caribbean and had amassed a considerable fortune by the time he died in 1982. Amazingly, Lansky never spent any time in prison. He was portrayed in the movies *Godfather II* (1974), *Mobsters* (1991), and *Billy Bathgate* (1991).

Hester Street on New York's Lower East Side: "The Street Their Only Playground," photographed by Jacob Riis around 1898. (© Museum of the City of New York. The Jacob A. Riis Collection.)

# The Genius of Yiddish Humor

## A Schtick for Every Occasion

*schtick schmuck schlemiel S-Words Yinglish klezmatic-style laughter Woody Allen nebbish schlepers shtetls Eastern Europe irony wryness self-m[illegible] gentl[illegible]sarcasm shnorer luft[illegible]entsh leydikg[illegible] [illegible] cantor sh[illegible] s[illegible] moyl[illegible]oged melamed Shol[illegible]m [illegible] vak Galitsianer Khel[illegible] (Chelm) Khelmer Khakhomim "wis[illegible] m[illegible]n of Khe[illegible]m" folklore farblondzhet Hasidim Misnagdim maskilim badkhonim Purimshpilers jokesters pranksters Hershele Ostropolyer Motke Khabad kanehore Vitsn un shpitsn oder anekdotn Isaac Meir Dick Sigmund Freud Jokes and their Relation to the Unconscious Immanuel Olsvanger Royte Pomerantsn "Red Oranges" How to Laugh in Yiddish Richard Raskin Life is Like A Glass of Tea Rabbinic Judgment Man versus God Ten Commandments Ultimate Jewish Mother Nu? Jewishness Ashkenazi Groucho Marx Isaac Asimov punchline who's counting? di fir kashes*

If you listen to the sounds of Yiddish for just a few minutes, you know that only a comedian could have put that **schtick** together. Why are **schmuck** and **schlemiel** and the other S-Words the most worn pages of the Yinglish daily lexicon? And whether or not we like to admit it, everyone of Yiddish descent secretly knows he or she harbors a humor gene that threatens to break out in **klezmatic**-style laughter at any moment.

Yiddish humor is often called "Jewish" humor, but this is clearly a mistake. The classic jokes and routines used by Jewish humorists and comedians past and present stem from Yiddish culture—the experience of Yiddish-speaking Jews in Eastern Europe. A one-liner by Woody Allen, for example, encapsulates the pessimism and paradox that are hallmarks of Yiddish humor: "It's not that I'm afraid of dying. I just don't want to be there when it happens."

Another (from Woody Allen's film *Bananas*) exhibits Yiddish humor's penchant for the darkly and comically absurd: "This trial is a travesty; it's a travesty of a mockery of a sham of a mockery of a travesty of two mockeries of a sham. I move for a mistrial." Allen's bumbling, stuttering, **nebbish** persona is itself a throwback to the **schlemiels** and **schleppers** that populated the **shtetls** of Eastern Europe. No similarly rich fund of humor has emerged from the Jews of Western Europe or the Middle East.

Yiddish humor, like the language itself, is characterized by irony, wryness, self-mockery, and gentle sarcasm. It is a humor developed in the confined and repressed environment of small East European villages and communities where Jews suffered for centuries from hostile Slavic neighbors and governments. This is the milieu of the **shnorer** or professional beggar, the **luftmentsh** or ineffectual dreamer, the **leydikgeyer** or perennial idler, the luckless **shlimazl**, the **shadkhn** or matchmaker, and the panoply of community functionaries that included the town rabbi, the town cantor, the **shames** or sexton, the **shoykhet** or ritual slaughterer, the **moyl** or circumciser, the **noged** or rich man, the **melamed** or religious teacher, and so on and on. Such an ensemble of stereotypes, found in every town and **shtetl**, provided rich fodder for countless humorous stories and anecdotes, as those mined and popularized by folk writers like Sholom Aleichem and Isaac Leib Peretz.

Comedian, actor, and director Woody Allen, 1971: quintessential roll-up of Yiddish humorous types—nebbish, schlemiel, schlepper. (© Hulton-Deutsch Collection/Corbis)

***

A shnorer, who regularly received a meal in a noged's house, showed up one day for dinner accompanied by a young man. The two walked into the dining room and sat down at the table.

"Who is this young man?" the rich man asked.

"He's my new son-in-law," the shnorer replied, "and I have agreed to provide him with bread and board for the first year."

***

A shnorer comes into a businessman's office and asks him for a handout. "Have pity," he says, "for a poor shoemaker whose family is on the verge of starvation."

"Seems to me," says the businessman, "that you came to me last week and presented yourself as a carpenter, not a shoemaker. Isn't that true?"

"True, true," says the shnorer, "but who can in these bad times support himself from just one job?"

***

Certain other types were derived from the character attributed to the inhabitants of particular towns, provinces, and regions. For example, a **Litvak** or Lithuanian Jew was invariably depicted as skeptical, shrewd, and logical; a **Galitsianer** or Galician Jew (inhabitant of a region in East Central Europe) was considered temperamental and hard to please; a **Khelmer** or **Khelmite** (a Jew of Khelm, a city in Poland) was considered a gullible simpleton or fool, and humorous stories about so-called **Khelmer Khakhomim** (wise men of Khelm) are widespread in Yiddish folklore.

***

Two wise men of Khelm are talking. Says one to the other: "I'll visit you tomorrow at noon. But if it will be raining at noon, I'll come to you in the evening."

"What if it will rain in the evening?"

"Then I'll come at noon."

***

A Litvak got **farblondzhet** one day and ended up in Khelm. Walking on the street, he sees two big Khelmites dragging a horse. "Where are you dragging him?" he asks the two men.

"To the attic," came the answer. "We have to feed the horse, and the hay and oats are in the attic."

The Litvak broke out laughing. "You stupid Khelmites!" he exclaimed. "You can bring the feed down to the horse, why are you **shleping** the poor animal up to the attic?"

That was a mistake. The Khelmites were so insulted by his calling them stupid that they left the horse alone and instead dragged the Litvak off to the jail, where they charged him with slander.

As he sat in the jailhouse, the Litvak figured out a way to escape. He said to the guard: "Listen, Reb **Yid**, I'm very hungry. Here, take these four kopecks and bring us a couple of fresh rolls we can share."

As soon as the guard left, the Litvak took off. But he was spotted running out of town, and was caught at the town's outskirts and hauled back to jail. This time, the guard was warned to stay put in the jailhouse and not leave it for any reason whatever.

Sure enough, an hour later the Litvak tried to trick him again. "Listen, Reb Yid, I'm really hungry this time. Please take these four kopecks and buy us a couple of fresh rolls we can share."

The guard gave a smile and answered: "Hey, you Litvak smart-aleck! You take me for a fool? You're not going to trick me again! I'm not budging from this jailhouse, see? If you want to have fresh rolls, you'll have to go yourself to the bakery!"

***

The hostility between **Hasidim** and **Misnagdim** (opponents of Hasidism), and not infrequently between rival Hasidic sects, also generated many jokes and anecdotes, as did the conflict between the **maskilim** (adherents of Haskalah or Jewish Enlightenment) and traditional Jews. Other types included the **badkhonim** or professional jesters who entertained at weddings, the *Purimshpilers* who staged humorous plays on the holiday of Purim, and the obligatory town fools and drunkards who provided merriment to alleviate the harsh life endured by shtetl Jews. Two legendary jokesters and pranksters of the 1700s were Hershele Ostropolyer and Motke Khabad. Hershele lived by begging as he wandered through Podolia, Poland, mingling with the Hasidim of the region. Motke Khabad traveled in the Northeast, spending much time in Vilna (Vilnius), the capital of Lithuania.

***

Someone asked Hershele Ostropolyer: "How are you doing?"

He answered: "Good."

"What do you mean, good?"

"I am good and hungry, and the wife is good and sick."

***

Hershele was known for his fondness for liquor. He used to say: "When I drink, I become a different person. And this different person, naturally, also wants a drink...."

On his deathbed, however, he surprised everybody by asking for a pitcher of water. "Why are you surprised," he said. "Don't you know that before death one has to make up with one's worst enemy?"

***

Motke Khabad had also a weakness for the bottle. The Vilna rabbi once scolded him: "Why do you drink? You have, **kanehore**, a wife with four little children!"

Answered Motke: "I drink because I want to drown in liquor all my troubles."

"So why haven't your troubles drowned by now?"

"Rabbi, they know how to swim!"

***

Motke once ate a sumptuous meal at a restaurant. As he was about to leave, the proprietor informed him that the meal cost two rubles. Since Motke did not even have a kopeck in his pocket, he told the proprietor:

"I am from out of town. Would you be good enough to tell me what one has to pay in the local court for slapping someone in the face?"

"I think it's five rubles."

"In that case," said Motke, "give me two slaps and I'll take three rubles in change."

***

The literature on Jewish (read "Yiddish") humor has been extensive, but almost all of it was published in the last century. Perhaps the earliest collection of Yiddish jokes was *Vitsn un shpitsn oder anekdotn* (Jokes and Wiles or Anecdotes), published in Vilna in 1875 by the Yiddish writer Isaac Meir Dick (1814–1893). Sigmund Freud, in his famous book, *Jokes and their Relation to the Unconscious* (1905), says this about Jewish humor: "I do not know whether there are many other instances of a people making fun to such a degree of its own character." In the 1930s and 1940s, the Polish-born folklorist Immanuel Olsvanger (1888–1961) collected and popularized Yiddish jokes in such books as *Royte Pomerantsn* (Red Oranges), published in 1935, and republished in English in 1965 with the subtitle *How to Laugh in Yiddish*.

A serious study of classic Jewish humor is Richard Raskin's *Life is Like A Glass of Tea* (1992, Aarhus University Press). In it the author, using the method initiated by Freud, analyzes six classic Jewish jokes and their variations, devoting a chapter to each. Here are four of the most commonly encountered types, reduced to their essentials, providing further insight into the workings of Yiddish humor.

1. *The Rabbinic Judgment joke*. A man comes with his wife to the rabbi to ask for a divorce. After hearing the man's side of the story, the rabbi says to him, "You're right."

He then asks the woman to tell her side of the story. When she is finished, the rabbi says to her: "You're right." At this point the rabbi's wife, who overheard him, shouts: "How can this be? Both of them couldn't be right!" To which the rabbi, after a moment's thought, answers: "You're right, too!"

2. *The Man versus God joke*. A man orders a pair of pants from a tailor. Six weeks pass before the tailor delivers the pants. Incensed, the man rebukes him: "It took God only six days to create the world, and you it takes six weeks to make a pair of pants!" "True," answers the tailor, "but just look at these pants. And then look at the world."

3. *The Ten Commandments joke*. Before approaching the Jews, God asked the Egyptians if they would accept His commandments. When they heard the commandment against killing, they said to God, "No,

## Matchmaker, Matchmaker, Make Me a Match...

Matchmaking is probably the oldest Jewish profession. According to folklore, from the time God matched up Adam with Eve, He has been arranging marriages on earth. Hence the saying, "marriages are made in heaven." But God also appointed helpers in this job, and these are your everyday matchmakers or marriage brokers.

The Yiddish word for a matchmaker is **shatkhn** (also spelled **shadkhn**), and Yiddish is replete with sayings and stories about matchmakers (**shatkhonim** or **shadkhonim** in Yiddish). Two favorite sayings are:

A shatkhn muz zayn a ligner.
*A matchmaker must be a liar.*

Bay a shatkhn iz nito keyn miese kale.
*With a matchmaker there's no homely bride.*

A female matchmaker is a **shatkhnte** in Yiddish. Perhaps the most famous shatkhnte in modern times was Yente the Matchmaker in the film version of *Fiddler on the Roof*. The part of Yente was memorably played by the Yiddish actress Molly Picon.

But traditionally most Jewish marriage brokers are males, and stories and jokes about them abound in Yiddish folklore.

***

A shatkhn once took an eligible bachelor to meet a young woman whom he had praised to the skies. As soon as the two were introduced, the bachelor pulled the broker aside and, barely containing his fury, whispered:

"What kind of **shtik** are you pulling? This woman is not only ugly, but is cross-eyed and walks with a limp!"

"It's all right," the shatkhn answered. "You don't have to whisper. She's also hard of hearing."

not for us." God then asked the Babylonians. When they heard the commandment against stealing, they too said "No." After shopping around some more, God finally asked the Jews if they would accept His commandments. "How much do they cost?" asked the Jews. "They cost nothing," said God. "I'm giving them away free." "In that case," said the Jews, "we'll take ten."

4. *The Ultimate Jewish Mother joke*. A little boy and his mother are walking along the beach when suddenly a huge wave sweeps the boy into the sea. The mother starts wailing to God and a minute later another wave miraculously washes the boy ashore. The mother looks at her son and then, frowning, looks up to heaven and says, "Nu? So where's his hat?"

At the end of the book, Raskin cites several commentators who try to define the term "Jewish joke." One commentator, for example, defines a Jewish joke as one which would be pointless if the Jewishness of the character were removed. The author rejects this as well as some other definitions on various grounds and suggests his own definition. Unfortunately, all the definitions fail to account for the one distinctive element in these jokes. And that is the historical fact that all of these jokes—and most of the ones to which the name "Jewish" is attached—sprang into the world's consciousness from the East European Jewish experience and through the medium of the Yiddish language. Once we accept the idea that these jokes are *Yiddish* jokes, we can reexamine and reinterpret them in the light of the special circumstances that brought about their creation.

This brings us back to the characteristics of Yiddish humor and the fact that a joke, in order to be classified as a Yiddish joke, must include some element that indicates its East European Ashkenazi origin. Each of the four classic jokes cited above contains at least one such element, and the same can be said for the remaining two classic jokes in Richard Raskin's study. Briefly, the other two jokes are exemplified by (1) the famous self-deprecating remark (often attributed to Groucho Marx) "I wouldn't want to belong to any club that would have someone like me as a member," and (2) the cryptic last words of the dying rabbi, "Life is like a glass of tea," that makes his disciples insist that he explain before dying the mystery behind the seemingly profound remark, to which the rabbi, with his last ounce of energy, replies, "Very well, so life is *not* like a glass of tea."

As these classic or standard jokes indicate, the genius of Yiddish humor lies chiefly in its absurd and paradoxical juxtaposition of contradictory elements. In a normal world, no rabbi would take the impossible position that both a plaintiff and a defendant are equally right; in a normal world, no one in his right mind would compare the making of a pair of trousers with the creation of the world; and in a normal world, no mother whose child's life has been miraculously spared would give a hang about his losing a hat.

And that is just the point: the life of Jews in the millennium-old Ashkenazi Diaspora culminating in the shtetls of Eastern Europe was anything but normal. The crusades, the blood libels, the shtetls and the ghettos, the Chmielnicki massacres of the 1600s, the rise and fall of false Messiahs, the growth of sectarianism, the struggle between new competing ideologies (Hasidism, Haskalah, Reform), and the menacing specter of modern, race-based anti-Semitism that ended in the Holocaust—all of these gave no respite or peace to the Jewish masses. The humor they created reflected the abnormality of their lives by its distortions of logic, fact, and reality. It is a humor of contradiction, confrontation, and denial.

In normal conversation, a question calls forth an answer. But in Yiddish humor, it often calls forth another question. As the joke goes: A Gentile once asked a Jew, "Why do Jews always answer a question with another question?" To which the Jew replied, "Why do you want to know? And who says this is so? And anyway, why shouldn't we answer a question with another question?"

A question, in Yiddish humor, can be wielded as a deadly weapon, hence probably its frequent use. Consider the following exchange:

> Mrs. Garfinkel: "What a wonderful dinner, Mrs. Finkelstein! Your cheese blintzes are so delicious I've eaten four of them!"
>
> Mrs. Finkelstein: "Actually it's seven, darling, but who's counting?"

The prolific writer Isaac Asimov once confessed that he was so enamored of this punchline that he used it whenever someone cited too small a figure for the number of books he had written. After stating the actual number of his published works (over 500), he would modestly add, "but who's counting?" The line, he said, always got a laugh.

## Yidisher Kop: Goldwynisms and Other Mind-Benders

**Der yidisher kop**—literally, the Jewish head—works in mysterious ways. Yiddish has countless down-to-earth but semi-cryptic expressions that are like koans to make you wake up and think: **Ikh hob im in der linker piate** (I have him in the left heel), meaning I don't care a whit about him; **Ikh darf es hobn vi a lokh in kop** (I need it like a hole in the head); and sayings like **Farvos iz keyn kashe nit un vorem iz keyn terets nit** (*Why* is not a question, and *because* is not an answer), and **Oyb mayn mume volt gehat reder volt zi geven a tramvay** (If my aunt had wheels she'd be a trolley car).

Some of the best-known mindbenders originated from the yidisher kop of Samuel Goldwyn (1882–1974), the famous Hollywood mogul who never lost his Yiddish accent and mindset. Like a Yiddish Yogi Bera ahead of his time, Goldwyn became famous for sayings like "Gentlemen, include me out" (on quitting an organization) and "A verbal contract isn't worth the paper it's written on." Here are some other classic Goldwynisms, which demonstrate the enduring and charming sarcasm of this famous Yiddish wit:

Don't pay any attention to the critics—don't even ignore them!

I can answer you in two words: im-possible.

Our comedies are not to be laughed at.

I don't want any yes-men around me. I want everybody to tell me the truth even if it costs them their jobs.

I read part of the book all the way through.

If I could drop dead right now, I'd be the happiest man alive.

Never let that bastard back in my office again—unless I need him.

Next time I want to send an idiot on some errand, I'll go myself.

Spare no expense to make everything as economic as possible.

The wide screen will only make bad films twice as bad.

They didn't release that film; it escaped.

We're overpaying him, but he's worth it.

Why should people go out and pay to see bad movies when they can stay at home and see bad television for nothing?

But asking questions goes far back in Jewish history. In a sense, it is the quintessence of Jewishness. The Talmud is replete with questions posed by the sages, many of which are left unanswered with a one-word Aramaic squelch, *teyku*, meaning "let it stand" (traditionally the word is seen as an acronym for the phrase "Elijah the prophet will come and answer the questions"). It is as if the sages felt that if it is a good question, why ruin it with a bad answer?

The most famous part of the Passover seder, or order of service, is what is known as the Four Questions (in Yiddish, **di fir kashes**). The Four Questions, usually asked by the youngest person at the table, begins with the question, "Why is this night different from all other nights?" A well-known joke relating to the Four Questions goes as follows:

> Sam Rabinowitz, a British subject, has achieved prominence in business and is consequently awarded an honorary knighthood by the Queen. After receiving the award, Sam steps forward, shakes the Queen's hand, and loudly says, "Oy, it's such a pleasure to make your acquaintance, Queen. You look just like in your *pitchers*. And how's the family? The grandchildren? And his majesty the Prince?" The Queen, speechless at first, looks about helplessly and finally cries out: "Why is this knight different from all other knights?"

The story doesn't end here, though. According to one version, when Sam hears her say this, he breaks into a big smile and exclaims, "well, whadya know, even the Queen knows di fir kashes!"

The longest variant of the "who's counting?" joke—with, incidentally, a different punchline—not only supports the notion that a Yiddish joke would be pointless if the Jewishness of the characters were removed, but tops it by being so thoroughly grounded in Jewish history and Yiddish culture that it couldn't possibly be told in any but a Jewish context. It goes as follows:

> During the Chanukah festival, when it is customary to eat potato latkes, a Hasidic Jew received in his house as a guest of honor the scion of a great Hasidic dynasty. When the host's wife placed on the table a large plateful of sizzling **latkes**, the distinguished guest took one, recited the appropriate blessing, and ate it. He then took another latke, and exclaimed, "I am taking this latke to recall the One God in heaven and upon earth!"

> After promptly consuming it, he took two latkes and exclaimed, "I'm taking two to recall Moses and Aaron!" He then took three and exclaimed, "I'm taking these three to recall the patriarchs, Abraham, Isaac, and Jacob! He then took four and exclaimed "I'm taking four to recall the matriarchs Sarah, Rebecca, Rachel, and Leah!"
>
> When he had reached the number twelve and exclaimed, "I'm taking twelve latkes to recall the twelve tribes of Israel!" the distraught host ran into the kitchen and shouted to his wife, "Quick, Miriam, remove the plate from the table! If you don't hurry, our guest may recall the six hundred thousand Jews who went out of Egypt!"

To sum up, Yiddish humor is a dark humor that thrives on contradiction and paradox. It is the opposite of the wholesome but insipid Norman Rockwell-type of humor one finds in the humor pages of the *Reader's Digest*. Yiddish humor is spicy, sharp, and not to everyone's taste. However, it has had a great influence on the routines of many American Jewish comedians like Groucho Marx, Fanny Brice, Molly Picon, George Burns, Milton Berle, Sid Caesar, Mel Brooks, Mort Sahl, Lenny Bruce, Woody Allen, Jackie Mason, Fran Drescher, and Jerry Seinfeld. It is worth noting that all of these—and many other—American Jewish comedians are of East European Ashkenazi descent. Their droll, pungent humor is in direct line with that of the characters in the stories of Sholom Aleichem and Peretz, and ultimately with the motley group of jesters and pranksters, like Hershele Ostropolyer and Moshe Khabad, who made the huddled masses in the European shtetls laugh through their tears.

## Yiddlish—Words That Sound Yiddish (But Never Were)

English words ending with *-el, -al, -le,* or *-il(e)* are Yiddlish—Y-i-d-d-l-i-s-h, not Yinglish or Yiddish (please pay attention)—words that sound Yiddish, but are not, and never were. For example, the English words *axle, facial, pestle, fossil, missile*. Compare them with Yiddish **bisl** (little), **pitsl** (small bit), and **shisl** (bowl). A Yiddlish word like *thistle* (prickly plant) could (but should not) be confused with Yiddish **tishl** (a small table).

Words ending with *-ish* are Yiddlish, too. Common examples are *peckish, raffish, sniffish, fetish,* which belong to the same species as Yiddish **goyish** (Gentile), **balebatish** (genteel), and **lekish** (dummy). Any word pronounced with <-ish>, no matter how you spell it, is part of this group. For example, *artificial, official, superficial* are all pronounced with the ending <-'fish-el>, which corresponds to the Yiddish **fishl** (small fish).

The Yiddlish word *famished* is a close kin to the Yiddish word **farmisht** (mixed up, confused). Note that both words have *-ish* in them.

Other noteworthy Yiddlish words include:

*bearish*. Compare the Yiddish male name **Berish**.

*bobble, bubble*. Compare Yiddish **bobele, bubele** (dear little grandma).

*Bubba*. Compare Yiddish **bobe** (grandmother).

*cactus*. Compare Yiddish **kakt** (excretes), **bakakt** (befouled).

*numbnuts, numnutz* (a numskull). Compare Yiddish **hotseplots** (hicktown).

*pish* (exclamation of contempt). Compare Yiddish **pishn, pishekhts, pisher** (piss; pisser).

*pots*. Compare Yiddish **pots** (fool; literally, penis).

*tumult*. Compare Yiddish **tumler** (literally, noisemaker) and **tsetumelt** (confused, disturbed).

# The Heart of Yiddish Vocabulary

## What Every Lover of Yiddish Needs to Know

Here is a list of popular Yiddish words and phrases that every admirer or lover of this vibrant language wants to know—from **bris** to **cheder**, **bar mitzvah**, **chuppah**, **peyes**, **sachel**, and more. Many of these words have become part of general English; for example **bagel**, **borscht**, **shul** (and are covered in more detail in "Yinglish 101"). Others, like **bobe mayse**, **hak a tshaynik**, and **kadokhes**, are borderline Yiddishisms in English, known well by those "in the know," but also gradually making inroads among the uninitiated.

**A Note on Spelling.** Where the English spelling of a word or phrase differs from the romanized Yiddish spelling, the romanized Yiddish is shown in square brackets immediately following the accepted English spelling; for example: ***chutzpah** [khutspe]. In addition, the asterisk * that precedes and highlights the English spelling denotes (1) those Yiddish-origin words that have entered mainstream English and now appear in English dictionaries; for example, ***chutzpah** [khutspe], ***bialy**, ***bris**, ***klutzy**, ***schmo**, and (2) those words that are still mid-stream in the vocabulary of Yiddish-English speakers, but which have an accepted English spelling; for example, ***bonditt** [bandit], ***bobkes** [bubkes]. The remainder of the popular Yiddish words or phrases *not* indicated by an asterisk are the romanized Yiddish spellings of words that generally have *not* yet entered the vocabulary of mainstream English; for example, **batamt**, **moyshe kapoyer**. But if you overhear Yiddish-English speakers, they are words you are bound to hear and that will tickle your fancy.

In the standard system of romanization for Yiddish, each letter or fixed combination of letters represents a single sound, and there are no "silent" letters. For example, the word **bobe** has two syllables, <ˈboh-beh>, and does *not* rhyme with English *robe*. The two-letter combination "kh" stands for the final guttural sound of English *loch* and German *ach*. The three-letter combination "tsh" stands for the sound of "ch" in *chin* and *much*. The combination "zh" stands for the sound of "z" in *azure*. The diphthong "ay" rhymes with the sound in *guy*; "ey" rhymes with the sound in *day*; and "oy" rhymes with the sound in *boy*. (For more on the romanization of Yiddish, see "Yiddish Basics" and "The YIVO Transcription Scheme" at the end of the book.)

**alevay** *adverb*. If only it should happen; would that it be so. Also spelled **halevay**.

**alte moyd** *noun*. A spinster (literally, old maid).

**alter bokher** *noun*. A bachelor (literally, old youth).

**alter kaker** *noun, vulgar*. An old geezer, especially a lecherous old man (literally, old shitter).

**alter teyrekh** *noun*. An old fool (literally, old Terah).

**azes ponim** *noun*. Impudent fellow; wise guy.

***bagel** [beygl] *noun*. Doughnut-shaped roll.

**balebos** *noun*; *plural* **balebatim**. Head of household; proprietor; congregant.

**baleboste** *noun*. Mistress of household; hostess; landlady.

***bar mitzvah** [bar-mitsve] (*often caps*) *noun*. Thirteen-year-old boy or his coming of age ceremony.

***bas mitzvah** [bas-mitsve] (*often caps*) *noun*. Twelve-year-old girl or her coming of age ceremony.

**batamt** *adjective*. Tasty, delicious; cute, sweet.

**batlen** *noun*; *plural* **batlonim**. Idler, loafer.

**beheyme** *noun*. Dumb animal; fool (literally, head of cattle, cow).

***bialy** *noun*. Flat baked roll with a depression in the center topped with onions.

*__blintze__ [blintse, blints] *noun, Jewish Cookery*. A pancake or crepe wrapped around a filling of cheese, fruit, etc. Also spelled **blintz**.

**bobe** *noun*. Grandmother.

**bobe mayse** *noun*. An old-wives' tale; fable; tall tale.

### bobe mayse

A phrase often used to dismiss a story—"That's a bobe mayse!"—meaning that it's an old wives' tale, a fable, a myth, a tall story. It is often translated as a "grandmother's tale," since the Yiddish word for grandmother is "bobe." This itself is a bobe mayse. The phrase was originally **bove mayse**, and it meant "the story of Bove." Bove was the Yiddish name of a knight, Buovo d'Antona, the hero of a popular Medieval Italian romance of chivalry based on the English chivalric hero Sir Bevis of Hampton. In 1507, a grammarian called Elye Bokher translated the Italian romance into Yiddish, using the poetic form of ottava rima, and entitling it *Bove deantone*. His book came to be widely known as the Bove-bukh. Over the years, as the stories of Bove's heroics described in the Bove-bukh were popularized by Jewish minstrels traveling across Europe, the phrase bove mayse, meaning a "Bove story," became transmuted by folk etymology into bobe mayse (literally, grandmother's tale). The phrase stuck, especially since the original tales of knights and damsels were, indeed, bobe mayses.

*__bobkes__ [bubkes] *noun*. Triflings, chicken feed, nothing (literally, goat or sheep dung).

*__bonditt__ [bandit] <bahn-ˈdeet *or* bon-ˈdeet> *noun*. A charming rascal or rogue (literally, bandit, robber).

*__borscht__ [borsht] *noun, Jewish Cookery*. Beet soup.

*__borscht circuit__ (sometimes caps). Also called **borscht belt**. Jewish resort area in the Catskills of New York.

*__boychik__ [boytshik] *noun, Slang*. Young fellow. Also spelled **boychick**.

*__bris__ *noun*. Jewish circumcision ceremony.

*__bubele__ *noun*. Darling, sweetheart. Also spelled **bubeleh**.

**bulvan** *noun*. Coarse, rude person, boor.

## Misconceptions About Yiddish

Is Yiddish really a language? Isn't it the same as German? Isn't it the same as Hebrew? Misconceptions about Yiddish abound. Here are the three most common ones clarified:

**Misconception #1.** Yiddish is not really a language, but a kind of jargon, without grammar and without rules of spelling and pronunciation.

**Fact:** Yiddish is as much a language as English, German, or Russian, having its own unique alphabet, sound system, and grammatical structure. Of course, there are dialectal varieties of Yiddish, just as there are in most languages.

**Misconception #2.** Yiddish is a language developed during the long European diaspora. With the revival of Hebrew as the national language of Jews, there is no longer a raison d'être for Yiddish and we should stop encouraging its use.

**Fact:** Even during the European diaspora, Hebrew was hardly forgotten. It was **loshn-koydesh** (the sacred tongue), the language of prayer, study, song, and scholarship. Yiddish, in contrast, was the Jewish vernacular, the language of everyday communication, the vehicle by which Jews interacted at home, at school, in business, and in the synagogue. Such a "natural" language has deep emotional content to its speakers, who use it as naturally as we use English. Besides, there is no reason why Hebrew and Yiddish cannot coexist, as indeed they do in Israeli cities like Benai Berak and Jerusalem.

**Misconception #3.** Yiddish is actually a form or dialect of German and the claim that it is entirely different from German is difficult to substantiate.

**Fact:** This canard amounts to about the same as saying that Italian is a form or dialect of Latin. No one denies that Yiddish is related to German; so are English, Dutch, and Danish. But just as English developed from a core of Anglian and Saxon dialects, so Yiddish emerged from a confluence of Middle High German dialects. Yet almost from its start Yiddish was written in the Hebrew alphabet and still remains the only Germanic language to be written in a non-Roman script. Yiddish became a distinctive language through a complex fusion of German, Hebrew, Aramaic, and Slavic elements.

*__challah__ [khale] <ʹkhah-leh> *noun, Jewish Cookery*. Traditional white Sabbath bread. Also spelled **challeh**, **hallah**.

*__Chanukah__ [khanuke] *noun*. The Feast of Lights. Also spelled **Hannukah**.

*__chasene__ [khasene] <ʹkhah-seh-neh> *noun*. Jewish wedding.

**chazer** [khazer] <ʹkhah-zer> *noun*. A glutton or **fresser**.

*__chazerai__ [khazeray] <khah-zeh-ʹrye> *noun*. Swill, filth; a mess; trashy food (literally, pig's feed). Also spelled **chazzerei**, **chozerei**.

*__chazzen__ [khazn] <ʹkhah-zen> *noun*; *plural* **chazonim** [khazonim] <khah-ʹzoh-neem>. A Jewish cantor.

*__cheder__ [kheyder] <ʹkhey-der> *noun*. Traditional religious elementary school.

*__chochom__ [khokhem] <ʹkhoh-khem> *noun*. A smart or wise person (often used ironically).

*__cholent__ [tsholnt] <ʹchoh-lent> *noun, Jewish Cookery*. A baked dish of meat, beans, and potatoes served on the Sabbath.

*__choson__ [khosn] <ʹkhoh-sen> *noun*. The bridegroom at a Jewish wedding (**chasene**).

**chotchke** *noun*. See **tchotchke**.

*__chremzel__ [khremzl] <ʹkhrem-zel> *noun, Jewish Cookery*; *plural* **chremzlach** [khremzlekh] <ʹkhrem-zlahkh>. Fried potato pancake, especially for Passover.

**chreyn** *noun*. See **khreyn**.

*__chuppah__ [khupe] <ʹkhoop-eh> *noun*. A wedding canopy or wedding ceremony. Also spelled **huppah**.

*__chutzpah__ [khutspe] <ʹhoots-peh *or* ʹkhoots-peh> *noun*. Impudence, brazen gall, nerve. Also spelled **chutzpa**.

**dafke** *adverb*. Deliberately; specifically; purposely, as in "I **dafke** go to this hotel on Pesach and no other because it serves the best **kneydlekh**."

*__daven__ [davenen] *verb*. To pray, especially the regular daily prayers.

**dibbuk** *noun*. See **dybbuk**.

*__dreck__ [drek] *noun*. Dung, excrement; worthless stuff, junk, trash.

*__dreidel__ [dreydl; *plural* dreydlekh] *noun*; *plural* **dreidels**. Spinning top, used especially on Chanukah.

*__dybbuk__ [dibek; *plural* dibukim] *noun*, *Jewish Folklore*; *plural* **dybbuks**. Evil spirit or soul of a dead person that enters a living person's body. Also spelled **dibbuk**.

**emes** *noun*. Truth. —*adjective*. True, real.

*__eppes__ [epes] *noun*. Something. —*adverb*. Somewhat.

**erev** *preposition*. On the eve of (Sabbath or holiday).

*__eruv__ [eyrev; *plural* eyruvim] *noun*; *plural* **eruvs**. Enclosure created to permit carrying objects on the street on Sabbath.

**farbisn** *adjective*. Embittered; mean; stubborn; hostile.

**farblondzhet** *adjective*. Lost; wandering aimlessly; bewildered. Also spelled **farblondjet**.

**farbrengen** *verb*. To spend time in company.

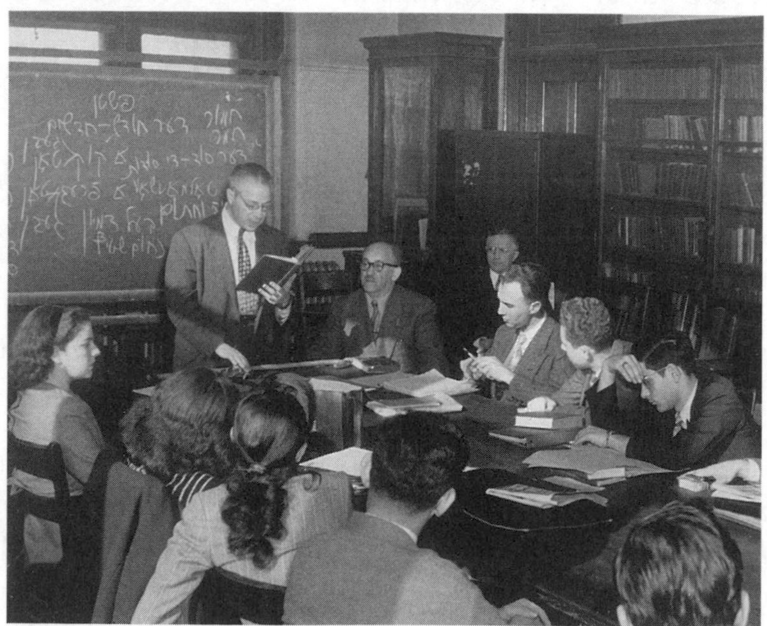

Max Weinreich (1894–1969), leading Yiddish linguist and author, teaching Yiddish at City College, New York, 1947. (YIVO Institute for Jewish Research)

***farfel** [farfl] *noun plural, Jewish Cookery*. Crisp fried pellets of matzo or noodles.

**fargesn** *adjective*. Forgotten.

**farklemt** *adjective*. All choked up; about to cry.

**farmisht** *adjective*. Mixed up; befuddled.

**farpatshket** *adjective*. Messed up.

**farshlofener** *noun*. A sluggish, sleepy person.

**farshtunken** *adjective*. Stinking.

**farts** *noun; plural* **ferts**. A fart. —*verb*, **fartsn**.

**fartshadet** *adjective*. Distracted, dazed.

***fartootst** [fartutst] *adjective*. Preoccupied; confused. Also spelled **fartutst**.

***faygele** [feygele] *noun, Slang, generally considered offensive*. A homosexual (literally, little bird).

***flanken** *noun, Jewish Cookery*. Boiled or stewed short ribs of beef.

**fleishig** [fleyshik] *adjective*. Made of meat or a meat product.

***fonfe** [fonfen] *verb*. To speak through the nose; hem and haw.

**frask** *noun*. A smack or slap in the face.

***fress** [fresn] *verb*. To stuff oneself on food; eat like a pig. —*noun*, ***fresser** [freser].

**frum** *adjective*. Religious; pious.

***futz around** *verb*. To mess around; screw around.

***Galitzianer** [galitsyaner] *noun*. A Jew from Galicia, region of Poland.

**ganef** *noun; plural* **ganovim**. A thief; *figuratively* a rascal, rogue. See **goniff**.

**gazlen** *noun; plural* **gazlonim**. A robber or swindler.

***gefilte fish** *noun, Jewish Cookery*. Chopped fish mixed with matzo meal and egg, cooked in broth and usually served cold.

***gelt** *noun*. Money; cash.

**genug** *adjective*. Enough.

**geshmak** *adjective*. Tasty, delicious.

**geshrey** *noun*. A shout or scream.

**get** *noun*; *plural* **gittin**. A bill of divorce.

**gevald** *noun*. A hue and cry; alarm; emergency. —*interjection*. Help! Also spelled **gevalt**.

**gezunt** *adjective*. Health, especially good health.

*__gilgul__ [gilgl; *plural* gilgulim] *noun*, *Jewish Folklore*; *plural* **gilguls**. A reincarnation; person or animal that is the incarnation of a dead being. Also spelled **gilgl**.

*__glatt kosher__ [glat kosher] *noun*. Strictly kosher.

### glatt kosher

The Yiddish word glat has two meanings: (1) smooth, as in a **glat tsungl**, "a smooth tongue," and (2) plain, as in **glat azoy**, "plainly, just so, for no reason."

Which of the two meanings fits into the phrase glat kosher (spelled in English *glatt kosher*)? Apparently neither, since the ordinary meaning of the phrase is "strictly kosher, ritually flawless." Not true. The Yiddish phrase derives from the first meaning, "smooth." According to Jewish law, a flaw (such as growth or perforation) found on the lungs of an animal after slaughter may render it **treyf** or unkosher. However, while there are flaws that are considered insignificant and are usually disregarded, a strict application of the law requires that the lungs be perfectly smooth, without the slightest irregularity. Hence smooth lungs indicate that the animal and its meat are strictly kosher. In general, meat may be either kosher or glatt kosher. If it's neither, it's—alas—treyf. And if you ask a rabbi's opinion about some flanken or schnitzel, the chances are it's going to be treyf. So better not ask.

*__glitch__ *noun*. A defect or bug in a system; a slip or skid. Also spelled **glitsh**.

*__golem__ [goylem] *noun*, *Jewish Folklore*. An artificial creature formed from clay; figuratively, a clumsy fellow, dummy.

*__gonnif__ [ganef] *noun*, *Slang*. Thief, rascal. Perferred English spelling for **ganef**.

***goy** (*feminine,* **goye**) *noun; plural* **goyim**. A non-Jew.

***goyish** *adjective.* Non-Jewish.

**grade** <'grah-deh> *adverb.* In reality; as a matter of fact, as in "I'm **grade** not interested in classical music and prefer pop."

***haimish** [heymish] *adjective.* Homelike; cozy. Also spelled **heimish**.

***hak a tshaynik** [hakn a tshaynik] *phrase.* To babble or nag constantly; (literally, to bang on a teakettle).

**halevay** *adverb.* See **alevay**.

***hamantash** [homentash; *plural* homentashn] *noun, Jewish Cookery; plural,* **hamantashen**. A triangular pastry with filling, eaten on Purim.

**hoyker** *noun.* A hump on the back; hunchback.

**huppah** *noun.* See **chuppah**.

**kaddish** [kadesh; *plural,* kadeyshim] *noun.* Mourners' prayer.

### kaddish

The universal Jewish prayer recited by one who has lost a parent, a sibling, a spouse, or a child. It's an ancient Aramaic prayer (the word **kaddish** means "holy" in Aramaic) that has nothing to do with death, but simply exalts and sanctifies God. Sometime in the early Middle Ages the custom arose to have mourners recite it in the synagogue after certain prayers; thereafter the kaddish became permanently associated with bereavement. In Yiddish usage, a couple's son, especially a firstborn son, is also called a kaddish (Yiddish **kadesh**, or **kadeshl**, "little kaddish"), in allusion to the fact that he would someday recite the kaddish after the passing of his father or mother. This is a great comfort to the parents, and many often refer in Yiddish to their son as **mayn tayerer kadeshl**, "my dear little kaddish."

**kadokhes** *noun.* A fever or seizure; figuratively, something or somebody worthless.

**kalike** *noun.* A cripple or misfit.

***kallah** [kale] *noun.* A bride at a **chasene** (Jewish wedding).

**kapelye** *noun.* A musical band.

**kapore** *noun.* A scapegoat; figuratively, a sacrifice or atonement.

## *Jewish Daily Forward:* The Voice of Yiddish in America

For the vast number of Jewish immigrants who came to America at the turn of the 20th century, one newspaper stood out as a beacon of hope and information: the *Jewish Daily Forward*, shortened informally to the *Forward*, after the Yiddish name *Forverts*. Founded in 1897, the paper was the largest Yiddish-language daily in the United States and at its peak reached a circulation of 250,000.

Its founding editor, Abraham Cahan (1860–1951), was an important Yiddish writer and novelist (for example, *The Rise of David Levinsky*). All the founders were immigrant followers of the socialist leader, Eugene V. Debs, and the paper stood for social justice, defending the rights of the newly arriving Jewish immigrants. They were a poor, underrepresented group, and the *Forward* covered the issues of their lives. Countless stories and editorials were written championing their cause in Lower East Side ghettos and New York City politics.

The *Forward* also provided a forum for numerous Yiddish writers and during the 20th century published most of the masters of modern Yiddish literature. Isaac Bashevis Singer, the Nobel Laureate, got his start in America writing for the paper. Singer serialized most of his novels in the paper before they were translated and published as books. Elie Wiesel, another Nobel Laureate, also published in the *Forward*. The paper has also published the work of other contemporary Jewish writers including Philip Roth, Joseph Heller, Chaim Potok, and Saul Bellow (another Nobel Laureate in Literature). The Pulitzer Prize-winning Holocaust cartoon "novel" *Maus* by Art Spegelman was first serialized in the *Forward*.

A more recent mission of the *Forward* has been the preservation of Yiddish writing and culture destroyed by Nazism. As the number of Yiddish-speaking readers declined, the paper began publishing on a weekly basis in 1983. In 1990 it began an English version. With the large number of Russian immigrants coming to New York in recent decades, a Russian edition was also started.

Now over a hundred years old, the *Jewish Daily Forward* continues to be a messenger for Yiddish-speaking people and part of a vital thread that keeps the language alive.

Source: www.forward.com; yiddish.forward.com

**kapote** *noun*. A long coat; kaftan.

**kapoyer** *adjective, adverb*. Reverse; topsy-turvy. See **moyshe kapoyer**.

***kasha** [kashe] *noun, Jewish Cookery*. Cereal or porridge, especially when made from buckwheat groats.

**khap** [khapn] *verb*. To catch; grab; snatch; grasp. You can **khap** a snooze, a bus, or a **ganef**.

**khazer** *noun*. See **chazer**.

**khazeray** *noun*. See **chazerai**.

**khnyok** *noun*. An unreasonable or narrow-minded person; a bigot.

**khreyn** *noun*. Horseradish. Also spelled **chreyn**.

***kibitz** [kibetsn] *verb*. To give unsolicited advice; meddle. —*noun*, **kibitzer** [kibetser].

**kile** *noun*. A hernia.

***kinder** *noun, plural*. Children. —*diminutive*, **kinderlekh**.

***kishke** *noun*. **1.** *Jewish Cookery*. Sausage casing stuffed with meat and spices. Also called **derma** or **stuffed derma**. Also spelled **kishka**. **2.** **kishkes** *plural, Slang*. Intestines; innards; guts.

***kittel** [kitl] *noun*. A man's white linen robe worn on Jewish holidays and solemn occasions.

Postcard with montage of mastheads of Yiddish newspapers in the United States, 1902–1907. (YIVO Institute for Jewish Research)

***klezmer** *noun (usually used attributively)*. **1.** Lively Yiddish folk music. **2.** *plural,* **klezmorim**. A band playing such music.

***klutz** [klots] *noun, Slang*. A dull, clumsy person; blockhead.

***klutzy** *adjective, Slang*; **klutzier**, **klutziest**. Like a klutz; clumsy —*noun*, ***klutziness**.

***knaidel** [kneydl] *noun, Jewish Cookery; plural* **knaidlach** [kneydlekh]. A dumpling made from matzo flour; matzo ball.

**knaker** <keh-ʹnock-er *or* keh-ʹnah-ker> *noun*. A big shot; wise guy.

**knipl** <keh-ʹnip-el> *noun*. Savings, nest egg (literally, a knot or money tied in a handkerchief).

***knish** <keh-ʹnish> *noun, Jewish Cookery*. A dumpling filled with cheese, potatoes, etc.

**kokhlefl** *noun*. A busybody (literally, cooking spoon).

**kop** *noun; plural,* **kep**. A head.

***kosher** *adjective*. **1.** Fit or permissible according to Jewish dietary laws **2.** *Slang*. Fit; satisfactory; legitimate.

***kreplach** [kreplekh] <ʹkrep-lekh> *noun plural, Jewish Cookery*. Triangular dumplings filled with meat, vegetables, etc. Also spelled **kreplech**.

***kugel** [kugl] *noun, Jewish Cookery*. A baked pudding made from potatoes, noodles, apples, etc.

***kvell** [kveln] *verb, Slang*. To be delighted; revel.

***kvetch** [kvetshn, kvetsh] *Slang, verb*. To complain; find fault; gripe. —*noun*. A habitual or perennial complainer; a **kvetcher** [kvetsher].

**kvitsh** *noun*. A shriek, scream, screech.

***landsman** *noun; plural,* **landsleit** [landslayt]. A fellow countryman or townsman; compatriot.

**landsmanshaft** *noun; plural,* **landsmanshaftn**. An association of **landsleit**.

***latke** *noun, Jewish Cookery*. A pancake fried in oil, popularly made from grated potatoes, especially for Chanukah.

***l'chaim** [lekhayim] *interjection*. To life! (a toast).

**lekekh** *noun, Jewish Cookery*. Cake, especially honeycake or spongecake.

**lekish** *noun*. A foolish or silly person; dummy.

**lemishke** *noun*. A simple, weak, or ineffectual person.

**leydikgeyer** *noun*. An idler, loafer (literally, empty walker).

***Litvak** *noun*. A native of Lithuania.

***lokshen** [lokshn] *noun, Jewish Cookery*. Noodles; as in **lokshen kugel**.

***lox** [laks] *noun*. Smoked salmon, usually eaten with bagel and cream cheese.

***macher** [makher] *noun*. Big shot; operator; doer.

**mame** *noun*. Mother; mom.

**mame-loshn** *noun*. The Yiddish language (literally, mother tongue).

***mamzer** *noun*. **1.** A bastard. **2.** A rascal or scoundrel. Also spelled **momzer**.

### mamzer

A mamzer is not a bastard, even though this is the usual translation given in books. At least, not exactly. Unless used as a coarse insult, the English word "bastard" means an illegitimate child, or one born to an unmarried mother. But in Yiddish, such a person is not considered illegitimate and not called a mamzer. In Yiddish, a mamzer is a child born of adultery or incest. So to call someone a mamzer in Yiddish is to charge his parents with a far more serious transgression than that of bringing him into the world without benefit of clergy. One therefore avoids using the word in Yiddish even as an insult; instead Yiddish uses the word playfully, to mean an impudent or devilish rascal or scoundrel, and even has several derivative words in this sense, **mamzerish** (devilishly cunning, very shrewd) and **mamzeray** (devilish or roguish action or trickery).

***matzo** [matse] *noun*. Unleavened bread, especially eaten on Passover. Also spelled **matzah, matzoh**.

**matzo brei** [matse brey] *noun, Jewish Cookery*. A dish of matzos and eggs, eaten for breakfast or as a snack.

***maven** [meyvn] *noun*. An expert or connoisseur. Also spelled **mavin**.

***mazel** [mazl] *noun*. Luck; fortune; destiny.

***mazel tov!** [mazl-tov] *phrase*. Congratulations! (Literally, Good luck!)

***megillah** [megile] *noun, Slang*. A long story Also spelled **megilla**.

### megillah

**Meaning a long, drawn-out story, this word derives from the Yiddish megile, where it means primarily a long letter or document, in allusion to the *megilas ester* (the scroll of Esther), referring to the Biblical book of Esther that is traditionally read in the synagogue from a parchment scroll on the festival of Purim. An extension of the term is found in the Yiddish phrase a gantse megile (a whole megillah) or a lange megile (a long megillah), meaning anything needlessly long or elaborate, such as a speech or lecture. In English, the phrase the *whole megillah* has come to mean "the whole thing," as in "I read the book and saw the movie, the whole megillah." Another, more recent, use in English is the phrase *big megillah*, meaning something or someone very big, or a big shot, as in "He thinks of himself as the big megillah in new technology."**

***mensch** [mentsh; *plural* mentshn] *noun*. A good person; a decent or trustworthy human being.

***meshuga** [meshuge] <meh-'shoo-geh> *adjective, Slang*. Out of one's mind; crazy. Also spelled **meshugga**.

***meshugana** [meshugene(r)] <meh-'shoo-geh-neh> *noun, Slang*. A crazy person; madman or madwoman. Also spelled **meshuggana**, **meshuggena**, **meshuggener**.

***meshugas** [meshugas] <meh-sheh-'gahs> *noun, Slang*. Something crazy; madness; craze. Also spelled **meshugaas**, **mishegas**.

**meshugoim** *noun plural*. Crazy people; lunatics.

**meydl** *noun*. A girl —*noun*, **meydele**. A little girl.

***mezuma** [mezumen] *noun, Slang*. Ready money; cash.

**mieskayt** *noun*. An ugly person or thing.

**milchig** [milkhik] *adjective*. Made of a dairy food or product.

**mise meshune** *phrase*. A bizarre, unnatural death.

***mishmash** *noun*. A mixture or hodgepodge; a mess. Also **mishmosh**.

***mishpocha** [mishpokhe] *noun*. A family, especially an extended family.

***mitzvah** [mitsve] *noun*. **1.** A commandment or precept. **2.** A good deed.

***mohel** [moyl] *noun*. A ritual circumciser.

**moyshe kapoyer**. **1.** *noun*. One who does everything backwards **2.** *adverb*. Backwards; topsy-turvy

### moyshe kapoyer

A moyshe kapoyer is one who does things backwards, the kind of **schlemiel** who puts the car in reverse when he means to put it in drive. He's also the fellow who deliberately or perversely buys a turkey the day after Thanksgiving. To do things moyshe kapoyer (or just kapoyer) is to do them ass-backwards. The original Yiddish term was **kapoyer** (*adverb*), derived from a Slavic word meaning reversed, topsy-turvy. The phrase moyshe kapoyer is an American Yiddish coinage, derived from the name of a dour and contrarian cartoon character created by the humorist B. Kovner in a series of cartoons that appeared during the 1920s in the *Forverts* (the *Jewish Daily Forward*). Kovner's coinage was influenced by the fact that the name **moyshe** (Moses) was already used in American Yiddish as a slangy synonym for an ignorant or boorish person, as well as in the derogatory personification of the common people **moyshe tokhes** (literally, Moses Bottom). Still, it was an inspired coinage that became permanently entrenched in Yiddish usage.

***naches** [nakhes] <ʹnah-khes> *noun*. Proud pleasure; delight and joy.

**nar** <nahr> *noun*; *plural* **naronim** <nah-ʹroh-neem>. A foolish person; a fool.

***nebbish** [nebish] *noun*, *Slang*. A pitiful or ineffectual person; sadsack. —*adjective*, **nebbishy**.

**nisl** *noun*; *plural* **nislekh**. A nut.

**nokhshleper** *noun*. Hanger-on, unwanted follower.

***noodge** [nudyen, nudzhen] *verb*. To nag, pester, or annoy. Also spelled **nudge**, **nudzh**. —*noun*. A pest or bore.

***nosh** [nashn, nash] *verb*. To nibble or snack. —*noun*. A nibble or snack.

***nosher** [nasher] *noun*. One who noshes a lot; a habitual eater.

***nosherei** [nasheray] *noun*. Food for snacking or nibbling; junk food.

***nu?** *interjection*. Well? So?

***nudge** *verb, noun*. See **noodge**.

***nudnik** *noun, Slang*. A pest, nag, or bore.

**nudzh** *noun, verb*. See **noodge**.

**ongeblozener** *noun*. A stuffed shirt (literally, puffed-up man).

***ongepotchket** [ongepatshket] *adjective*. Messed or muddled up.

**ongeshtopt** *adjective*. Stuffed; loaded, especially with money.

***oy!** *interjection*. Oh! Ah!

***oy vey!** *interjection*. Oh dear!; goodness me!

***pareve** *adjective*. Neutral; neither meat nor dairy, as fruit and vegetables. Also spelled **parve**.

**paskudne** *adjective*. Mean; nasty; gross.

**paskudnyak** *noun*. A gross, revolting, or obnoxious person.

***patsh** *noun*; *plural* **petsh**. A slap or smack —*verb* [patshn]. To smack.

***patshke** [patshken] *verb*. To mess up or mess around; play around.

***peyes** *noun*. Sidecurls; sidelocks, as those worn by Hasidic Jews.

***Pesach** [peysekh] *noun*. Passover.

***pirogen** [pirogn, *singular* pirog] *noun, Jewish Cookery*. Dumplings with a filling of meat, potatoes, etc.

***pisher** *noun, Slang*. **1.** A little squirt. **2.** A nobody (literally, a pisser).

**pisk** *noun*. A mouth, especially a big mouth.

**pitsl**, **pitsele** *adjective*. Very small; tiny.

***plotz** [plats] *verb*. To burst or explode from anger, laughter, etc.

**ponem** *noun*. A face.

**pots** *noun, Vulgar*; *plural* **pets**. A jerk; prick (literally, penis). See **putz**.

**potsh** *noun, verb*. See **patsh**.

**prost** *adjective*. Coarse; common; vulgar.

**prostak** *noun*. A coarse or vulgar person.

**pupik** *noun*. Navel; gizzard; bellybutton.

***Purim** *noun*. The Feast of Lots.

**pushke** *noun*. A charity box.

***putz** [pots] *noun, Slang*. A jerk; prick (literally, penis) —**putz around**. To mess around.

***rugelach** [rugelekh] *noun plural, Jewish Cookery*. A pastry dessert with a filling of chocolate, fruit, etc. Also spelled **rogelach**.

***sachel** [seykhl] <ˈsey-khel> *noun*. Brains; intelligence; common sense.

***schlemiel** [shlemil] *noun, Slang*. A clumsy person; bungler; simpleton. Also spelled **shlemiel**, **schlemihl**.

### schlemiel

**The origin of this word for a perennial bungler or loser is a matter of controversy. In Yiddish, the word is traced back to Western Europe (France, Germany), so it must have traveled a long way to become part of Eastern Yiddish. It first surfaced in England in the 1890s and in America in the 1920s.** ***The Dictionary of Americanisms,*** **published in 1951, includes the word and suggests that it may have come from the name of Peter Schlemihl, the main character in a German story, Peter Schlemihls Wunderbare Geschichte (Peter Schlemihl's Wonderful Story), published in 1814 by the German poet Adelbert von Chamisso (1781-1838). The story is an allegory about an impoverished young man, Peter Schlemihl, who gives up his shadow to the devil in exchange for a purse full of money. The lack of a shadow exposes Peter to public contempt and despite his wealth he becomes an outcast from society. However, both the** ***Oxford English Dictionary*** **and** ***Webster's Third International Dictionary*** **dismiss this derivation and trace the Yiddish word's origin to the Biblical name of Shelumiel, the chief of the tribe of Simeon, who is identified in the Talmud with another Biblical figure, Zimri, a Simeonite prince killed for fornicating with a Midianite woman. If this is indeed the ultimate source of schlemiel, then the name given by von Chamisso to his unfortunate hero may have been borrowed from the Yiddish word.**

***schav** *noun, Jewish Cookery*. A cold, cream-of-sorrel soup.

***schlep** [shlepn, shlep] *Slang; verb,* **schlepped, schlepping**. To drag; plod; lug. —*noun*. **1.** A bum; tramp; nonentity **2.** A long, tiresome trip.

***schlepper** [shleper] *noun*. **1.** A person who schleps **2.** A bum or tramp.

***schleppy** *adjective, Slang;* **schleppier, schleppiest**. Of or like a **schlep** or **schlepper**.

***schlimazel** [shlimazl, shlemazl] *noun, Slang*. A luckless person; a ne'er-do-well; a loser. Also spelled **schlimazl, shlimazel**.

***schlock** [shlak] *noun, Slang*. Something shoddy, junky, or inferior. Also spelled **shlock**.

***schlockmeister** *noun, Slang*. One who sells cheap or inferior goods.

***schlocky** *adjective, Slang;* **schlockier, schlockiest**. Cheap; junky; inferior. Also spelled **shlocky**.

***schlub** *noun*. See **zhlob**.

***schlump** [shlump] *Slang, noun*. A slovenly person; slob. —*verb*. **1.** To drag or droop, as in walking **2.** To act or work sluggishly. Also spelled **shlump**.

***schmaltz** [shmalts] *noun*. Excessive sentimentality; mawkishness (literally, rendered fat).

***schmaltzy** *adjective, Informal;* **schmaltzier, schmaltziest**. Overly sentimental; mawkish.

***schmatte** [shmate] *noun, Slang*. A rag; a cheap or shoddy dress or outfit. Also spelled **shmatte**.

***schmear** [shmirn, shmir] *Slang, verb*. **1.** To smear **2.** To bribe. **3.** To beat, as an opponent —*noun*. **1.** A smear, as of butter **2.** A bribe.

***schmegegge** [shmigege] *noun*. A simpleton; a half-wit or nitwit. Also spelled **shmegegge**.

***schmendrick** [shmendrik] *noun*. An insignificant person; nonentity. Also spelled **shmendrick**.

***schmo** *noun, Slang; plural* **schmoes**. A foolish or silly person; jerk. Also spelled **schmoe**.

***schmooze** [shmus, shmues] *verb;* **schmoozed, schmoozing**. To con-

**YIVO Institute for Jewish Research**

Founded in Berlin in 1925 and later headquartered in Vilna, Lithuania, the YIVO Institute for Jewish Research houses one of the world's major collections of Eastern European and American Yiddish culture. YIVO is an acronym of its original name, *Yidisher Visnshaftlikher Institut* (Jewish Scientific Institute). The Institute moved to New York City in 1940 to escape the Nazis and to preserve its extensive collection. YIVO has been dedicated to saving and transmitting Eastern European Jewish culture with a significant focus on Yiddish language, culture, and music especially before World War II. It is a place where Ashkenazi Jews can learn about the lost world of their families before the Nazi depredations.

YIVO's library has over 350,000 volumes; its archives contain over 22 million documents, including photographs, posters, films, recordings, and videotapes. Its collections preserve the primary records of Jewish daily life with such items as family trees, telephone directories, theater and political posters, the Bund Jewish labor movement, Yiddish children's literature, and rabbinical works dating back to the 16th century. YIVO offers intensive Yiddish-language study, library, and archive access, and a donation site for Jewish and Yiddish-related materials.

In 1999 it joined the Center for Jewish History to consolidate four major Jewish research institutions into one large, 125,000-square-foot facility in New York City. They include: the YIVO, The American Jewish Historical Society, The Leo Baeck Institute, and the Yeshiva University Museum. The Center houses the most extensive collection of Jewish cultural history outside of Israel.

Source: www.yivoinstitute.org

verse idly; chat. *—noun.* Idle conversation; chitchat. Also spelled **schmoose**.

*__schmuck__ [shmok] *noun, Slang.* A fool; prick (literally, penis).

*__schmutz__ [shmuts] *noun, Slang.* Dirt; filth; smut. *—adjective,* **schmutzy**; **schmutzier**, **schmutziest**.

*__schmutzig__ [shmutsik] *adjective.* Dirty; filthy; soiled. Also spelled **schmutzik**.

*__schnook__ [shnuk] *noun, Slang.* An insignificant fool; poor devil.

*__schnorrer__ [shnorer] *noun, Slang.* A beggar or moocher. Also spelled **shnorer**, **shnorrer**.

*****schnoz** [shnoyts] *noun, Slang*. A nose, especially a long or prominent one. Also spelled **shnoz, schnozz.** Also **schnozzle, schnozzola.**

*****schtick** [shtik] *noun, Slang*. An act or routine, as by a performer (literally, piece, bit). Also spelled **schtik, shtick.**

*****schtup** [shtupn] *verb, Slang* (*vulgar*); **schtupped, schtupping.** To fornicate (literally, to push). Also spelled **shtup.**

**sha!** *interjection*. Hush! Quiet!

*****shadchen** [shadkhn, shatkhn; *plural* shadkhonim, shatkhonim] <′shahd-khen> *noun*. A marriage broker; matchmaker.

**shames** <′shah-mes> *noun*; *plural* **shamosim** <shah-′moh-seem>. **1.** A synagogue caretaker; beadle. **2.** An assistant.

**Shavuos** [shvues] *noun*. The Festival of Weeks; Pentecost.

*****shegetz** [sheygets] *noun*; *plural* shkotzim [shkotsim] (*often disparaging*). **1.** A male non-Jew. **2.** An irreligious Jew. **3.** A troublemaker; scoundrel.

*****sheitel** [sheytl; *plural* sheytlen, sheytlekh] *noun*. A wig worn by an Orthodox woman in public to cover her hair.

**shidekh** *noun*. A marital arrangement; a match, as by a **shadchen.**

**shiker** *noun*. A drunkard.

*****shiksa** [shikse] *noun*. A non-Jewish girl or woman, especially an attractive one.

**shkotzim** *noun plural*. See **shegetz.**

**shmatte** *noun*. See **schmatte.**

**sholem aleykhem** *phrase*. Hello (literally, peace unto you).

**shoyte** *noun*. A fool.

**shpilkes** *noun*. Pins and needles; jitters (literally, pins).

**shtarker** *noun*. A strong or tough fellow; a muscleman.

*****shtetl** *noun*; *plural* **shtetls** or **shtetlach** [shtetlekh]. A Jewish town or village in Eastern Europe, especially before World War II.

**shtikl** *adjective*. A piece or bit.

**shtup**. See **schtup.**

**shul** *noun*. A synagogue.

## The National Yiddish Book Center

One of the great rescue stories in history began a little over twenty years ago. In 1980, a twenty five-year-old graduate student by the name of Aaron Lansky discovered that thousands of Yiddish books were being discarded or destroyed—not by neo-Nazi book burners, but by Jews who could no longer read the language of their parents and grandparents. Lansky felt so strongly that the priceless Yiddish books had to be saved for posterity, he issued a public appeal for old Yiddish books.

He succeeded beyond anyone's imaginings. When he issued his call in 1980, it was estimated that only about 70,000 Yiddish volumes were extant and recoverable in all of North America. That many were recovered within six months! Today the National Yiddish Book Center's collection of Yiddish books exceeds one and a half million volumes, and an average number of 500 Yiddish books continue to arrive each week. There are over two hundred **zamlers** (volunteer book collectors) collecting Yiddish books for the center throughout the United States and Canada.

The National Yiddish Book Center's headquarters is located in Amherst, Massachusetts, in a remarkable building whose exterior and interior recall the old wooden synagogues of Russia and Poland. The building houses a book repository, containing a core collection of 120,000 Yiddish books and 150,000 folios of Yiddish and Hebrew sheet music; the Steven Spielberg Digital Yiddish Library, which has preserved and made permanently available 14,000 titles; three exhibition halls with rotating exhibits; a reading library; a theater; a book processing center; and a shipping and receiving section. The center runs an internship program for college students and a summer program in Yiddish culture. It has established or strengthened Yiddish library collections in over 450 university and research libraries. And it publishes a critically-praised English-language magazine, *Pakn Treger* (Pack Carrier), whose contributors include many distinguished scholars and writers such as Robert Alter, Hillel Halkin, Jonathan Rosen, and Ruth Wisse.

The Center's list of "The 100 Greatest Works of Modern Jewish Literature" is a widely hailed selection of the hundred books that best record Jewish experience and sensibility over the past 150 years. The complete list, with annotations and essays by the judges, has been published in the *Pakn Treger* and made available online.

Source: www.yiddishbookcenter.org

**shvits** *noun*. Sweat. —**shvitsbod** *noun*. A Turkish bath.

**shvitser** *noun*. **1.** A hard worker. **2.** An aggressive person (literally, one who sweats much).

***simcha** [simkhe] <'sim-kheh> *noun*. A joyous celebration, such as a bris or chasene (literally, joy).

**smetene** *noun*. Sour cream.

***strashe** [strashen] *verb*. To threaten.

***Sukkos** [sukes] *noun*. The Festival of Tabernacles or Booths.

**taam** *noun*. Taste, especially a good taste. Also spelled **tam**.

**take** <'tah-keh> *adverb*. Indeed; really, as in "He's **take** the nicest guy you'll ever meet." "Do you mean it? **Take**?"

***tayglach** [teyglekh] *noun plural*. Small spicy honey cakes.

***tchotchke** [tshatshke] *noun*. A trinket or bauble. Also spelled **chotchke**.

**tkhine** <teh-'khee-neh> *noun*. A Yiddish prayer or supplication, chiefly for women.

***toches** [tokhes] *noun*. The behind; buttocks. Also spelled **tochis**, **tuchis**.

***tref** [treyf] *adjective*. Not kosher. Also spelled **trayf**.

**tsatske** *noun*. **1.** A toy, bauble, or ornament. (Related in meaning to **tchotchke**.) **2.** A spoiled or indulged child; brat. **3.** Cutie; an over-dressed or sexy woman.

***tshep** [tshepn] *verb*. To bother or pester; pick on.

**tsore** *noun*. A calamity, plight.

***tsuris** *noun*. Troubles; problems. Also spelled **tsores**, **tsouris**.

***tuchis** *noun*. See **toches**.

***tummel** [tuml] *noun*. Big noise or commotion.

***tummler** [tumler] *noun*. An M.C. or entertainer, as at a borscht-belt resort (literally, noisemaker).

*__tush__ *noun, Slang*. Also, **tushie**, **tushy**. Buttocks; **toches**.

*__tzaddik__ [tsadik] *noun*. **1.** A righteous person **2.** A Hasidic leader; grand rabbi.

*__tzimmes__ [tsimes] *noun*. **1.** A stew of fruit or vegetables **2.** A big fuss or to-do; a federal case. Also spelled **tsimmes**.

**umbatamt** *adjective*. Tasteless.

**vits** *noun*. A joke. Also spelled **vitz**.

**yakhne** *noun*. A busybody or shrewish woman.

**yakhsn** *noun*. A person who has or claims pedigree or privilege. See **yikhes**.

*__yarmulke__ [yarmlke] *noun*. A skullcap. Also spelled **yarmulka**.

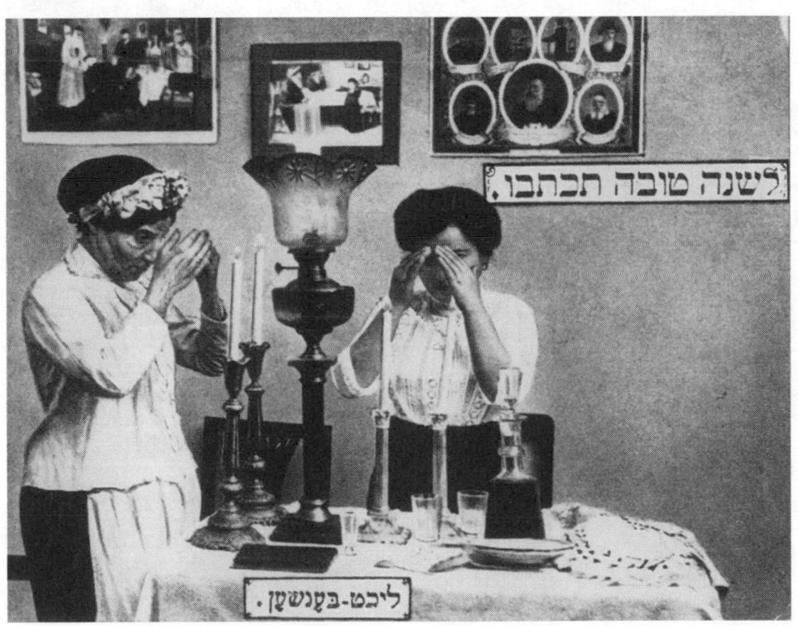


Blessing the Sabbath candles, a New Year's greeting card, Warsaw, undated. (YIVO Institute for Jewish Research)

***yenta** [yente] *noun, Slang*. A busybody or gossip.

***yeshiva bocher** [yeshive bokher] *phrase*. A yeshiva student.

***yid** *noun* [*plural* yidn]. A Jew. —*Slang (often disparaging)*; *plural* **yids**. A Jew.

## Weather-Prophets (Veter-Neviim)—A Glimpse of Contemporary Yiddish

Contrary to Polonius's famous advice to Laertes, the Yiddish language is both a borrower and a lender. As a borrower, it has liberally appropriated an extensive vocabulary from Hebrew, Aramaic, Slavic, and English. Its acquisitive characteristic is perhaps best illustrated by the way it borrows popular and scientific terms from modern languages. Yiddish sometimes takes an English word and simply Yiddishizes it (English *addict* becomes Yiddish **der adikt**). Or it translates it (English *aircraft* becomes Yiddish **luftshif**); or partially translates it (English *weatherman* becomes Yiddish **veter-novi**, literally, weather-prophet). But it can also be innovative, as when it calls a beep over the phone a **pips**; a burglar alarm a **gevaldglok** (literally, emergency bell); and a call girl a **lebmeydl** (playgirl) on the model of **lebyung** (playboy). Here is a list of up-to-date Yiddish words culled from various contemporary sources, especially the Yiddish periodical *Afn shvel* (organ of the League for Yiddish, Inc.), and Weinreich's *Modern English-Yiddish Yiddish-English Dictionary*.

| English | Yiddish |
|---|---|
| addict | der adikt |
| aircraft | di luftshif |
| area code | di kodnumer; *plural* kodnumern |
| astronaut | astronoyt |
| beep | der pips; *plural* pipsn |
| call forward | der klung-ibershik |
| call girl | lebmeydl; *plural* lebmeydlekh |
| cell phone | der tselularer telefon; *informal*, di tselke |
| checking account | tshek-konte |
| civil rights | birgerrekht |

***Yiddish** *noun*. The Germanic language of Ashkenazic Jews (chiefly of East European origin or descent), written in Hebrew letters and containing many Hebrew, Aramaic, and Slavic words. *—adjective*. Of or pertaining to Yiddish. *—noun*, **Yiddishism**. *—noun*, **Yiddishist**.

| English | Yiddish |
|---|---|
| computer | der kompyuter |
| credit card | kreditkartl; *plural* kreditkartlekh |
| depression | di depresie |
| down payment | der adroyf |
| drug | der narkotik; *informal*, dos fartoybekhts (dope) |
| electronic | elektronish |
| e-mail | blitspost; *formal*, elektronish post |
| fax machine | di telekopirke |
| heart attack | der hartsatak; *plural* hartsatakes |
| jet plane | der dzhet eroplan |
| missile | der raket, der misl |
| page, *verb* | pazhirn |
| pager | der pazhir |
| pay phone | der tsol-telefon |
| recycle | ibernitseven |
| security guard | der zikherkeyt-hiter |
| stroke | der moyekh-atak |
| sunburn | der zunopbren |
| switchboard | di shlisbret |
| tape recorder | di rekordirke |
| televise | televizirn |
| television | televizie |
| touch-tone phone | der kvetsh-telefon |
| voice mail | di kol-post |
| weatherman | der veter-novi; *plural* veter-neviim |
| Web site | vebzaytl |

***Yiddishkeit** [yidishkeyt] *noun*. **1.** Jewishness **2.** Judaism. Also spelled **Yiddishkeyt**.

**yidene** *noun*. **1.** A Jewish woman. **2.** A wife. (Literally, female Jew.)

**yikhes** *noun*. Pedigree; status.

**yingl** *noun*. A boy. —*noun*, **yingele**. A little boy.

***Yinglish** *noun*. A blend or combination of Yiddish and English.

**yold** *noun*. A simpleton; fool.

**yontev** *noun*; *plural* **yontevs, yontoyvim**. A Jewish festival or holiday.

**yortsayt** *noun*. The anniversary of someone's death, especially that of a parent or close relative. Usually spelled **yahrzeiht** in English.

### yortsayt

**This Yiddish word, meaning the anniversary of a person's death, especially of a parent or close relative, is one of the most widely known Yiddishisms. Besides English, Spanish, French, and other European languages, it has also entered Hebrew. In English, the usual spelling is yahrzeit, which is an Anglicized form of German Jahrzeit, which is itself a Germanized form of Yiddish yortsayt.**

**The Yiddish word also includes the meaning "ceremonial observance of a yortsayt," as by lighting a twenty-four-hour memorial candle and reciting the kaddish in the synagogue. In addition, the anniversary of the death of any great or famous person is called a yortsayt. Which raises the question:**

**Why doesn't English (and other languages) have a word to designate, say, Shakespeare's or George Washington's death anniversary or yortsayt? How about *deathday*? Other suggestions are welcome.**

***zaftig** [zaftik] *adjective, Slang*. **1.** Juicy; luscious **2.** Full and shapely; voluptuous. Also spelled **zoftig**.

***zayde** [zeyde] *noun*. Grandfather. Also spelled **zeyde**.

**zets** *noun*. A punch; blow.

***zhlob** *noun, Slang*. A gross or boorish person; slob. Also spelled **zhlub, schlub**.

**zup** *noun*. Soup. "From **zup** to **nislekh**" means "from soup to nuts."

## Frumspeak: The Yiddishized English of the Orthodox

The following is an excerpt from an English periodical published in the United States for a modern Orthodox Jewish readership:

> The yeshiva bocherim are dancing,...it is time to b'dek the kallah. Hush, the chossen, Aaron Shlomo, approaches.... He is her besherte.... (*Jewish Press*)
>
> Translation of the above: "The yeshiva youths are dancing, ...it is time to cover the bride [a custom in which the groom covers the bride's face with a veil just before the wedding ceremony]. Hush, the groom, Aaron Shlomo, approaches.... He is her predestined mate...."

In the American Orthodox Jewish community this is a perfectly natural passage, since it reflects the speech of modern English-speaking Jews of East European descent. This manner of speaking and writing, in which any number of Yiddish words are freely mixed with English words, has been formally called *American Orthodox Jewish English* and informally *Frumspeak,* frum being the Yiddish word for "religious."

Frumspeak is peppered with Yiddish words and phrases like *aderabe* (on the contrary), *agmes nefesh* (upset, aggravation), *al regel akhas* (briefly; literally, on one foot), *amorets* (ignoramus), *apikoyres* (atheist, heretic), *azoyns un azelekhes* (something unique; literally, such and such), *avade* (certainly), *a yor mit a mitvokh* (a long time; literally, a year and a Wednesday), *make ash un blote from* (make mincemeat of; literally, make ashes and mud from).

A special kind of Frumspeak—that of Orthodox yeshiva students (and their teachers), which includes many common Yiddish words that have perfectly good English equivalents—has been called *Yeshivish,* a Yiddish adjective meaning "characteristic or typical of yeshivas." A dictionary published in 1995 by Chaim M. Weiser, entitled *Frumspeak: The First Dictionary of Yeshivish,* is a serious attempt to list and define many of the Yiddish usages of English-speaking yeshiva students.

Frumspeak and Yeshivish are fertile fields for new borrowings from Yiddish and new coinages based on Yiddish. These usages help keep Yiddish alive in an English setting and thereby stimulate the study and use of the Yiddish language.

# Yiddish Literature

## Out of the Shtetl to World Renown

*Diaspora Germanic Hebrew-Aramaic East European ivre-taytsh Hebrew-German Abraham Joseph Moses Talmud Midrash golden age folk-songs lullabi… parables stori…s incantations minstrels songs st… …riting Yiddish Codex Mirk…es hamishne Anshel of Cracow Sefer shet Rav A… King Arthur Round Table Bove-…ukh Bo… of Bove Elia Levita Medieval romance Shmuel-Bu…h Book of Samuel Tsene-Urene Rabbi Jacob ben Isaac Ashkenazi megillahs Esther Ruth Song of Songs Ecclesiastes Lamentations …ytsh …umesh German Pentateuch Mayse-bukh Book of Stories Basle Elchanan Jewish Pope penny booklets tkhines supplications daily life holidays childlessness travel husband mates children protection evil Glikl bas Yehuda Leyb Die Kuranten Amsterdam Hasidism Haskalah Yiddish Enlightenment kabbalah rebbes tzaddikim. shtetls Moses Mendelssohn Israel Baal Shem Tov Besht, Shivchei ha-Besht Praises of the Besht Sipurei Maasiyos Tales of*

As Jews wandered during the long Diaspora after the expulsion from the Land of Israel (70 C.E.), many settled in Europe. Over the last thousand years Yiddish evolved from its origins as a fusion of Germanic, Hebrew-Aramaic, and East European languages and dialects into a secular Jewish tongue. Yiddish literature is a relatively recent phenomenon, emerging about 150 years ago and flourishing in Europe and America up until World War II. Since then, two new generations of Yiddish writers, poets, and critics have continued building a body of work in the United States and Israel that, so far, is little known outside the rarefied world of Yiddish writers, teachers, and scholars.

From its onset, Yiddish writing was expressed in both religious and secular works. The Bible and its interpretations were translated and explained in a formal written variety of Yiddish known as **ivre-taytsh** (literally, Hebrew-German). Heroes like Abraham, Joseph, and Moses were glorified in rhyming, epic tales. Newer literary forms in prose, such as parables and sermons, interpreted biblical passages. Yiddish liturgy also flourished in many forms, including prayer books translated from Hebrew and religious poetry associated with the Jewish holidays. Yiddish also developed an ethical literature with books on conduct that were based on Hebrew sources. These were written for the average person and often used exemplary tales and parables found in the Talmud and Midrash.

This chapter provides a very brief sketch of the development of Yiddish literature, focusing on its classic, golden age in the late 19th to the early and mid-20th century. The bibliography at the back of the book offers sources for more in-depth study.

## Early Yiddish Literature

From its inception, Yiddish relied on the oral tradition to disseminate and perpetuate non-sacred folksongs, lullabies, parables, stories, and incantations. Jewish minstrels roamed across Germany and other countries as early as the 12th century, spreading and reinterpreting their material through song and storytelling. Yiddish writing during this early period also focused on making Jewish sacred texts available and intelligible to a wider audience. The earliest preserved Yiddish manuscript, known as the Cambridge Yiddish Codex (it was discovered in the early 1950s in the Cambridge University Library), dates from 1382 and includes four epic poems based on the Bible. But the Codex also contained a rhymed fable about a dying lion, which in the view of some scholars represents a transition from works of religious content to works reflecting a wider cultural sphere. Little has been preserved between then and the appearance of Yiddish printed books in the 16th century. The first printed book containing Yiddish was a concordance and glossary of the Bible, the *Mirkeves hamishne*, by Anshel of Cracow, published in 1534. In this work, all the Hebrew words listed alphabetically are translated and annotated in Yiddish. A well-known second edition, titled *Sefer shel Rav Anshel* (Rav Anshel's Book), appeared in 1584, also in Cracow.

Jewish minstrels often incorporated variations of the stories of King Arthur and his Round Table. The most popular knightly romance, *Bove-bukh* (Book of Bove), composed in rhyme by the grammarian Elye Bokher (Elia Levita), was a Yiddish rendition of a Medieval Italian romance whose hero, Buovo d'Antona, was based on the English knight Sir Bevis of Hampton. The *Bove-bukh* was published in 1541 and it remained in print for over 400 years. A famous Yiddish religious epic was the *Shmuel-Bukh* (Book of Samuel), published in 1544. It told the story of God's intervention on behalf of the Jewish people with David as its main hero. The *Tsene-Urene* (popularly called Tsenerene) by Rabbi Jacob ben Isaac Ashkenazi (1550–1625) was an important Yiddish rendering of the Pentateuch, the weekly Prophetic portions, and the five **megillahs** or scrolls (Esther, Ruth, Song of Songs, Ecclesiastes, and Lamentations). Though not aimed at women, the Tsenerene gave women access to Jewish sacred texts (since the study of the Torah and Hebrew was restricted to the men) and thus became extremely popular among women. The book, whose Pentateuch was also known as **taytsh-khumesh** (literally, German Pentateuch), included commentaries, parables, allegories, short stories, and other texts expounding on ethical and religious issues.

Other ethical Yiddish books, using moralistic tales, were printed as guides for Jewish men and women seeking a virtuous life. A classic of this kind is the *Mayse-bukh* (Book of Stories), published in Basle in 1602. It contained 255 anonymous stories, folk tales, and legends that had been transmitted orally for centuries. Many of the stories came from the Talmud and Midrash; others were medieval tales of ghosts, werewolves, and vampires; still others were stories about legendary figures, as that of Elchanan, the "Jewish Pope." This story is about Elchanan, the son of Rabbi Simon the Great, who is kidnapped by a Christian maid. The maid hands him over to a monastic teacher who raises the boy as a Christian, so that eventually Elchanan becomes a priest, then a cardinal, and finally the Pope. All along Elchanan knows that he is a Jew and one day he arranges to meet his father, to whom he reveals himself. Finally, unable to live as a Christian, he leaps from a tower to his death and becomes a Jewish martyr.

From the 16th to the 18th century inexpensive, "penny booklets" known as **tkhines** (literally, supplications) were very popular as collections of devotional prayers for women (see "Tkhines—Yiddish Women's Prayers"). Beginning with their first publication in 1590, tkhines covered many topics from daily life and holidays to special situations (for example, childlessness, dangers of travel, finding a husband or mates for one's children, or protection from the evil eye). Two noteworthy non-devotional Yiddish works from this period include a diary of Jewish life in Sweden by the founder of the Swedish Jewish community, Aaron Isaac (1730–1816), and the *Memoirs* of Glückel of Hameln (1645–1724), written between 1699 and 1719 but not published until 1896. Both represent important documentation of Jewish life in the 17th to 18th century. In 1686 *Die Kuranten*, a Yiddish semiweekly, was published in Amsterdam and carried local news as well as details of Jewish life in foreign places.

The 18th century saw the flowering of Yiddish literature concomitant with the rise of the **Haskalah** and **Hasidic** movements. Both movements served to raise awareness of Jewish culture but from widely different

## Glikl bas Yehuda Leyb—An Early Yiddish Woman Writer

Glikl bas Yehuda Leyb (1646–1724), also known as Glückel of Hameln, the name given to her by her 19th-century German editor, was an important writer known for her *Memoirs*, one of the earliest publications in Yiddish by a woman writer. Her writings provide a period glimpse into the life of a strong and affluent German-Jewish woman who was an advisor and partner to her first and second husbands. Sections include her growing up, her years of study, marriage, widowhood, raising her children, business practices, and religious observances of Jews. The book provides an invaluable and rare portrait of the culture and history of Central European Jews of the 17th and early 18th centuries. Her writing also offers modern scholars the opportunity for linguistic and literary analysis of older Yiddish.

Her *Memoirs* were penned primarily as a personal family document and not originally planned for publication. She began writing them at the age of 46 after the loss of first husband (Hayyim of Hameln) and as documentation for her large family of 12 children. She completed five sections by 1699 and then, after a break of 16 years, completed the last two sections. Glikl was well traveled, and the *Memoirs* depict Jewish life in cities like Hamburg, Berlin, Hanover, and Amsterdam. Glikl studied in a traditional Jewish **cheder** (religious school) and was well versed in the Talmud and Yiddish ethical books. She used traditional parables and folktales to make religious or moral points and adapted popular devotional prayers (from a penny booklet of **tkhines**). Though the original manuscript was lost, her descendants had made copies, and in 1896 the *Memoirs* were published in the original Yiddish.

perspectives. The Haskalah, or Jewish Enlightenment, encouraged Jews to become part of the modern European secular world. The Haskalah was an intellectual and cultural revolution, and the German philosopher and writer Moses Mendelssohn (1729–1786) was its main spokesman. He wrote in German, using Western classical imagery, and argued for Jewish acceptance of European ideas. Mendelssohn urged his followers to replace Yiddish with German to further their integration. In Western Europe, where they were culturally more accepted by the Christian public, Jews were quick to shed Yiddish and adopt European languages for daily life and creative expression. This separated them from their brethren in Eastern Europe who were generally poorer, uneducated and oppressed, especially in the Pale of Settlement, under the Russian czars. The Haskalah's proponents in Eastern Europe disapproved of Yiddish as a vulgar and inferior form of German. Ironically, they were also obliged to use Yiddish to reach the Jewish masses, who understood no other language.

**Hasidism** was a popular religious movement deeply influenced by the mystical teachings of **kabbalah** and centering on charismatic spiritual leaders known as **rebbes** or **tzaddikim**. Followers of Hasidism (see "Hasidism and Kabbalah—The Yiddish Connection") were primarily found in the poor **shtetls** of Eastern Europe. Hasidism was a counterpoint to the Haskalah and sought to revitalize Jewish life by providing Jews with a direct emotional and mystical experience of their religion. Anyone could directly commune with God. For the Hasidim, piety and religious exaltation transcended scholarship and material accomplishment. Hasidism saw Yiddish as the language of the people and created its own literature, with countless stories, parables, and mystic tales, to further Hasidic ideals.

In a sense, Yiddish literature was at the center in the conflicts between the Haskalah and Hasidism. The former had a rational, modern view of life, the latter was mystical and romantic. As Western European Jews embraced the modern, pragmatic world, Jewish writers adopted the languages where they lived (Germany and France, for example), and Yiddish writing went into decline. But while Yiddish faded in these countries, it flourished in Eastern Europe as the language of the simple and poor who were embracing the values of Hasidism.

The founder of Hasidism, a contemporary of Moses Mendelssohn, was a mystic and a miracle worker known as Israel Baal Shem Tov (1700–1760). Besht, as he is often called (an acronym for Baal Shem Tov), was revered by the poor of the shtetls, who were drawn to his vision that God and His joy were everywhere and in everything. The Baal Shem Tov's preaching was part of the Yiddish oral tradition and he left no writings. But his remarkable tales were transcribed by his followers in collections such as the *Shivchei ha-Besht* (Praises of the Besht), published in 1815. Rabbi Nachman of Bratzlav (1772–1811)

## Golem, the Yiddish Frankenstein

Cyborgs, terminators, Pinocchio, and Frankenstein all have one thing in common—the notion of bringing inanimate objects to life. But Jewish folklore and mysticism preceded these stories with the creation of the **golem**. Here was a creature made from dust and clay and brought to life by magic and ritual. Golem comes from the Hebrew word *gelem*, which means raw material, and in Yiddish a golem means a lifeless clod. And let's not forget Adam: God's golem made from dust.

As the story goes, in the old city of Prague during the late 1500s, lived the famous Rabbi Judah Loew (1520–1609). Jews had lived in Prague for over 600 years, confined to a ghetto where most spoke Yiddish. Although Jews were generally treated fairly well by the local aristocracy, they were still subjected to periodic harassment, attacks, and even murder.

European Catholics were often stirred up by a vicious legend that claimed that Jews ritually murdered Christian children and used their blood to make matzo during Passover. Jews were also falsely accused of desecrating holy wafers with this blood. This evil and totally unfounded "blood libel" was often used to arouse anti-Semitic pogroms for political or religious purposes.

A great sage and a practitioner of the mystic Jewish tradition known as **kabbalah**, Rabbi Loew was concerned for the safety of his people and wanted to protect them. Working with his two sons-in-law, he used the kabbalah to breathe life into a creature he made out of clay: the golem thus became a protector of the community whenever summoned by Rabbi Loew.

There are different versions of the myth but in most Rabbi Loew loses control over his golem. In one version the golem developed an ego and became uncontrollable. In another, Rabbi Loew's wife used the golem for mundane housework. The golem worked without supervision and continued to fill a barrel with water even after it overflowed, flooding their home (a possible basis for the "Sorcerer's Apprentice," seen in Walt Disney's *Fantasia*). The higher purpose and purity of the golem's mission was lost and it became necessary for the rabbi to stop his creation.

As part of the kabbalistic ritual of bringing the golem to life, the word *emes* (truth) was written on its head. Rabbi Loew erased the first letter (aleph in Hebrew) so that what remained was the word *mes*, which means dead. The golem then collapsed and returned to inanimate clay. Rabbi Loew hid it in the attic of the Altneuschul (Old-New Synagogue) of Prague amongst the old books, where it eventually dried to dust. This 13th-century synagogue still stands (the oldest in Europe) and legends say the golem's dust still waits to return to life.

The moral of the story of the golem was that only God could create life. Man's attempts to play God are dangerous and could spin out of control. This message was repeated in Mary Shelley's gothic novel, *Frankenstein*, with Dr. Victor Frankenstein's monster terrorizing the village. Shelley may have been influenced by the golem myths that were popular in the early 19th century.

On a deeper kabbalistic level, the creation of a golem is also seen as an alchemical process and spiritual quest. Here the golem could be considered a reflection of its creator and thus a lower form of him or herself. This golem form could then enable its creator to see the darker forces within and exorcise them as part of the path to his/her greater awareness and redemption.

The golem has been the subject of many plays, stories, including ones by I.B. Singer and Cynthia Ozick, and a few classic European movies from the 1920s and 1930s. In Michael Chabon's 2001 Pulitzer-prize-winning novel, *The Amazing Adventures of Kavalier & Clay*, the coffin of the golem hides the hero Joe Kavalier in his escape from Nazi-occupied Prague to America. And in 2002, H. Leivick's original Yiddish play, "The Golem," first produced in Moscow in 1924, again stirred the imagination of audiences in New York City in a new adaptation.

was an important disciple of the Baal Shem Tov and his great-grandson. Rabbi Nachman's stories, *Sipurei Maasiyos* (later known as *Tales of Rabbi Nachman of Bratzlav*), were a unique expression of religious, symbolic mysticism; some serious, others humorous or ironic. They too were transcribed by his disciples.

The stories of the Baal Shem Tov and Rabbi Nachman had an enormous impact on the development of modern Yiddish poetry and prose. They idealized these Hasidic founders and were derived from Yiddish oral traditions or religious, mystical stories, often drawn from folk literature. These works had a lasting and seminal influence on modern writers such as I. L. Peretz and Isaac Bashevis Singer.

Apart from the Haskalah and Hasidism, other elements influenced the development of Yiddish literature through the growth of Jewish cultural awareness. These included anti-Semitism and the emerging movements of socialism and Zionism. The vicious pogroms of the 18th and 19th centuries heightened Jewish self-consciousness, vulnerability, and isolation. The Jews of Eastern Europe, who were either **Hasidim** or **Misnagdim** (traditional Jews who opposed Hasidism), knew they would never become part of their surrounding culture as their Western European counterparts did.

Thus the unique conditions of 19th-century life created a cultural divide between Western and Eastern European Jews. The latter were long familiar with oppression, and many living in the Pale of Settlement were ripe for emerging political movements. Many young **maskilim** (adherents of the Haskalah) were attracted to Socialism, drawn by its ideas of justice, political and social freedoms, and better working conditions. Activists formed the Bund (see "When the Labor Movement Spoke Yiddish—The Bund") to help organize Jewish political and social efforts. As a secular, socialist organization, the Bund favored the use of Yiddish as the language of the Jewish masses. An emerging audience of poor, working-class Jews encouraged Yiddish writers to explore themes that examined social issues. Many of these younger writers gathered in cosmopolitan cities, like Warsaw, Vilna, and Odessa, creating a stimulating atmosphere of intellectual and progressive ideas. These cities saw a flowering of creative literary output between 1900 and the outbreak of World War I.

Zionism, with its call for a return to the ancient Jewish homeland, was another emerging movement and added to the complexity of Jewish entry into the modern world. Zionists saw the shtetl as a place of social, religious, and psychological confinement that Jews needed to evolve beyond. A Jewish homeland was the solution, but Zionists preferred Hebrew, not Yiddish, as the national language. The ideals of Zionism appealed to many Jews, but they also created conflict between those immersed in Yiddish language and culture and those looking to leave it behind. Thus the Zionist cause was not the foremost of issues for 19th-century Yiddish writers who were helping to define and create modern Yiddish literature.

# Modern Yiddish Literature

The 19th century saw a flowering of Yiddish writers who chose to write in this "unworthy" language of exile in order to propagate the ideas of Haskalah among the masses. A Russian Jew, Israel Axenfeld (1787–1866), wrote one of the first Yiddish novels, *Dos Shterntikhl* (The Headband). An ardent maskil (adherent of the Haskalah), his novels and plays satirized shtetl life, especially the customs and practices of Hasidim, while Western European life was depicted as culturally advanced. His contemporaries included Joseph Perl (1773–1839), Issac Meir Dick (1814–1893), and Isaac Joel Linetzky (1839–1915). Perl was a leading maskil in Galicia whose Yiddish satires and parodies ridiculed Hasidim and their movement. His most famous work is *Megale Temirim* (Revealer of Secrets), published in 1819. It is a parody of Hasidic stories, written in the form of a correspondence between Hasidim engaged in concocting various plots against maskilim or other Hasidic sects. Dick was a prolific writer who disseminated the ideas of Haskalah through realistic and often melodramatic stories written in an idiomatic Yiddish. Linetzky, another maskilic and anti-Hasidic writer, is noted for his satiric novel *Dos Poylishe Yingl* (The Polish Boy).

Though there were other authors, Yiddish's Classical Age is defined by three great writers: Sholem Yankev Abramovitsh, better known as Mendele Mokher Seforim (Mendele the Bookseller, after the name of his most famous character); Sholom Aleichem; and Isaac Leib Peretz.

## *Mendele Mokher Seforim*

Mendele Mokher Seforim (1835–1917) is revered as the "grandfather of Yiddish literature" for his innovations in laying a new literary framework for Yiddish. His work realistically portrayed Jewish life with honesty and without judgment, and depicted the world of the shtetl with all its poverty and decay; all its joy and poetry. Mendele was born in Belorussia (Belarus) and came from a comfortable family of Lithuanian rabbis. He initially wrote in Hebrew and was a proponent of the Haskalah.

But as he wrote in his *Complete Works*: "I tried to compose a story in simple Hebrew, ground in the spirit and life of our people at the time. At that time, then, my thinking went along these lines: Observing how my people live, I want to write stories for them in our sacred tongue, yet most do not understand the language. They speak Yiddish. What good does the writer's work and thought serve him, if they are of no use to his people? For whom was I working? The question gave me no peace but placed me in a dilemma." (Quoted in *The Oxford Book of Jewish Stories*, edited by Ilan Stavans, New York: 1998.)

After spending ten years writing in Hebrew, in the 1860s he began writing in Yiddish, continuing for two decades. Mendele's novels and stories from this period were for the Jewish masses and include: *Dos Vintshfingerl* (The Magic Ring), *Dos Kleyne Mentshele* (The Little Man), and *Fishke der Krumer* (Fishke the Lame). Mendele's work ultimately challenged the Haskalah position that Jews needed to give up aspects of their identity in order to be accepted by Christian society. *In Di Kliatshe* (The Mare, 1873), a powerful satire, Mendele allegorically depicts the Jew as a despised beast of burden, suffering as the world's scapegoat. Yet this abused animal has dignity and a moral superiority that demands justice rather than mercy from its tormentors. The story is narrated by "Crazy Yisrulik" (Yisrulik dem meshugenem), who also tells the story "Di Byabak" (The Marmot), also written in 1873. In this tale Yisrulik is granted his wish and is transformed into a marmot, who then encounters and converses with the angel Gabriel. Yisrulik was the second narrative figure used by the writer after Mendele the Bookseller.

Mendele's work could be critical of Jewish patrician society and often placed him in conflict with community leaders. Two contrasting themes in his writing reflect his own ambivalence: satiric and/or critical treatment of the ghetto Jew afflicted by stagnation, ignorance, and isolation, contrasted by a sympathetic love and defense of his people. Mendele boldly opposed Russian anti-Semitism and Jewish persecution and often used symbolism and allegory to depict these conditions. These works had a profound stylistic and thematic influence on Yiddish literature, examining Jewish life with criticism, satire, pathos, and humor.

Mendele's work and life exemplify the broad spectrum of the historical and linguistic development of Jewish culture in the 19th century. His writing developed a new realism in fiction and nonfiction. He wrote in Hebrew and Yiddish, often emphasizing one language over the other for specific genres. He depicted the major cultural forces the Jew faced in entering the modern world: Haskalah and assimilation; the shtetl with its anti-Semitism and social oppression; Zionism with its call for Jewish nationalism. Mendele's legacy invited both praise and criticism. His depiction of East European Jews was acclaimed as a sober rendering of their often harsh lives, yet others felt he reinforced negative Jewish stereotypes. Mendele forged a new literary path, and created a modern portrait of an ancient people faced with ambivalence and contradictions on the threshold of a radically changing world.

**In "The Calf," a short story about a boy and his animal, Mendele Mokher Seforim weaves realism and allegory with the threads of conflict between Jewish tradition and youthful spontaneity.**

**I was a child, and like a child thought that the whole world was a copy of my village, that all places were the same and there was only one way of doing things. Everywhere people prayed, recited psalms, studied the Mishnah, pored over the Gemara, sat is small stores, yawned, chatted, gossiped, leaned on canes. Human beings and beasts were part of the same order. Boys were led off to cheder, beast led out to pasture. The rebbe had his plaited whip, the shepherd his crook, boy or calf it did not matter, so long as it was a living thing. Lucky the boy who could gain the favor of some mongrel, which would follow him around, bark when told, attack at command. Every boy was ready to give up not only his noonday meal but his very soul for such a dog.**

**Source:** *A Treasury of Yiddish Stories,*
**edited by Irving Howe and Eliezar Greenberg**
**(revised edition, Viking Penguin, 1989)**

## *Sholom Aleichem*

Born Sholom Rabinovitz (1859–1916), he took the pseudonym, Sholom Aleichem, to hide his life as a Yiddish writer, which his family opposed. Like Sholem Yankev Abramovitsh's alter ego and pseudonym Mendele the Bookseller, Sholom Aleichem's pen name, meaning "How do you do?" (literally, Peace unto you) in Hebrew and Yiddish, was chosen to create a humorous fictional alter ego. As his audience and popularity grew, Sholom Aleichem's name became synonymous with someone who makes fun of himself and others.

Sholom Aleichem came from a small town in Ukraine and had a Hasidic background. At fifteen, his fertile imagination and humor were

Sholom Aleichem (1859–1916), "the Yiddish Mark Twain," as a young man, late 1800s. (YIVO Institute for Jewish Research)

already documented in his first writings. Though poor by birth, he became wealthy through marriage. He used his resources not only to allow him to write but also to further other Yiddish writers and Yiddish literature. Between 1888 and 1890 he was the patron and publisher of *Di Yidishe Folksbibliotek* (The Popular Jewish Library), the first Yiddish literary annual. Though it only published two issues, it made a deep impact on Yiddish writing by publishing the works of the Yiddish literary triumvirate of Mendele, Sholom Aleichem, and Peretz, as well as other popular Yiddish writers.

"The Popular Jewish Library" played a seminal role in elevating Yiddish literature above its negative reputation by offering an alternative to the poorly-written stories and novels that were then popular. Unfortunately, through a series of bad investments, in 1890 Sholom Aleichem lost the journal and his fortune and was thereafter constantly plagued by money problems despite the success of his writing. The 1890s were probably the hardest years of his life as he constantly moved trying to avoid his creditors. Even with diminished literary output he was able to create the first monologue of *Tevye der Milkhiger* (Tevye the Milkman), who eventually became his most famous character and creation, immortalized in the musical *Fiddler on the Roof*.

Sholom Aleichem's work recreates the lives of the characters inhabiting the world of the Pale of Settlement (see "Shtetl Life"). In his stories, Voronka, the town of his youth, became the village of Kasrilevke. Here he portrays the **simkhes** (joys) and **tsores** (troubles) of the poor and oppressed who struggled to survive by using their wits and humor. His characters were embraced and loved by his readers and captured the period's social and historical reality. His themes avoided sentimentality, yet evoked tears and laughter. Sholom Aleichem's use of the feuilleton (a short story or serialization appearing on the first page of newspapers) allowed him to stay in touch with his readers and they become part of the common folklore. They also provided needed income for his shaky financial situation. Ironically, even though his writing made his publishers wealthy, Sholom Aleichem often lived in dire straits.

His feuilletons included *Di Ibergekhapte Briv oyf der Post* (Letters Stolen from the Post Office, 1883–84), an exchange between a dead man and his crazy friend, and *Kontor Gesheft* (Counting-house Business, 1885), a series of letters set in the business world and describing a network of absurd events that were constantly changing. The comic character Menakhem-Mendl, featured in stories written between 1892 and 1909, is a striking portrait of a man plagued by bad luck, chasing riches that continually elude him. Through these pieces, Sholom Aleichem painted a broad satire of newly rich urban Jews, the swindlers and **ganovim** who preyed on them, and the symbolic uncertainty of Jewish life. The stories were a major influence on Ilf and Petrov's famous novel *The Twelve Chairs* (1928), a picaresque tale of **luftmentshn** narrated through letters written by the characters to their wives.

Sholom Aleichem's most memorable creation is Tevye der Milkhiger, a simple milkman who is like a Jewish Don Quixote. Tevye is constantly challenged by tests and trials: losing his daughters who choose their mates through modern love rather than tradition; assailed by Russian anti-Semitism and pogroms; caught between conniving relatives and his own unselfish instincts. Yet Tevye places his trust and faith in God through an ongoing dialogue with the Almighty about the state of the world and his fellow humans. Tevye is a classic Jewish archetype guided by spiritual independence and goodwill who relies on humor as an antidote to life's hardships. In the Tevye stories Sholom Aleichem navigates this simple character through normal events which turn into catastrophes (for example, a daughter's conversion to Christianity; another daughter's marriage to a revolutionary). These tragic events force Tevye to find deep, inner moral reserves to resume life with a positive attitude and a spiritual perspective. Though seemingly a naive Jew, Tevye draws on a higher wisdom fed by his faith in God, yet which also questions God's justice.

One of the many delights in reading *Tevye der Milkhiger* is Tevye's routine quotations and deliberate misquotations of Biblical and Talmudic statements on just about anything. He describes, for example, his son-in-law, Motl the Tailor, as one who "spent day and night **al hatoyre v'al hoavoyde**, putting patches on pants with needle and thread." Tevye is quoting here ironically the Yiddish phrase meaning "on the Torah and on divine service," from a saying of Simeon the Just in the *Ethics of the Fathers*: "The world rests on three things: on the Torah, on divine service, and on kind deeds."

Or, when he invites Menakhem-Mendl to his house and asks his wife Golde for some refreshments for his guest, Tevye says, "**Kol dikhfin yeysey veyitsrakh**—one can't dance on an empty stomach," misquoting as a joke the first passage read at the Passover seder: **Kol dikhfin yeysey veyeykhol, kol ditsrikh yeysey veyifsakh**, "All who are hungry—come and eat, all who are needy—come and celebrate the Passover." Tevye's misquote says, in effect, "Let those who are hungry come and be needy."

Sholom Aleichem has left us an indelible portrait of Jewish life in transition from the shtetls of Eastern Europe to the modern world. His characters have a zest for life, a sense of humor, and healthy skepticism that enable them to transcend the mean particulars of their daily life. They epitomize Jews surviving in a hostile environment with death and cultural disintegration all around them. Though the world of Sholom Aleichem is now lost forever, his writing has memorialized life in the Pale of Settlement, a unique chapter in Jewish history. His cast of characters—from peasants to patricians, Gentiles to Jews—continue to inspire us to persevere and renew ourselves spiritually in a world beset with evils.

From the chapter "Heyntige Kinder" (Today's Children) in Sholom Aleichem's *Tevye der Milkhiger* (Tevye the Milkman):

In regard to what you were saying about today's children: *Children have I raised and exalted* [Isaiah 1:2]—you bring them into the world, suffer for them, sacrifice yourself for them, work hard day and night, and for what? One thinks, maybe I should raise them this way and maybe that way, everyone according to his ideas or his means. To Brodski [a wealthy industrialist], of course, I can't propose a match, but neither am I obligated to lower myself completely, because, upon my word, I'm not just anybody. We don't come, as my wife, may God bless her, says, from tailors and shoemakers, so I figured that I'll do well with my daughters. Why? First of all, God blessed me with beautiful daughters, and a pretty face, as you yourself say, is half a dowry. And secondly, I am today, with God's help, not the same Tevye I once was, so I can count on the best match even in Yehupets, wouldn't you say? And yet there's a God in the world, a compassionate and gracious God, who shows His great wonders summer and winter, up and down, and He says to me: "Tevye, don't talk yourself into foolish fancies and let the world run as it does!" ...Listen to what can happen in this great world of ours, and who runs into all the luck? Tevye schlimazel.

## *Fiddler on the Roof*

The movie and play, *Fiddler on the Roof*, introduced millions of English-speaking people to the world of the 19th-century Russian **shtetl**. Here Teyve the Milkman spoke to God, his family, and the audience, spilling out his hopes, fears, and dreams as he dealt with the details of daily life in a poor Jewish village. This was the fantastic world created by Sholom Aleichem (1859–1916), who achieved enormous success for his work and is recognized as one of the main founders of modern, secular Yiddish literature.

*Fiddler on the Roof* enjoyed enormous success as a Broadway hit in 1964 and then as a Hollywood film in 1971 starring Topol as Teyve. Daily survival, the task of marrying off seven daughters, the arrival of the modern age into a traditional society, and the questioning of God's plan, all capture the emotional heartbeat of Yiddish life. With his brilliant evocation, Sholom Aleichem created characters who have become archetypes of ordinary Jewish people living in the vanished world of the shtetl. For this he is revered as the "Jewish Mark Twain" and his writing lives on, beyond a Yiddish audience.

Zero Mostel in the role of Tevye, in the play *Fiddler on the Roof*, New York, 1964. It ran for 3,242 performances at the Imperial Theater. (YIVO Institute for Jewish Research)

## Isaac Leib Peretz

I.L. Peretz (1852–1915) is the third of the great classical Yiddish writers and the one considered the more literary and probing realist of the trio. Whereas Mendele and Sholom Aleichem wrote about shtetl life and were loved by the masses as folk heroes, Peretz appealed to the intellectuals who lived in the thriving cities. His writing was a call for self-determination and resistance against Jewish humiliation. Peretz was ultimately an optimist who believed that progress was the path to greater Jewish freedom and enlightenment. He understood that shtetl Jews had to examine and alter their beliefs in order for them to be emancipated. Peretz believed in his roots as a Jew, but saw his religion as needing to evolve beyond its traditional strictures to advance the progress of the Jewish people.

Peretz was born into a respected family in the Polish small town of Zamosc. Though raised as an Orthodox Jew, he was eager for secular knowledge even at an early age. He learned Polish, Russian, German, and French so he could read in those languages and be exposed to larger worlds. His family married him off at eighteen in the hope of his settling into a traditional Jewish life. But Peretz was not suited for these constraints and rebelled against his family's wishes, eventually divorcing his wife and marrying his sweetheart. He published poems and lyrics in Hebrew and Polish through the 1870s. At twenty five, Peretz became a lawyer and spent ten years building a successful practice in Zamosc, during which time he wrote little. Peretz was initially a proponent of the Haskalah, and was intensely involved in Russian and Polish issues. He initially felt Yiddish was only a temporary vehicle to reach the masses and not a permanent language for Jews. The murderous Russian pogroms of 1881 altered his views about Yiddish as he found himself identifying more deeply with his underprivileged brethren. He began to write in Yiddish, and in 1888 submitted his long poem, *Monish*, to Sholom Aleichem's *Folksbibliotek* journal. It is considered the first major Yiddish poem, with themes of the earthly and spiritual forces pulling at Monish (a pious youth facing a religious crisis), who symbolizes the Jewish artist struggling against the attractions of secular culture.

In 1886 Peretz became the target of false and unspecified accusations, and his license to practice law was revoked by the government. He moved his family to Warsaw, where for the rest of his life he was

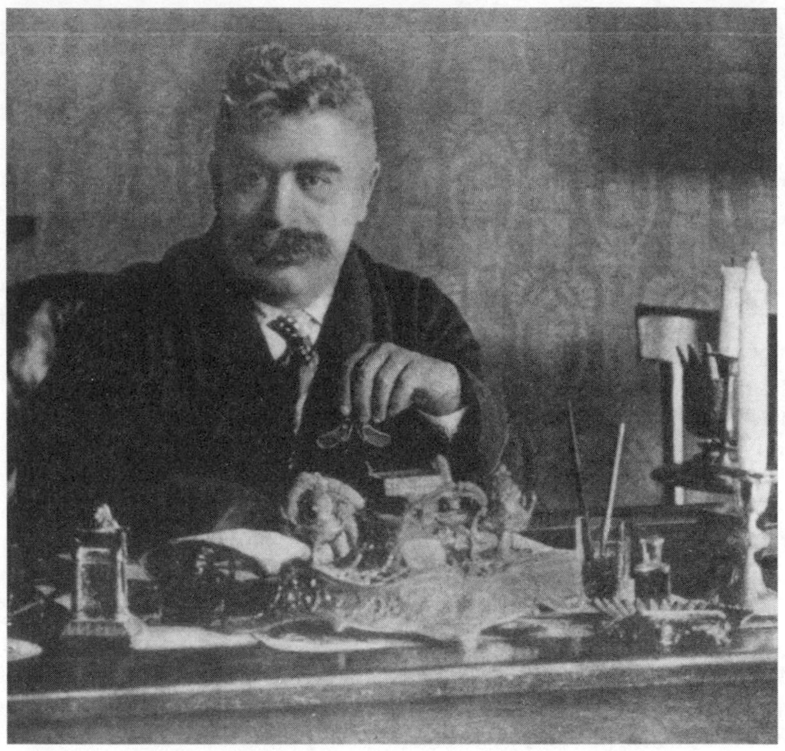

I. L. Peretz (1852–1915), master of modern Yiddish literature, Warsaw, probably at the turn of the century. (YIVO Institute for Jewish Research)

employed by the city's Jewish community. Here he entered the literary life of this cultured city, resumed his writing in earnest, and was active in its social and political affairs. His essays condemned anti-Semitic acts but were also critical of the poverty and intolerance found in the Jewish community. He was the publisher of *Yontev Bletlekh* (Holiday Pages), which argued for enlightenment and socialist ideals. He was also editor of *Di Yidishe Bibliotek* (The Jewish Library), which published a wide array of articles on secular subjects including science. Writing in both Hebrew and Yiddish, he became a literary and intellectual magnet to younger Yiddish writers, many who later became well known (for example David Pinski, Abraham Reisen, Sholem Asch, Joseph Opatoshu).

Peretz wrote poems, essays, plays, and novels, but his short stories and sketches are considered his most astute and powerful work. Though not a Hasidic follower or folk writer, he drew on Hasidic tales to further his own literary conceptions. Peretz's stories layered symbolism and psychological realism, creating a new literary aesthetic in Yiddish literature. His characters, such as Khaim the Porter or Shmerl the Woodcutter, transcended their poverty and oppression with a faith in a higher reality where justice would prevail even after death. The themes of forgiveness, self-sacrifice, modesty, and purity are embedded in his stories.

One of his most famous stories, "Bontshe Shvayg" (Bontshe the Silent), illustrates some of these themes. Bontshe is a victim of poverty and degradation who never complains about his miserable lot in life, so that when he dies he goes straight to heaven, greeted by a chorus of angels, and is invited by the highest judge of the heavenly tribunal to ask for anything he wants as his just reward. And what is Bontshe's greatest wish? "What I'd like most of all," says Bontshe, "is a warm roll with fresh butter every morning." Hearing this, the judges and angels hang their heads in shame, while the prosecutor breaks out in contemptuous laughter. Bontshe came to symbolize the passive, ignorant, and hopeless condition of the typical shtetl Jew.

Another classic neo-Hasidic story is Peretz's "Oyb Nit Hekher" (If Not Higher). This is the story of a Litvak, a skeptical Lithuanian Jew, who is determined to disprove the fervent belief of the Hasidim of Nemirov that their charismatic rebbe ascends to heaven during the Ten Days of Penitence to plead with God on their behalf. Sneaking into the Nemirov rabbi's room one night and hiding under his bed, the Litvak sees the rabbi arising before dawn, dressing himself in peasant clothes, and going into the woods. There the rabbi chops up a tree with an axe and takes the bundle of wood to the broken-down shack of a sick old woman. Pretending to be Vasil, a peasant, he brings the wood inside and proceeds to make a fire in the oven. And as he puts each stick of wood into the oven, he recites a part of the day's **selichos** or penitential prayers. After witnessing this anonymous act of charity, the Litvak becomes a disciple of the rabbi, and thereafter, whenever he hears a Hasid mention that during the Ten Days of Penitence the rabbi of Nemirov goes up to heaven, the Litvak adds quietly, "if not higher."

As one of the three founders of modern Yiddish literature, Peretz contributed new ideas where doubt mingled with faith, where symbolism mixed with psychological realism, where traditional stories were retold in a modern context. For Yiddish readers and writers, Peretz's work was the stage where the intellect struggled with all the contradictions of the modern human condition and strove to achieve transcendence.

**From the short story "The Dead Town" by I.L. Peretz:**

**What's poor and what's rich? We make a living. The paupers beg in the town or in the countryside, but mostly in town. Whoever stretches out his hand gets something. Others look for a soft touch; for example, a middleman haunts the streets in search of a bargain. The Almighty does not desert us. Orphan boys have their "eating days" at the tables of householders and study at the synagogue. Orphan girls become servants and cooks, or go elsewhere to earn their bread. Widows, divorcees, grass widows, sit over their fire ovens and with their heads circled by smoke dream that fully baked rolls grow on trees.**

**...A pauper lives on hope; a merchant on air; and the man who works the soil—the gravedigger, I mean—he never lacks.**

*******

**But suppose the man was no man, his life was no life, and he did neither good nor evil, because he could not do anything, because he had no choice and slept away his whole life as if in a dream? What shall be done with such a soul? Hell? For what? He never harmed a fly. Paradise? For which good deed? He never troubled himself to do anything.**

**Source:** ***A Treasury of Yiddish Stories*,**
**edited by Irving Howe and Eliezar Greenberg**
**(revised edition, Viking Penguin, 1989)**

## The 20th Century

Mendele, Sholom Aleichem, and Peretz laid the foundations for modern Yiddish literature and by the time of their deaths, during World War I, Yiddish writers had found a wide, receptive audience. In Poland, stimulated by writers like Peretz, Warsaw became the Yiddish literary center for younger writers such as David Pinski (1872–1959), noted for his epic novel *Dos Hoyz fun Noyakh Edon* (The House of Noah Edon, 1931); Sholem Asch (1880–1957), author of such popular historical novels as *Kiddush Hashem* (Martyrdom, 1919) and the trilogy *Farn Mabul* (Before the Flood, 1921–31); the poet and short-story writer Abraham Reisen (1876–1953), author of the beautiful and moving poem "May Kemashmalon" (What Does It Tell Us); and the novelist Israel Joshua Singer (1893–1944), master of such family sagas as *Di Brider Ashkenazi* (The Brothers Ashkenazi, 1936), and *Yoshe Kalb* (1932).

The period between 1900 and World War I saw a continuing immigration of East European authors to America. New York City became almost as important as Warsaw as a center for Yiddish writers. Numerous Yiddish newspapers, such as the *Jewish Daily Forward* (see "*Jewish Daily Forward*: The Voice of Yiddish in America"), published their stories and serialized their novels. The immigrant experience became fertile ground for Yiddish storytellers. Some looked back with nostalgia to the Old World; others drew on the present, creating serious or humorous sketches of immigrant characters trying to adapt to a strange, new world. Important writers from this period include: Joseph Opatoshu (1886–1954; for example, *In Poylishe Velder* (In Polish Woods, 1921) and Abraham Cahan (1860–1951; for example, *The Rise of David Levinksy*, 1917), who was editor of the *Jewish Daily Forward*. Israel Joshua Singer's younger brother, Isaac Bashevis Singer, also came to New York City. He was one of the few to find an English-speaking and then worldwide audience for his work. Isaac Bashevis Singer's success exceeded that of any contemporary Jewish writer and he was given the Nobel Prize in 1978 for his unique expressionist and even surreal Yiddish vision (see "The Yiddish Nobel: Isaac Bashevis Singer").

As the turmoil leading up to World War II continued, Jews in Europe kept fleeing social upheaval and persecution. As entry into America became more difficult, many immigrated to places like South Africa, Australia, and Latin America. Here too, Yiddish readers eagerly awaited new work from abroad. After the Russian Revolution (1917), the Soviet Union seemed to offer a greater freedom and hope for Jews. They had fought in the Revolution, hoping that its socialist ideals would end czarist oppression. Many Yiddish writers and poets flourished in the initial atmosphere of tolerance and experimentation. But as Stalinism's deadly shadow spread, there was a resurgence of anti-Semitism, and the blossoming of Yiddish Soviet writers was doomed to elimination in the gulags and by firing squads. Notable writers, many who were executed, included Moshe Kulbak (1896–1940), for example, the novel *Zelmenianier*, 1931; David Bergelson (1884–1952), for example, the novel *Nokh*

## The Yiddish Nobel: Isaac Bashevis Singer

Though Yiddish literature had a golden age from the 1850s to the 1940s, with writers like Sholem Yankev Abramovitsh, creator of Mendele Mokher Seforim (Mendele the Bookseller), Sholom Aleichem, I.L. Peretz, and Sholem Asch, it was Isaac Bashevis Singer (1904–1991) who captured the imagination of readers worldwide. His translated stories and novels struck a universal chord, especially in America, and introduced his readers to the world of Yiddish culture. Singer wrote about the lost world of the Jewish shtetls and ghettos of pre–World War II Poland.

Singer was born in the village of Radzymin, Poland. His father was a poor Hasidic rabbi and spiritual mentor for a small congregation where strict pieties and religious joy intermingled. Singer's only real education was during the four years he spent with his mother at the home of her father, the rabbi of Bilgoray—a classic shtetl environment. The language of the home and streets was Yiddish. The family settled in Warsaw, a cosmopolitan city with a thriving Jewish ghetto. In Warsaw, Singer frequented the Writers Club where his older brother, Israel Joshua Singer, was a well-known and respected writer (for example, *The Brothers Ashkenazi*, 1936). In Warsaw Isaac Bashevis honed his writing skills and, with the rise of Nazism, followed his brother to New York in 1935. In America he continued writing in Yiddish even though some of the themes were now about Jews struggling to make sense of this New World.

Singer's work is inhabited by individuals caught in the contradictions of the human condition. Good and evil, the old world and the new, morality and sexual passions all define their conflicts. His characters are often obsessed and caught between the dilemmas of their passions, their self-destructive behaviors, and their creative potentials. In this intense world, where mysticism and folklore, pogroms and weddings, **dybbuks** and demons, and reality and illusion all mix, Singer's characters dance like figures in a Marc Chagall painting.

Singer's early years in America were difficult. Israel Joshua preceded him and had established success with his Yiddish audience and Isaac was often in his brother's shadow. But eventually Isaac Bashevis secured a growing readership with the weekly serialization of his work in the largest Yiddish newspaper in America, the *Jewish Daily Forward* (see "*Jewish Daily Forward*: The Voice of Yiddish in America"). Yiddish was the only language Singer really knew well and he deliberately chose to write in it to make sure that its Old World values wouldn't disappear. He was well versed in philosophy, from the writings of the Talmud to the ideas of Spinoza and Kant, and he would often embellish philosophical thoughts with Yiddish humor or pathos (for example, *The Spinoza of Market Street*).

Singer's work has broad themes. He draws on tales of the supernatural taken from Jewish superstitions, where demons and ghosts all interact with the living, and brings medieval sensibilities alive (for example, *Satan in Goray*). He depicts the simpleminded Jew struggling to survive (*Gimpel the Fool*), or the disbelieving Jew questioning God after the Holocaust (*Shadows on the Hudson*). Singer wrote sweeping epics of the old Jewish families wrenched and split by modern pressures (*The Manor, The Estate*). He also wrote children's stories (*Zlateh the Goat*) and fairytales with simple, endearing themes.

Singer was awarded the Nobel Prize for Literature in 1978 honoring his unique vision and the power of the Yiddish language to enthrall readers worldwide.

*Alemen* (After All), 1913; and Peretz Markish (1895–1952), for example, the novel *Dor Ayn, Dor Oys* (Generation In, Generation Out; 1929). The Soviet promise of a home for Yiddish literature was never realized.

The Nazi Holocaust decimated the Yiddish-speaking population of Europe along with its writers, poets, and artists. Those who were lucky escaped to America, Palestine, or other countries. The work of some Yiddish writers survives this period, including those of the poet Yitzkhok Katzenelson (1886–1944) and the writer Emanuel Ringelblum (1897–1944). Both took part in the Warsaw ghetto uprising and documented their brutal experiences for posterity.

Prior to formation of the State of Israel (1948), Palestine was not an important center for Yiddish writing. Many early Zionists believed that Hebrew should be the dominant language, and Yiddish was often regarded with disdain, even though it was spoken widely by Ashkenazi Jews. Early pioneers were drawn to the kibbutznik way of life and included Yiddish writers emigrating from Europe. These included writers and poets such as Barahman Lev (1910–1970), Yoel Mastboim (1884–1957), Abrahman Rives (1900–1962), and the woman poet Rikudah Potash (1906–1965). After statehood greater efforts were made to recognize Yiddish with centers of study and publications. Much of the Yiddish writing in Israel after the Holocaust centered on stories, novels, and memoirs recounting the hardships of survival in Europe. Yiddish scholarly activity now concentrated mainly on Israeli universities. Since 1994, the scholarly journal *Khulyot* (Links), featuring articles in Hebrew and Yiddish dealing with Yiddish writing and writers, has been published jointly by faculties of the Universities of Haifa and Tel-Aviv (see "Hebridish: Yiddish in Israel").

Prior to World War II, Poland, Russia, and America were the three centers of Yiddish writing. After the war, Poland lost 90 percent of its Jews. Russia's anti-Semitic policies silenced most Jewish writers and many migrated to Israel up through the breakup of the Soviet Union. Only America remained as a vital center for Yiddish literature, especially as European refugees arrived immediately after the war. Yiddish centers, like YIVO (See "YIVO Institute for Jewish Research") were repositories of Yiddish culture, and Yiddish studies were introduced in some American universities. In general, however, there has been a steady decline of Yiddish writers in America, and with the death of

Issac Bashevis Singer (1991) a dominant Yiddish literary voice was lost. Nevertheless, a young, vital, mostly American-born generation of Yiddish writers has sprung up phoenix-like in the wake of the Holocaust. The work of this group was first exhibited in 1989, in an anthology titled *Vidervuks* (Regrowth), published jointly by the League for Yiddish and the Yugentruf organizations.

*Vidervuks: a nayer dor yidishe shraybers* (Regrowth: A New Generation of Yiddish Writers) features the work of twenty young poets, short-story writers, and essayists, born after the Holocaust in such diverse places as Argentina, Canada, Israel, Poland, Russia, and the United States. Among them are emerging figures in Yiddish cultural circles such as Leybl Botwinik, David E. Fishman, Paul Glasser, Itzek Gottesman, Avrom Novershtern, Leye Robinson, David G. Roskies, and Gitl Schaechter-Viswanath. The anthology was named after a Yiddish literary group called Vidervuks that appeared some eighty years ago in post-World War I Kiev. Its name symbolized a rebirth of Yiddish literary activity after the pogroms of 1917–20. If the recently reincarnated Vidervuks will live up to its promise, it will constitute a rebirth of Yiddish cultural activity in the 21st century.

Thus, though contemporary Yiddish literature is often described as a dying art, it continues to make its presence known. As the Nobel Laureate Isaac Bashevis Singer said:

> Why do I write in a dying language? I like to write about ghosts. Nothing fits a ghost better than a dying language. Ghosts love Yiddish—they all speak it. I believe in resurrection and the Messiah will soon come, and millions of Yiddish speaking corpses will rise from their graves one day and their first questions will be: "Is there any new Yiddish book to read?"
>
> Source: "Isaac in America," WNET Public Television, 1985.
> (From Singer's remarks when receiving the Nobel Prize, not found in his speech from Nobel Archives.)

## Body of Golden Rings: Women Yiddish Poets by Kathryn Hellerstein, Ph.D.*

Women have been publishing poems in Yiddish since at least the late 1500s, when Yiddish was the language of daily life for most of Ashkenazic Jewry in Europe. Today, over 400 years later, women are still publishing poems in Yiddish. The first of these poets, or at least those whose poems have survived the years, were a few exceptional pious girls and women, some the daughters of rabbis or printers, all more literate than most other Jewish women. They published and probably lived in Cracow, Halle, Prague, and Amsterdam. The women who today write poetry in Yiddish work as teachers, business women, professional writers, and performers, and conduct their daily lives in English or Hebrew, in the United States, Canada, Australia, and Israel.

Among the first was Royzl Fishls, daughter of a printer. In 1586, soon after her father's death, Royzl introduced a Yiddish version of the Psalms with her own poem explaining that the printer has died and his daughter has taken over his work. Such early Yiddish translations and prayer-poems were written to give the girls, women, and uneducated men who could not read the sacred language of Hebrew access to the holy texts that governed their daily lives.

After the Haskalah (Jewish Enlightenment) in the mid-19th century, Yiddish poetry developed from its devotional and folk origins into secular forms in the nascent Yiddish theater and the socialist movement. Men dominated the Yiddish literary world—following in the steps of the great fiction writers Sholem Yankev Abramovitsh (known by the name of his most famous character, Mendele Mokher Seforim, Mendele the Bookseller), Sholom Rabinovitz (better known as Sholom Aleichem), and I.L. Peretz. Yet women such as Roza Goldshteyn (1870–?), involved in the Jewish Bund and the early labor movements in Eastern Europe and America in the 1890s and 1900s, wrote poems in the political genre of their male contemporaries, such as the Labor Poets Morris Rosenfeld and David Edelstadt.

In the 1920s, though, a different kind of poem began to emerge from women. In Poland, Miriam Ulinover (1890–1944) published poems in her book, *Der bobes oytser* (Grandmother's Treasure) (Warsaw, 1922) that preserve women's religious life and language of earlier generations. Ulinover deliberately wrote in the folk idiom

*Senior Fellow in Yiddish and Jewish Studies, Department of Germanic Languages and Literatures, University of Pennsylvania. Translations from the Yiddish © Kathryn Ann Hellerstein.

and simple language of her great-grandmother, yet her poems speak from a distinctively modern perspective.

With a bold, urban voice, Kadya Molodowsky (1894–1975), publishing poetry, fiction, drama, essays, and journalism from 1927 in Warsaw through 1975 in New York, also bridges tradition and modernity. In a 1927 poem, entitled "Froyen-lider I" (Women-Poems I), she writes of a young woman's struggle with the traditional Jewish roles and laws for women:

The women of our family will come to me in dreams at night and say:
Modestly we carried a pure blood across generations,
Bringing it to you like well-guarded wine from the kosher
Cellars of our hearts.

(Women-Poems I, lines 1–4)

The young woman replies to the accusations of her ghostly female ancestors with a question:
And why should this blood without blemish
Be my conscience, like a silken thread
Bound upon my brain,
And my life, a page plucked from a holy book,
The first line torn?

(Women-Poems I, lines 15–19)

As the modern, secular woman untied the binding piety of "blood without a blemish," she found that her poetry in Yiddish retained the essence of Jewish tradition.

In the 1920s, in New York, some women poets were connected to the modernist literary movements, the *Yunge* and the *Introspectivists*. Fradl Shtok (1890–1930?), Celia Dropkin (1887–1956), and Anna Margolin (1887–1952) arrived in New York between 1907 and 1914 from Galicia and White Russia. Fradl Shtok's sonnets and lyrics subverted the conventions of love and beauty with a wicked touch, as in these stanzas from "Dusks":

Fly about in the sunset, you bee,
Your body of golden rings
Is shimmering into my eyes,
Is luring me to sing.
You fly in rings around me, too,
Intolerably tiresome,
Bringing no honey, for I know
You want to leave me venom.

After Shtok published a collection of Yiddish short stories in 1919 and a novel in English in 1927, she fell silent. Celia Dropkin's poems present the complexities of a woman's erotic life. Her 1935 book, *In heysn vint* (In the Hot Wind) includes poems she published in the 1920s, such as "My Guest," a poem that gives hospitality a new face:

You are welcome, welcome, my guest.
Throw down the load of your life,
Undress yourself, rest
In my light-filled house.
Wash your hands, your feet,
Sit at the table with me,
Quiet your hunger, your thirst
At my breast, at my breast.

Considered the quintessential modernist, Anna Margolin wrote poems as sleek and hard as bronze sculptures, such as "Years," which was collected in her 1929 book, *Lider* (Poems):

Like women, much loved yet never sated,
Who walk through life with laughter and with anger
In their eyes of fire and agate—
So are the years.

And they were also like actors
Who mouth Hamlet half-heartedly for the market,
Like noblemen in a proud country
Who seize the rebellion by the nape.

And see, how demure they are now, my God,
And mute as a crushed clavier,
And grasp at anyone's impulse and mockery as love,
    And seek you, not believing in you.

My mother's old *tkhine*-book lies on the garden bench.
And I'm still waiting under the cherry tree—
The clay pitcher is full of water, clear and cool,
And my left hand tilts it toward the lips of the dream.

But why, then, is the shepherd of my father's sheep
Named not Jacob, but Ivan—and from his belt an ax
Flashes, and in his bosom lies a sack
Ready for my mother's Sabbath dress?

In 1977, in California, the Ukrainian-born poet Malka Heifetz Tussman (1893–1987) wrote "In Spite," protesting the Holocaust:

In spite of the destroyers,
To spite them, I will not cry openly,
I will not write down my sorrow
On paper.

Tussman asserted her faith in life by writing new poems that make Yiddish expand beyond the words printed on a page:

To register words
With ink—
Not enough for me.

Letters in words
Double one on the other
To make shades of color.

(Not Enough, 1980)

Philadelphia-born Rukhl Fishman, a student of Tussman's in Los Angeles who moved to Israel at age nineteen, in 1954, characterized her own writing in Yiddish as urgent and natural as the harsh desert climate in the opening poem of her 1966 book, *Derner nokhn regn* (Thorns After Rain):

Like sun on my heated neck,
Like thorns after rain,
Sharp and clean,
Unavoidable—
Poems come.

Despite the decline in the secular Yiddish-speaking population, a number of women continue to write poetry in Yiddish. Some were born in Europe, before World War II, and grew up speaking Yiddish, such as Rivke Basman-Ben-Haim and Hadassah Rubin, who came to Israel after the war; Beyle Schaechter-Gottesman, who lives and writes in New York City; and Chava Rosenfarb, in Toronto. Others were born after the war, in Australia (Hinde Burstin), in the United States (Gitl Schaechter Viswanath), and in England (Leye Robinson). These women of the post-war generation exemplify an unusual commitment to the continued growth of poetry in Yiddish at a moment when most of the people among whom they live do not speak, understand, or read the language.

That they choose to write poetry in Yiddish is not, however, an anomaly. Many earlier Yiddish poets and writers, female and male, turned to Yiddish after initially writing in other languages, such as German (Moyshe-Leyb Halpern), Russian (Dovid Edelshtat, Celia

Dropkin), Polish, English, or Hebrew (Mendele Mokher Seforim, Sholom Aleichem, I.L. Peretz). While many of the earlier generations of writers may have chosen Yiddish for ideological reasons, it was also a logical choice for most of them. Yiddish was their **mame-loshn** (mother tongue) and the vernacular language of the Jewish population in which they lived. Poets who write in Yiddish today face a different set of circumstances. Whether in the United States, Canada, Australia, or Israel, most Jews do not speak Yiddish as their primary language, with the exception of some Orthodox and Hasidic communities.

Women writing poetry in Yiddish at the beginning of the 21st century face the same problem as their male colleagues, a question that overwhelms the differences of gender. For whom are they writing? In a strange way, they are like the earliest devotional poets, who set down their lines for other women who could not write their own, who were, in effect, silenced by their culture. The recent Yiddish poets speak for those silenced by history—the Jewish children never born after the war in Europe, and also the Jews of today who have forgotten the Yiddish language.

## A Catskills Recommended Reading List

### Fiction

Allegra Goodman, *Kaaterskill Falls* (Dial Press, 1998)

Terry Kay, *Shadow Song* (Pocket books, 1994)

Thane Rosenbaum, "Bingo by the Bungalow," story from collection *Elijah Visible* (St. Martin's Press, 1996)

Philip Roth, *The Professor of Desire* (Farrar, Strauss & Giroux, 1977)

Isaac Bashevis Singer, *Enemies: A Love Story* (Farrar, Strauss & Giroux, 1972)

Art Spegelman, *Maus II* (Pantheon Books, 1991)

Herman Wouk, *Majorie Morningstar* (Doubleday, 1955)

### History

Stefan Kanger, *A Summer World: The Attempt To Build a Jewish Eden in the Catskills* (Farrar, Strauss & Giroux, 1989)

Alf Evers, *The Catskills: From Wilderness to Woodstock* (Overlook Press, 1982)

### Memoirs

Phil Brown, *Catskill Culture: A Mountain Rat's Memoirs of the Great Jewish Resort Area* (Temple University Press, 1998)

Tania Grossinger, *Growing Up at Grossingers* (D. McKay Company, 1975)

Source: "Yesterday's Borscht and Knishes Return as Today's Reading List," by Joseph Berger, *New York Times*, August 31, 2000

# Yiddish Proverbs and Sayings

## For Fools and Wise Mentshn

Almost every culture has its proverbs, maxims, and truisms that succinctly encapsulate popular beliefs and values. Many are similar the world over; others are unique to a people's experience. Proverbs have an ancient history in the Jewish literary tradition going back to the Old Testament and Solomon's Book of Proverbs. Aphorisms continued to be compiled in the Talmud (body of Jewish law and tradition); Midrash (interpretation of scripture); and wisdom literature (for example, Book of Solomon). These proverbs still continue to be read and studied by students and scholars to further elucidate what it means to be an aware and just person.

Yiddish developed its own language rich in **shprikhverter** (folk sayings) that captured the soul of **shtetl** life. These sayings continue to illuminate the great truths about the human condition with simplicity, humor, and bite. Despair and tragedy were polished with hope and wit, using irony and brevity to turn many proverbs into gems of perception. These sayings helped Jews to transcend a pessimism that could have easily broken their spirit through millennia of oppression. During the thousand years that Yiddish evolved, life's circumstances resulted in many perceptive individuals coming up with the appropriate proverb. Youth and age, parents and children, fools and wise men, poor and rich, love and marriage, enemies and friends—you're sure to find a few that will become your favorites!

# Fools and Wise Mentshn

**A kluger veyst vos er zogt, a nar zogt vos er veyst.**
*A smart person knows what he says, [but] a fool says what he knows.*

**A kluger farshteyt fun eyn vort tsvey.**
*From one word, a smart person grasps two.*

**Az a nar varft arayn a shteyn in vaser, kenen es tsen khakhomim nit aroysnemen.**
*If a fool throws a stone into a well, ten wise ones can't get it out.*

**Vi men darf hobn moyekh, helft nit keyn koyekh.**
*Where brains are needed, brawn doesn't help.*

**Bay ferd kukt men af di tseyn, bay a mentshn afn seykhl.**
*With a horse one looks at the teeth, with a person one looks at the brains.*

**Af a sheynem iz gut tsu kukn, mit a klugn iz gut tsu lebn.**
*Someone beautiful is good to look at; someone smart is good to live with.*

**Sheynkeyt fargeyt, khokhme bashteyt.**
*Beauty fades, wisdom stays.*

**Far gelt bakumt men alts akhuts seykhl.**
*Money can get you everything except brains.*

**Az men vil zayn tsu klug banarisht men zikh gor.**
*One who wants to be too smart makes a complete fool of himself.*

**Es felt im mebl in boydem.**
*He needs furniture in the attic. (He's got bats in the belfry.)*

**A gantser nar iz a halber novi.**
*A complete fool is a half-prophet.*

**An eyzl derkent men in di lange oyern, a nar in der langer tsung.**
*You recognize a donkey by the long ears, a fool by the long tongue.*

**A kranker vet gezunt vern, a shiker vet zikh oysnikhtern, ober a nar vet blaybn a nar.**
*Someone sick will get well, someone drunk will sober up, but a fool will remain a fool.*

**Der kluger bahalt dem seykhl, der nar vayzt zayn narishkeyt aroys.**
*The smart person conceals intellect, the fool reveals stupidity.*

## Poor and Rich

**Az men hot nit keyn broyt iz erger vi der toyt.**
*Having no bread is worse than being dead.*

**Keyner veyst nit vemen der shukh kvetsht.**
*Nobody knows whom the shoe pinches.*

**Fun glik tsum umglik iz a shpan; fun umglik tsu glik iz a mayl.**
*From good to bad luck is a step; from bad to good luck is a mile.*

**Orem iz nit keyn shand, ober nit keyn groyser koved oykh.**
*Being poor is no disgrace, but it's no great honor either.*

**Az es kumt tsonveytok, fargest men kopveytok.**
*When a toothache comes, one forgets a headache.*

**An oreman hot nit vos tsu farlirn.**
*The poor have nothing to lose.*

**Az an oreman est a hun, iz er krank oder der hun.**
*If a poor person eats chicken, either he or the chicken is sick.*

**Eyner hot nit keyn apetit tsum esn, der anderer hot nit keyn esn tsum apetit.**
*One has no appetite for food; [while] another has no food for his appetite.*

**Tsores mit yoykh iz gringer tsu fartrogn vi tsores on yoykh.**
*Troubles with soup are easier to bear than troubles without soup.*

**Af dray zakhn shteyt di velt: af gelt, af gelt, un af gelt.**
*On three things the world stands: on money, on money, and on money.*

This proverb is a cynical parody of a famous saying from the Ethics of the Fathers (part of the Mishnah or Oral Law), "*The world stands on three things: on Torah study, on Divine Service, and on kind deeds.*"

**Ver es hot di matbeye hot di deye.**
*Whoever has the dough has the say-so.*

**Az men iz raykh iz men sheyn, klug, un men ken zingen.**
*One who is rich is good-looking, smart, and knows how to sing.*

**Gelt geyt tsu gelt.**
*Money goes to money.*

**An oysher hot faynt koved vi a kats hot faynt smetene.**
*A rich person hates honor like a cat hates cream.*

**Orem un raykh zenen in keyver glaykh.**
*Poor and rich are alike in the grave.*

**Takhrikhim makht men on keshenes.**
*There are no pockets in shrouds.*

**Az men volt zikh kenen oyskoyfn fun toyt, voltn di oremelayt gut parnose gehat.**
*If the poor could die for the rich, they'd make a good living.*

## God and Humankind

**Got lozt zinken, ober nit dertrinken.**
*God lets one sink but not drown.*

**Der vos git lebn git oykh tsum leben.**
*He who gives life also gives a living.*

**Got hot lib dem oreman un helft dem nogid.**
*God loves the poor and helps the rich.*

**Got shikt di refue far di make.**
*God sends the remedy before the malady.*

**Mit eyn hant shtroft Got un mit der anderer bentsht er.**
*God punishes with one hand and blesses with the other.*

**A mentsh trakht un Got makht.**
*Man proposes and God disposes. (Literally, A person thinks and God does.)*

> *A variant is* **A mentsh trakht un Got lakht.** *(Literally, A person thinks and God laughs.)*

**Az Got vil, shist a bezem.**
*If God wills it, even a broom can shoot.*

Yiddish theater poster, New York, during the heyday
of American Yiddish culture, around 1920.
(American Jewish Historical Society, Waltham, Massachusetts,
and New York, New York.)

**Got veyst vos er tut.**
*God knows what He does.*

**Vos bashert, dos vert.**
*What will be, will be. (Literally, What is predestined, that will be.)*

**Bay Got zenen ale glaykh, orem un raykh.**
*God doesn't care which is which, poor or rich. (Literally, To God they are all the same, poor and rich.)*

**Yeder eyner far zikh; Got far undz alemen.**
*Everyone is for himself; God is for all of us.*

**Fun dayn moyl in Gots oyern.**
*From your mouth to God's ears.*

## Youth and Age

**A yung beyml beygt zikh, an alt brekht zikh.**
*A young tree bends, an old one breaks.*

**Vi eyner tsu zibn, azoy tsu zibetsik.**
*As one is at seven, so at seventy.*

**A yunger ken, an alter muz.**
*A young person can, an old one must.*

**Kinder un naronim zogn dem emes.**
*Children and fools tell the truth.*

**Vos di alte kayen, tuen di yunge shpayen.**
*What the old chew, the young spit out.*

**Zorgn un yor makhn groy di hor.**
*Worries and years make the hair gray.*

**Vos elter alts kelter.**
*The older one gets, the colder one gets.*

**Alt zol men vern, ober nit zayn.**
*One should get old, but not be old.*

**Far yugnt lebt men nisht; far elter shtarbt men nisht.**
*One doesn't live because of youth; one doesn't die because of old age.*

**Az men lebt, derlebt men.**
*As long as one lives, one lives to see everything.*

**Vi lang di oygn zenen ofn darf a mentsh hofn.**
*Where there's life, there's hope. (Literally, While the eyes are open, a person may hope.)*

**A mentsh vert geboyrn mit kulyikes un shtarbt mit ofene hent.**
*A person is born with clenched fists and dies with open hands.*

**Tsu shtarbn hot men alemol tsayt.**
*One always has time for dying.*

**S'iz gut tsu shikn a foyln nokh dem malekhamoves.**
*It's good to send someone lazy for the angel of death.*

## Parents and Children

**Got hot nit gekent zayn imetum, hot er beshafn mames.**
*God couldn't be everywhere, so He created mothers.*

**Kinder un gelt iz a sheyne velt.**
*Children and money make a beautiful world.*

**Bay a tate un mame iz keyn kind nit iberik.**
*To a father and mother no child is superfluous.*

**Bay a mame iz nito keyn mies kind.**
*To a mother no child of hers is ugly.*

**Kinder hobn iz laykhter vi kinder dertsien.**
*It's easier to have children than to raise them.*

**Kleyne kinder lozn nit shlofn; groyse kinder lozn nit lebn.**
*Small children don't let you sleep; big ones don't let you live.*

**Der tate shelt, ober es tut im vey dos harts.**
*The father curses, but his heart aches.*

**Eyn tate ken oyshaltn tsen kinder, ober tsen kinder kenen nit eyn tate oyshaltn.**
*One father can support ten children, but ten children can't support one father.*

## Yiddish First Names: From Alter to Yentl

Apart from Yiddish names derived from Hebrew—such as Yankev (from Hebrew Yaakov, Jacob); Itzik (from Hebrew Yitzchak, Isaac); and Yoshe (from Hebrew Yosef, Joseph)—the oldest Yiddish first names derived from Jewish dialects of Old Italian and Old French. Among them were the female names Yentl, derived from Old Italian Gentile, meaning "genteel, noble"; Shprintse, from Old Italian Speranza (hope); and Dreyzl, from the Old Italian and Latin name Drusilla. Among the male names were Bunim, from Old French Bonhomme (good man); Fayvish, from a Romance form of Latin Phoebus (the sun); and Bendet or Beynush, both derived from Old Italian Benedetto (blessed). These names are still borne by descendants of European Jews.

Many more Yiddish given names, however, are based on German. Such names include the male names Alter (old), Zelig (happy), Leyb (lion); and the female names Blume (flower), Golde (gold), and Royze (rose).

After Yiddish speakers were forced by the Crusades to move eastward into Slavic countries, they adopted first names from various Slavic languages. Most of these, however, were female names, since the Hebrew and Yiddish names of males (used for calling them up to the Torah-reading) were considered sacred and not lightly changeable. Some of these female names were Zlate (from Czech for gold, translating Yiddish Golde); Charne (from Polish for black); and Dobre (from Russian for good, translating Yiddish Gute, Gite).

Yiddish given names of males are often double, combining a sacred (Biblical) name and a corresponding vernacular name. The two names may be equivalent in meaning, as Tsvi Hersh (deer), Dov Ber (bear), Asher Zelig (happy). Or, the vernacular name may derive from the sacred name, as Shlomo Zalmen (Solomon), Shmuel Zanvil (Samuel), and Yisroel Iser (Israel). Or, they may be traditionally related, as Naftoli Herts (Naftali deer, based on Genesis 49:21) and Binyomin Zev (Benjamin wolf, based on Genesis 49:27). Or, they may be alliterative, as Avrom Aba, Menakhem Mendl, and Noson Note.

Double female names are rarer, and combined arbitrarily. Typical examples are Shifra Beyla (Hebrew and Romance for beauty), Khaye Golde (Vivian Aurelia), Leye Rifke (Leah Rebecca).

**A mame muz hobn a groyse fartekh di khesroynes fun di kinder tsu fardekn.**
*A mother must have a large apron to cover up her children's faults.*

**Az der tate shenkt dem zun, lakhn beyde; az der zun shenkt dem tatn, veynen beyde.**
*When a father gives to his son, both laugh; when the son gives to his father, both weep.*

**S'iz nito a guter toyt un nito a shlekhte mame.**
*There's no such thing as a good death or a bad mother.*

**Eltern lernen oys di kinder redn; kinder lernen oys di eltern shvaygn.**
*Parents teach children to talk; children teach parents to keep quiet.*

**Kleyne kinder, kleyne tsores; groyse kinder, groyse tsores.**
*Small children, small troubles; big children, big troubles.*

**Mames trern un tatens shmits kumen in lebn shtark tsu nits.**
*Mother's tears and father's spanks are of great use in their children's lives.*

**Fun der mames klap vert dem kind nit keyn lokh in kop.**
*From a mother's blow a child won't get a hole in the head.*

## Beauty

**Beser a bis fun a sheynem eyder a kush fun a miesn.**
*Better a bite from a beautiful person than a kiss from a homely one.*

**Ale kales zenen sheyn; ale meysim zenen frum.**
*All brides are beautiful; all the dead are devout.*

**Tsu sheyn iz amol a khisorn.**
*Too beautiful is sometimes a defect.*

**Es iz laykhter tsu makhn a barg klener eyder a mies ponem shener.**
*It's easier to make a mountain smaller than to make a homely face beautiful.*

**Kuk af di meydl, nit af di kleydl.**
*Look at the girl, not at her dress.*

**Kheyn shtaygt iber sheyn.**
*Grace outshines looks. (Literally, Charm rises above beauty.)*

**Kheyn un mazl koyft men nit in krom.**
*Charm and luck can't be bought in a store.*

**A miese moyd hot faynt dem shpigl.**
*A plain-looking girl hates the mirror.*

**A khisorn: di kale iz tsu sheyn.**
*A defect: the bride is too pretty.*

*Intended as a put-down to spoilsports who manage to find fault in everything, even a beautiful bride!*

## Love and Marriage

**Tsedoke gebn un lib hobn ken men nit neytn.**
*Charity and love can't be forced.*

**Di libe iz blind.**
*Love is blind.*

**Ganovim un farlibte hobn lib fintsternish.**
*Thieves and lovers like the dark.*

**A tropn libe brengt amol a yam trern.**
*A drop of love can sometimes bring a sea of tears.*

**Kleyne meydlekh tseraysn di shertsn, groyse meydlekh tseraysn di hertsn.**
*Little girls tear dresses, big girls tear hearts.*

**Alte libe zhavert nit.**
*Old love doesn't rust.*

**A harts iz a shlos; men darf dem rikhtikn shlisl.**
*A heart is like a lock; one needs the right key to open it.*

**Hob mikh veyniker lib, nor hob mikh lang lib.**
*Love me less, but love me long.*

**Dos harts zet beser fun dem oyg.**
*The heart sees better than the eye.*

**Az men tut a shidekh muz men zen mit vemen vet men dernokh tsegeyn.**
*Before marrying someone, be sure you know whom you may later divorce.*

## Vishniac and Riis: Photographers of Shtetl and Slum

Life for Jews in the **shtetls** of Eastern Europe or the immigrant ghettos of America was too often characterized by harsh conditions and desperate poverty. Two photographers, Roman Vishniac and Jacob Riis, dedicated themselves to portraying this life and captured a world that has disappeared forever.

**Roman Vishniac** (1897–1990) was born near St. Petersburg and was highly educated, achieving a medical degree. He also worked as a photojournalist who, at great personal risk, documented Jewish life in Germany and Eastern Europe as the Nazis consolidated power. Hiding his camera under his coat, Vishniac took over 16,000 photos. He was jailed numerous times by the Nazis and was lucky to survive.

Moving unnoticed amongst his people Vishniac recorded their daily lives and expressions. His books, *A Vanished World* and *Children of a Vanished World* are testaments to his dedication and vision. His work is deeply moving and sad, freezing for posterity the tragedy of a world and people experiencing their last moments. Vishniac understood what lay ahead when he wrote: "I knew that Hitler had made it his mission to exterminate all Jews, especially children and women.... I was unable to save my people, only their memory."

After Vishniac immigrated to America he became a pioneer in color photomicroscopy and time-lapse cinematography. A true Renaissance man, he brought artistry to the microscopic world of science and to his disciplined record of shtetl life.

**Jacob Riis** (1849–1914) arrived in New York City from Denmark in 1870 and worked as a photojournalist and writer. His portraits of poor immigrants and their living conditions made him one of the foremost social crusaders at the turn of the 20th century. His highly acclaimed book, *How the Other Half Lives*, played a pivotal role in advocating reforms against the exploitation and neglect of the poor of all races. Though not Jewish himself, Riis's portraits of "Jewtown" and the Jewish garment sweatshops captured the poverty and crowding of Lower East Side Jews with indignation and compassion.

Unlike the Jews in Vishniac's photos, Riis' subjects survived. They were the lucky ones who saved enough to escape the oppression of the shtetls. And though many still had to endure hardship in America, their descendants became successful and found a life of opportunity that shtetl Jews could have never imagined.

**Az di kale iz nit sheyn, hot zi andere mayles.**
*If the bride is not beautiful, she has other qualities.*

**A shadkhn muz zayn a ligner.**
*A matchmaker must be a liar.*

**Vi dos vayb is a malke, azoy iz der man a melekh.**
*As the wife is queen, so the husband is king.*

**A vayb makht fun der man a nar oder a har.**
*A wife makes of her husband either a fool or a master.*

**Sheyn iz di libe nokh a geshmake vetshere.**
*Lovely is love after a tasty supper.*

**Tsvishn man un vayb iz nor Got a shoyfet.**
*Between husband and wife only God is a judge.*

## Health

**Gezunt iz beser fun gelt.**
*Health is better than wealth (literally, better than money).*

**Di shrek fun toyt iz erger vi di toyt aleyn.**
*The fear of death is worse than death itself.*

**Nifter pifter, abi me lebt un hot parnose.**
*Dead, shmed, as long as you can make a living.*

**A mentsh iz amol shtarker vi ayzn in a mol shvakher vi a flig.**
*A person is sometimes stronger than iron and sometimes weaker than a fly.*

**Az men iz nor gezunt iz men shoyn raykh.**
*If one is healthy one is already wealthy.*

**A dokter tor men nit vintshn a gut yor.**
*One must not wish a doctor a good year.*

**A dokter un a kabren zenen shutfim.**
*A doctor and a gravedigger are partners.*

**Di tsayt iz der bester royfe.**
*Time is the best healer.*

**Az a kranker geyt tsum dokter vert dos ershte geholfn der dokter.**
*When a sick person goes to the doctor, the first to be helped will be the doctor.*

**Beser a gezunter oreman eyder a kranker oysher.**
*Better poor and healthy than sick and wealthy.*

**Eyder dray vokhn krank iz beser dray yor gezunt.**
*Three years healthy is better than three weeks sick.*

**Freg nit dem royfe, freg dem khoyle.**
*Don't ask the doctor, ask the patient.*

**A krankn fregt men, a gezuntn git men.**
*A sick person one asks [before offering], but to a healthy person one just gives.*

## Enemies and Friends

**Beser tsen gute fraynd eyder eyn soyne.**
*Better ten good friends than one enemy.*

**Far keyn soyne ken men zikh nit oyshitn.**
*One cannot protect oneself from an enemy.*

**Freg baym soyne eyn eytse un tu farkert.**
*Ask an enemy advice and then do the opposite.*

**Beser a bis fun a fraynd eyder a kush fun a faynd.**
*Better a bite from a friend than a kiss from a foe.*

**Khavershaft iz shtarker fun brudershaft.**
*Comradeship is stronger than brotherhood.*

**A guter fraynd iz beser fun a fraynd.**
*A good friend is better than just a friend.*

**Beser a guter soyne vi a shlekhter fraynd.**
*Better a good enemy than a bad friend.*

**Az me leygt zikh mit a hunt, shteyt men oyf mit a fley.**
*If you lie down with a dog, you'll get up with a flea.*

**Az du vest zikh khavern mit a ganef vestu aleyn vern a ganef.**
*If you make friends with a thief, you'll become a thief yourself.*

**Naye fraynd bakum, alte nit farges.**
*Acquire new friends, [but] don't forget old ones.*

## Advice to the Wise

**Az men redt zikh oys dos harts, vert laykhter.**
*If you pour out your heart, you feel lighter.*

**Nit alts vos men veyst meg men zogn.**
*Not everything one knows must be told.*

**Zog nit alts vos di veyst, gloyb nit alts vos du herst.**
*Don't tell everything you know, [and] don't believe everything you hear.*

**Di tsung is on beyner—un zi tsebrekht beyner.**
*The tongue has no bones—but it can break them.*

**Vi men leygt nit arayn, nemt men nit aroys.**
*[When] you put nothing in, you can't take something out.*

**A klap iz laykhter tsu bekumen vi tsu gebn.**
*A blow is easier to receive than to give.*

**A patsh fargeyt, a vort bashteyt.**
*A slap passes, a word remains.*

**Az di velt zogt, muz men gleybn.**
*If the world says so, [you'd] better believe it.*

**Gleyb eyn oyg mer vi tsvey oyern.**
*Trust one eye more than two ears.*

**Der bester lign iz der emes.**
*The best lie is the truth.*

**A ligner darf hobn a gutn zikoren.**
*A liar must have a good memory.*

**Gey pavolye, vestu gikher onkumen.**
*Go slowly, you will get there quicker.*

**Gebentsht zenen di hent vos tuen zikh aleyn.**
*Blessed are the hands that do things themselves.*

**A geshlogenem vayzt men keyn shtekn nit.**
*Don't show a stick to one who has been beaten.*

**Ven men muz, ken men.**
*When one must, one can.*

**Vilst nit hobn keyn umkoved, yog zikh nit nokh koved.**
*If you don't want dishonor, don't chase after honor.*

**Oyb me git dir, nem; oyb me nemt fun dir, shray gevalt!**
*If they give you, take; if they take from you, scream bloody murder!*

**Oyb du rekhnst gornit, vestu hobn a sakh koynim.**
*If you charge nothing, you'll have a lot of customers.*

**Shpay nit in brunem, vest nokh fun im darfn vaser trinken.**
*Don't spit into the well from which you might have to drink.*

**Men ken nit tantsn af tsvey khasenes af eyn mol, un men ken nit zitsn af tsvey ferd mit eyn tokhes.**
*One can't dance at two weddings at the same time, nor sit on two horses with one behind.*

**A hunt on tsen is oys hunt.**
*A dog without teeth is no longer a dog.*

## When the Labor Movement Spoke Yiddish—The Bund

Over a hundred years ago, in Vilna, Lithuania, The General Jewish Workers Alliance of Poland and Russia (**Der algemeyner yidisher arbeter-bund in poyln un rusland**) was established. It came to be known as the Bund and its goal was to fight for the political freedom of Jews and to overthrow the Russian czar. This was the beginning of a Jewish socialist party that played a crucial role in the development of a worldwide labor movement and the rights of Jewish workers.

Yiddish was vital to the growth of the Bund: its activists knew it was a universal way to reach poor Jews throughout Russia. **Dokeyt** became the Bund's credo—Yiddish meaning hereness. Dokeyt meant to struggle for one's rights in the here and now. It was a rallying cry to create organizations that promoted the welfare of the Jewish proletariat and focused on Yiddish as the living, national language of Jews. The Bund promoted Yiddish culture and education as an organizational tool and through it Yiddish was elevated beyond a lowly vernacular. With Yiddish as the **mame-loshn**, the Bund led demonstrations and strikes, fought against anti-Semitism and pogroms, and agitated for the rights of the Jewish minority.

During the early decades of the 20th century, the Bund was at the forefront in the development of modern labor unions. The organization helped poor working Jews in the **shtetls** and ghettoes of Eastern Europe fight for their rights and take pride in their culture.

The Bund organized and promoted Yiddish study groups, publications, schools and camps, sports clubs, and cultural organizations. The Bund also developed academic courses, theater groups, and libraries. Bund publishing included central party organs, daily local papers and periodicals, and the YAF (*Yidishe arbeter froy*), which promoted the rights of working Jewish women.

With the immigration of poor Jews to America between 1880 and 1910, the ideals of the Bund found a new home and Jews played a prominent role in labor rights. Papers like the *Jewish Daily Forward* in New York helped spread the Bund message. The Bund faced opposition from the Left and Right as it fought to affirm Jewish secular identity. The socialism the Bund espoused, including being the sole representative of Jewish workers, often did not find favor with other groups. Under the leaders of the Russian Revolution Bund activities were suppressed and their leaders killed.

Between the two World Wars, the Bund flourished especially in Poland, where 10 percent of the population was Jewish. As anti-Semitism and restrictions increased in Poland, the Bund fought for social justice and Jewish autonomy. But with the rise of Nazism, the Bund's leaders were killed in Hitler's death camps. This annihilation was the death knell for Jews and the Bund in Europe.

Though some of the Bund's followers became important figures in American labor (for example, David Dubinsky, Sidney Hillman), it failed to become a mass movement in the United States as Jews found unprecedented freedom and opportunity. But Jews played a central role in the 20th-century history of American labor, especially in the foundation of the International Ladies Garment Workers Union and the Amalgamated Clothing and Textile Workers. In the 1930s, American Jewish labor leaders were integral in the fight for labor reforms. They helped secure the National Labor Relations Act that made social security, workers compensation, and unemployment insurance part of United States law.

The Bund is now history, but its ultimate legacy was to meld socialism to Jewish history using Yiddish language and culture. Ironically, the Bund's demise is partly related to the success of Jewish immigrants in America and their children's assimilation.

# Yiddish Expressions

## Abi Gezunt! and More

*Abi gezunt As long as you're healthy Alter kaker An old fogy or lecher Arumgeflikt Robbed Plucked on all sides Balebatishe yidn Respectable Jews Bashert Fated or predestined A bisl A little Bist meshuge Are you crazy [illegible]ber Absolutely nothing [illegible] with liver Es gezunterheyt Eat in good health [illegible] starting up again Farbisener farbiser A bitter, truculent person A farshlepte krenk An endless, dragged-on affair An obnoxious or complaining individual Farshteyst Do you understand A gantser knaker Big shot Gebentsht mit kinder Blessed with children Gey avek Go away Gey kakn afn yam Go crap on the sea Gezunt vi a ferd Strong as a horse A groyser gornisht Big good-for-nothing Hak mir nit keyn tshaynik Don't bang me on the teakettle Ikh hob es in drerd To hell with it Kenehore May no evil eye befall Kush mir in tokhes Kiss my ass Khap a gangBeat it Lang lebn zolt ir May you live long A lebn af dir A life upon you Mazl tov Good luck A meydl mit a kleydl A girl showing off her*

Many of our Yiddish-speaking relatives spoke **tsebrokhener** English (fractured English). Yet when it came to the right Yiddish expression for a particular situation or person, a mellifluous stream of phrases, expressions, allusions, and metaphors flowed off their tongues. Often we didn't quite know what they were saying, but their intonation, hand movement, and body language left us in stitches. **A farshlepte krenk** not only meant a dragged-out illness, but the person constantly complaining about it. **Oy gevald!** or **Oy vey!** are Yiddish expressions that are now almost part of our English vernacular. And only a people who have had thousands of years to refine their experience of **tsores**, could come up with expressions like **Ikh zol azoy visn fun tsores!** (I should know as little about troubles!) or **Zol ikh azoy visn fun tsores!** (I haven't got the faintest idea! Literally, I should so know from troubles as I know about this!), or compare troubles to chopped liver, as in **gehakte tsores** (literally, chopped troubles, meaning utter misery).

Yiddish expressions have a wonderful rhythm and pointed directness that enhance their humor, sarcasm, and pungency. Here are some of the more popular expressions that will give you a chance to practice your own **tsebrokhener** Yiddish.

By expressions we mean any word, phrase, or idiom that is commonly heard in the regular give-and-take of Yiddish speakers. There are thousands of expressions in Yiddish, but we have room only for a small sampling—to give you an idea what to expect or look for when you fall into the company of a roomful of people **schmoozing** in **mame-loshn.**

## A

**Abi gezunt!**
*As long as you're healthy!*

**Af mir gezogt!**
*I wish it could be said about me!*

**Af tsulokhes.**
*For spite.*

**Afn himl a yarid!**
*Much ado about nothing! Impossible! (Literally, A big fair in heaven.)*

**Akurater mentsh.**
*Meticulous person.*

**Alevay!**
*Variant of* **Halevay!**

**An alte makhsheyfe.**
*An old witch.*

**Alte moyd.**
*A spinster (literally, old maid).*

**An alter bakanter.**
*An old acquaintance.*

**Alter bokher.**
*A bachelor (literally, old youth).*

**Alter kaker.**
*An old fogy (literally, old crapper).*

**An alter trombenik.**
*An old blowhard.*

**Aroysgevorfene gelt.**
*Money wasted, squandered, or thrown away.*

**Arumgeflikt!**
*Robbed! Milked! (Literally, Plucked on all sides!)*

**Arumshleper.**
*A person who runs around; a person without home or roots.*

**Az okh un vey!**
*Tough luck! Too bad! Misfortune!*

**Aza yor af mir.**
*I should have such good luck. (Literally, Such a year upon me.)*

**Azes ponem.**
*Impudent fellow.*

**Azoy?**
*Really?*

**Azoy geyt es!**
*That's how it goes!*

**Azoy gikh?**
*So soon?*

**Azoy vert dos kikhl tsebrokhn!**
*That's how the cookie crumbles!*

## B

**Balebatishe yidn.**
*Respectable Jews; men of substance and good standing in the community.*

**Bal-nes.**
*Miracle worker.*

**Es tut mir bang.**
*I'm sorry. (Literally, It makes me sorry.)*

**Es vet helfn vi a toytn bankes!**
*It won't help (any)! (Literally, It will help like blood-cupping on a dead body.)*

**Baredn yenem.**
*To gossip about another.*

**Bashert.**
*Fated or predestined.*

**Bashert zayn.**
*To be destined by fate.*

**Ben toyre.**
*Learned Jew; scholar.*

**A bisl.**
*A little.*

**Bist meshuge?**
*Are you crazy?*

**Biz hundert un tsvantsik.**
*You should live till 120; long life to you.*

**Biz hundert azoy vi tsvantsik.**
*Live till 100 like a twenty-year-old.*

**Zol dikh khapn baym boykh!**
*You should get a stomach cramp!*

**Zol es brenen!**
*The hell with it! (Literally, Let it burn!)*

**A brokh!**
*Oh hell! Damn it! A curse!*

**A brokh iz mir!**
*Woe is me!*

**A brokhe.**
*A blessing.*

**A brokhe levatole.**
*A waste; lost labor (literally, a blessing made in vain).*

## D

**Danken Got!**
*Thank God!*

**Dayge nisht!**
*Don't worry!*

**Dergey di yorn.**
*Pester, nag (literally, trample on someone's years).*

**Dos gefelt mir.**
*This pleases me.*

**Dos harts hot mir gezogt.**
*My heart told me. I predicted it.*

**Dos iz alts.**
*That's all.*

**Drek af dem teler.**
*Mean-spirited; valueless (literally, crap on a plate).*

**Drek mit leber.**
*Absolutely nothing; worthless (literally, crap with liver).*

**Drey arum.**
*Run around.*

**Drey mir nit keyn kop!**
*Don't bother me! (Literally, Don't twist my head!)*

## E

**Ekh!**
*A groan; a disparaging exclamation.*

**Ek velt.**
*End of the world.*

**An emese mayse.**
*Absolutely true; true story.*

**Er est vi nokh a krenk.**
*He eats as after a sickness.*

**Es gefelt mir.**
*I like it. (Literally, It pleases me.)*

**Es gezunterheyt!**
*Eat in good health!*

**Es hot zikh oysgelozn a boydem!**
*Nothing came of it! (Literally, There's nothing up there but an attic.)*

**Es iz (tsu) shpet.**
*It is (too) late.*

**Es ken gemolt zayn.**
*It's conceivable. It's possible.*

**Es makht mir nit oys.**
*It doesn't matter to me.*

**Es past nit.**
*It's not becoming. It's not fitting.*

**Es vert mir fintster in di oygen.**
*I am fainting! (Literally, It's getting dark in my eyes.)*

**Eybershter in himl!**
*God in heaven!*

## F

**Du fangst shoyn on?**
*Are you starting up again?*

**Farbisener** *(masculine)*, **farbisene** *(feminine)*.
*A bitter, truculent person.*

**Farbrenter** *(masculine)*, **farbrente** *(feminine)*.
*Ardent; zealous.*

**Fardayget.**
*Worried; full of care or anxiety.*

**Fardinen a mitsve.**
*Earn a merit for a good deed.*

**Fardrey zikh dem kop!**
*Go drive yourself crazy!*

**Farmakh dos moyl!**
*Shut up! Be quiet! (Literally, Shut your mouth!)*

**Farmutshet.**
*Worn out, fatigued, exhausted.*

**Farshnoshket.**
*Loaded, tipsy, drunk.*

**A farshlepte krenk.**
*An endless, dragged-on affair; also, an obnoxious or complaining individual (literally, a protracted illness).*

**Farshteyst?**
*Do you understand?*

**Farshtunken.**
*Smelling bad, stinking.*

**Farshvitst.**
*Sweaty.*

**Fartshadet.**
*Confused, bewildered, befuddled, as if by gas fumes.*

**Ikh fayf af dir!**
*I despise you! Go to the devil! (Literally, I whistle on you!)*

**Feh!**
*Ugh! Yuck! Disgusting!*

**Fintster un glitshik.**
*Miserable (literally, dark and slippery).*

**Folg mikh!**
*Obey me!*

**Folg mikh a gang!**
*It's quite a ways! Why should I do it? It's hardly worth the trouble!*

**Er frest vi a ferd.**
*He gorges himself like a horse.*

**Zol er tsebrekhn a fus!**
*May he break a leg! He should break a leg!*

## G

**Ganeyvishe shtiklekh.**
*Sneaky or crooked actions.*

**A gantse megile.**
*A long story (sarcastic); a big deal (literally, a whole megillah).*

**A gantser knaker.**
*Big shot.*

**A gantser mentsh.**
*A whole person; a grown-up (usually in praise of a child or youngster).*

**Gebentsht mit kinder.**
*Blessed with children.*

**A gebentshte boykh.**
*Literally, a blessed stomach or womb. (Said of a woman with a fabulous child or children.)*

**Geb mir nit keyn eynhore.**
*Don't give me the evil eye!*

**Gebn shoykhed.**
*To bribe.*

**Geb zikh a treysl.**
*Get a move on. (Literally, Give a shake.)*

**Genug iz genug!**
*Enough is enough!*

**A gevaldike zakh!**
*A terrific thing!*

**Gey avek!**
*Go away!*

**Gey fayfn afn yam!**
*Go peddle your fish elsewhere! (Literally, Go whistle on the sea.)*

**Gey gezunterheyt.**
*Go in good health.*

**Gey in drerd arayn!**
*Go to hell! (Literally, Go into the ground!)*

**Gey kakn afn yam!**
*Get lost! (Literally, Go crap on the sea.)*

**Gey plats!**
*Go split your guts! (Literally, Go blow up!)*

## Blessings in Yiddish

Is it a reflection of the bitter life led by Jews through much of their history that curses tended to be more prevalent among them than blessings? (For proof, see "Yiddish Curses.") Nevertheless, blessings are given in Yiddish in many different contexts, especially the following:

In response to a sneeze:

**Tsu gezunt!**
*To health!*

**A lebn of dir! or Lang leben zolstu!**
*A long life to you!*

After the name of a beloved person:

**Zol er (*feminine*, zi) lang lebn un zayn gezunt!**
*May he/she have a long life and be healthy!*

To a child:

**A gezunt dir/im in kepele!**
*Health upon your/his little head!*

To an elderly person:

**Got zol aykh nor gebn gezunt un koyekh!**
*God should give you only health and strength!*

On closing a business deal:

**Zol zayn mit mazl un brokhe!**
*It should be with luck and blessing!*

At a bris, bar mitzvah, or wedding:

**Ir zolt/Du zolst hobn nakhes fun di kinder!**
*You should have pleasure and joy from the children!*

**Ir zolt/Du zolst derlebn tsu zen nor nakhes fun zey!**
*You should live to see only pleasure and joy from them!*

To a sick person:

**Got zol aykh/dir shikn a refue shleyme!**
*God should send you a complete cure!*

**Ir zolt/Du zolst hobn a refue shleyme!**
*You should have a complete cure!*

**To a mourner:**

**Ir zolt/Du zolst mer keyn tsar nit hobn!**
*You shouldn't have any more grief!*

**Me zol zikh trefn nor of simkhes!**
*We should meet only on happy occasions!*

**At a yahrzeit (anniversary of a death), as a toast:**

**Di neshome zol hobn an aliye!**
*May the soul of the deceased have an ascent [to heaven]!*

**On the New Year:**

**Mir zoln derlebn iber a yor in freydn!**
*We should live another year in joy!*

**At a birthday or anniversary celebration:**

**Got zol aykh/dir gebn glik un parnose un lange yorn!**
*God should give you good fortune and livelihood and long years!*

**Yiddish characteristically also uses blessings interjectionally as a rhetorical device, without any expectation of response. For example:**

**Der zeyde, zol er zayn gezunt un shtark...**
*Grandfather, may he be well and strong...*

**Gezunt zolt ir zayn, vos tshepet ir zikh tsu mir?**
*You should be well, why do you bother me?*

**Do voynt myn tokhter, bit hundert un tsvantsik, mit ir man, zol gezunt zayn.**
*Here lives my daughter, till a hundred and twenty, with her husband, may he be well.*

**Similarly, gezunterheyt (in good health) is used in a formulaic manner after an imperative verb in many locutions, such as:**

**For gezunterheyt!**
*Travel in good health!*

**Es gezunterheyt!**
*Eat in good health!*

**Gey gezunterheyt!**
*Go in good health!*

**Shlof gezunterheyt!**
*Sleep in good health!*

**Gey shlog dayn kop in vant!**
*Go bang your head against the wall!*

**Gey shoyn, gey!**
*Go already! Scram! Don't be silly!*

**Gey strashe di vantsn!**
*You don't frighten me! (Literally, Go threaten the bed bugs.)*

**Es geyt nit!**
*It doesn't work!*

**Gezunt vi a ferd.**
*Healthy or strong as a horse.*

**A gezunte moyd.**
*A buxom, healthy woman.*

**Gezunterheyt.**
*In good health.*

**Gleyb mir!**
*Believe me!*

**Gotenyu!**
*Oh God!*

**Got in himl!**
*God in heaven!*

**Got tsu danken!**
*Thank God!*

**Got zol ophitn!**
*God forbid!*

**A groyse gdile!**
*Big deal (sarcastic)!*

**A groyser gornisht.**
*Big good-for-nothing.*

**A groyser pots** (*taboo/curse*)**.**
*A big prick.*

**A gut vort.**
*A bon mot or clever remark; also, a concise Torah commentary (literally, a good word).*

**A gute neshome.**
*A good soul; gentle person.*

## H

**Hak mir nit in kop!**
*Stop bending my ear! (Literally, Stop banging on my head!)*

**Hak mir nit keyn tshaynik.**
*Don't get on my nerves. (Literally, Don't bang me on the teakettle.)*

**Hakn a tshaynik.**
*To make dull, long-winded and/or annoying conversation. (Literally, To bang on the teakettle.)*

**Halevay!**
*If only! Would that it be so!*

**Her zikh ayn!**
*Listen here!*

**A heymish ponem.**
*A friendly face.*

**Hit zikh!**
*Look out!*

**Hob derekh erets.**
*Have respect.*

**Hob nit keyn dayges.**
*Don't worry.*

**Hobn tsu zingen un tsu zogn.**
*Have no end of trouble (literally, to sing and to say).*

**Host bay mir an avle!**
*So I made a mistake! So what!*

## I

**Ikh hob dikh in bod!**
*To hell with you! (Literally, I have you in the bath house!)*

**Ikh hob dir!**
*Drop dead! (Literally, I have you!)*

**Ikh hob es in drerd!**
*To hell with it!*

**Ikh veys nit.**
*I don't know.*

## K

**Gebn kadokhes.**
*Give nothing (literally, give someone malaria or a fever).*

**Kak im on!** *(taboo/insult)*
*Defecate on him! The hell with him!*

**Kak zikh oys!** *(taboo/insult)*
*Go take a crap!*

**Ikh darf es af kapores.**
*It's good for nothing! I have no use for it. (Literally, I need it for [Yom Kippur] scapegoats.)*

**Ken zayn.**
*Maybe; could be.*

**Kenehore** <kan-eh-ˈhor-eh>.
*(May) no evil eye (befall).*

**Zol dir klapn in kop!**
*It should bang in your head (the way it is bothering me)!*

**Es klemt baym harts.**
*It pulls at the heartstrings.*

**A kleyner gornisht.**
*A little prig (literally, a little nothing).*

**A klog iz mir!**
*Woe is me!*

**A klots kashe.**
*A foolish or pointless question.*

**Kom derlebt.**
*Narrowly achieved (literally, hardly lived to see).*

**Kom vos er krikht.**
*He's barely able to crawl; he's a slowpoke.*

**Kom vos er lebt.**
*He's barely alive.*

**A kop af di pleytses.**
*Good, common sense (literally, a head on the shoulders).*

**Kush mir in tokhes! (***taboo/insult***)**
*Kiss my ass!*

## Kh

**Khamer eyner!**
*You blockhead! You dope! You ass!*

**Khap a gang!**
*Beat it! (Literally, Catch a way; catch a road!)*

**Khap nit!**
*Take it easy! Not so fast! (Literally, Don't grab!)*

**Khas vekholile!**
*God forbid!*

**Khaym-yankl.**
*A simple-minded person; a nebbish (literally, a common Yiddish name).*

**Khoshever mentsh.**
*Man of worth and dignity; elite person; respected person.*

**Khosn-kale.**
*Bride and groom; engaged couple.*

**Khoyzek makhn.**
*Make fun of, ridicule.*

## L

**Lakhn mit yashtsherkes.**
*A forced or false laugh; to laugh through tears (literally, laugh with lizards).*

**Lang lebn zolt ir!**
*May you live long!*

**A lebediker.**
*A lively person.*

**A lebn af dayn kop!**
*Well said! Well done! (Literally, A long life upon your head!)*

**Lebn a khazerishn tog.**
*Living high off the hog.*

**A lebn af dir!**
*Bless you! (Literally, A life upon you!)*

**Zolstu azoy lebn!**
*You should live so!*

**Zolst lebn un zayn gezunt!**
*You should live and be well!*

**A lung un leber af der noz!**
*Stop talking yourself into illness! (Literally, Don't imagine a lung and a liver upon the nose!)*

**Ikh hob dikh lib!**
*I love you!*

**Lig in drerd!**
*Get lost! Drop dead! (Literally, Lie under the ground!)*
**Ikh darf es vi a lokh in kop!**
*I need it like a hole in the head!*

**Loz mikh tsu ru!**
*Leave me alone! (Literally, Let me be in peace!)*

## M

**Mame, mamele, mameshe.**
*Endearments for mother: mama, mommy, mom.*

**Mayn bobes tam.**
*Bad taste; old-fashioned taste (literally, my grandmother's taste.)*

**Mayn khayes geyt oys!**
*I'm dying for it! (Literally, My life goes out!)*

**Mazl tov!**
*Good luck!*

**Ikh bin dikh nit mekane.**
*I don't envy you.*

**A metsie fun a ganef.**
*It's a steal (literally, a bargain from a thief).*

**A meydl mit a veydl.**
*A pony-tailed girl (literally, a girl with a tail).*

**A meydl mit a kleydl.**
*A girl showing off her (new) dress.*

**Me ken brekhn!**
*You can vomit from this!*

**Me ken lekn di finger!**
*It's delicious! (Literally, You can lick the finger!)*

**Me krekhts, me geyt vayter.**
*You complain, but you keep going.*

**Me lost nit lebn!**
*They don't let you live!*

**Me redt zikh oys dos harts.**
*You talk your heart out.*

**Meshuge af toyt!**
*Crazy as a loon! Really crazy! (Literally, Crazy to death!)*

**Me zogt.**
*It is said.*

**A mise meshune.**
*An unnatural death.*

**In mitn drinen.**
*All of a sudden, suddenly.*

**Zi (er) farmakht nit dos moyl.**
*She (he) doesn't stop talking. (Literally, She [he] doesn't close the mouth.)*

**Mutshen zikh.**
*To sweat out a job (literally, to wear oneself out).*

# N

**Na!**
*Here! Take it! There you have it!*

**Nakhes fun kinder.**
*Pleasure from the children.*

**Nar eyner!**
*You fool, you!*

**Er bolbet narishkeytn.**
*He babbles nonsense.*

**A nekhtiker tog!**
*Forget it! Nonsense! (Literally, A yesterday's day!)*

**Nem zikh a vane!**
*Go take a bath! Go jump in the lake!*

**Nisht neytik.**
*Not necessary.*

**Nishkoshe.**
*Not bad.*

**A nishtikeyt!**
*A triviality; a nothing!*

**Nit do gedakht!**
*May this never happen here! God forbid!*

**Nit gefonfet!**
*No fooling! No doubletalk!*

**Nit getrofn!**
*Wrong guess! So I guessed wrong!*

**Nit gut.**
*Not good; lousy.*

**Nit haynt, nit morgn!**
*Not today, not tomorrow!*

**Nit keyn farshlofener.**
*A lively person (literally, not a sleepy one).*

**Nit ahin, nit aher.**
*Neither here nor there.*

**Nit kosher.**
*Impure food, not kosher. Anything unfit or illegitimate.*

**Nito farvos!**
*You're welcome! Don't mention it! (Literally, No reason for it.)*

**Nokh nisht.**
*Not yet.*

**Nor Got veyst.**
*Only God knows.*

**Nosn tsum emes.**
*A big sneeze.*

**Nu?**
*So? Well?*

**Nu, shoyn!**
*Move, already! Hurry up! Let's go! Aren't you finished?*

**Er iz shoyn do, der nudnik!**
*The nuisance is here already!*

## O

**Ober yetst (*or* itst)?**
*But now?*

**Oder a klap, oder a farts.**
*Either too much or not enough (literally, either a wallop or a fart).*

**Okh un vey!**
*Woe it is!*

**On lange hakdomes!**
*Cut it short! (Literally, Without long introductions!)*

**Ongepatshket.**
*Cluttered; disordered; scribbled; sloppy; muddled; overly done.*

**Ongeshtopt mit gelt.**
*Very wealthy (literally, stuffed with money).*

**Onzaltsn.**
*To give one the business; bribe; soft-soap; sweet-talk (literally, to pour on salt).*

**Opgeflikt!**
*Done in! Suckered! Milked!*

**Opgekrokhene skhoyre.**
*Shoddy merchandise.*

**Opgelozen(er).**
*Careless dresser.*

**Zol Got ophitn!**
*God forbid!*

**Oy, a shkandal!**
*What a scandal!*

**Oy, gevald!**
*Cry of anguish, suffering, frustration, or for help.*

**Oy oy!**
*Yes, oh yes! And how!*

**Oykh a bashefenish!**
*Also a creature (sarcastically or in pity)!*

**Oykh mir a lebn!**
*This too is a living! This you call a living?*

**Oykh mir a —.**
*Humorous, disparaging remark, meaning "not much of a [something]." For example, "Dumb and Dumber—*oykh mir a *film."*

**Oysgemutshet.**
*Worked to death; tired out.*

**Oysgeputst.**
*Dressed up, overdressed; overdecorated.*

**Oys shidekh!**
*The marriage is off!*

**Oysshteler.**
*Show-off, braggart.*

**Oyverbotl.**
*Absent-minded, mixed up; senile.*

**Oy vey iz mir!**
*Woe is me!*

## P

**Es past nit.**
*It's not right.*

**Patern.**
*To spoil or waste.*

**Patshken.**
*To mess or bother with.*

**Pisk melokhe.**
*Big talk, little action (literally, mouth work).*

**Plats!**
*Burst! Bust your guts out!*

**Plogn zikh.**
*To suffer.*

**Proste layt.**
*Simple people, common people; vulgar, ignorant, "low-class" people.*

**Proster mentsh.**
*Vulgar man; boor.*

**Zol vaksn tsibeles fun dayn pupik!**
*Onions should grow from your bellybutton!*

## R

**Hob rakhmones!**
*Have pity!*

**Raysn di hoyt.**
*Skin someone alive (literally, to tear the skin).*

## Tkhines—Yiddish Women's Prayers

Among East European Jewry, women did not participate in the study of Bible, Talmud, and Midrash: though conducted in Yiddish, these studies were reserved for men. But alongside the more structured and fixed world of Hebrew prayer, a second liturgy of **tkhines** was created for women and their families in the everyday language of Yiddish.

Tkhines were published anonymously, and for some time it was disputed whether women authored any. But recent scholarship has clearly established that women, mostly from prominent rabbinical families, composed many of these now-classic Yiddish prayers. Tkhines were also uplifting to those "men who were like women" in not being able to read or speak Hebrew. Thus, tkhines through its "passionately emotional personal prayer" gave voice to a wide circle of both men and women—not unlike the personal prayers of Jewish mystics of the time, composed in the non-sacred language of Yiddish in order to attain a more direct and intimate relation with God.

From the daily life of pious women arose beautiful Yiddish tkhines that still resonate to this day:

> This [the woman] says when she puts the loaf of *berkhes* [*hallah*] into the oven:
>
> > Lord of all the world, in your hand is all blessing. I come now to revere your holiness, and I pray you to bestow your blessing on the baked goods. Send an angel to guard the baking, so that all will be well baked, will rise nicely, and will not burn, to honor the holy Sabbath (which you have chosen so that Israel your children may rest thereon) and over which one recites the holy blessing—as you blessed the dough of Sarah and Rebecca our mothers. My Lord God, listen to my voice; you are the God who hears the voices of those who call upon you wholeheartedly. May you be praised to eternity.

Tkhines continue to inspire many, and a modest revival of this form of prayer is going on among Hasidic as well as Conservative and feminist Jewish women today.

Source: *Voices of the Matriarchs: Listening to the Prayers of Early Modern Jewish Women,* by Chava Weissler (Boston: Beacon Press, 1998).

## A Modern Tkhine for Easy Labor

Written by Rabbi Geela Rayzel Raphael, when a student at the Reconstructionist Rabbinical College in 1993, loosely based on a traditional **tkhine** recited before biting off and eating the *pitom* or blossom end of a citron to assuage labor pains and help delivery.

> Mother of the Universe and all Universal Knowledge, our tradition has taught us that Eve suffered on account of her eating of the fruit. I know, however, that our eyes have been opened as a result of her courageous act. Eating of the Tree of Knowledge, although a disobedient act, gave us the ability to discern injustice and oppression. We see and are aware of your justice and mercy as well as the wounded places in the world.
>
> Eve, the crown of Your creation, was assertive and strong as she ran wild with the wolves. She delivered her children with strength. As I eat this pitom, may I be infused with Eve's birthing powers. Let my labor be only mild pangs of discomfort, yet may I labor for the revelation of Your presence in the world. Primal Earth Mother Eve tended and cared for Your garden as I care for my child. May this child grow to be conscious of your world and environment as Eve did. Let this child blossom as a garden blooms in the springtime. May this child grow to respect Your creation—treasuring the sweetness and tartness just like the etrog (citron).

Source: "Techinah for Easy Labor" by Geela Rayzel Raphael, in *Voices of the Matriarchs: Listening to the Prayers of Early Modern Jewish Women*, by Chava Weissler (Boston: Beacon Press, 1998).

**Redn on a mos.**
*To chatter without end (literally, to talk without measure).*

**Redn tsu der vant.**
*To talk in vain (literally, to talk to the wall).*

**Redn zikh eyn a krenk.**
*To talk oneself into an illness.*

**Ribifish, gelt afn tish!**
*Don't ask for credit! Cash on the barrelhead!*

**Riboynesheloylem.**
*God in heaven; Master of the Universe.*

**Rikhtiker kheyfets.**
*Real article; the real McCoy.*

**Ruf mikh knaknisl!**
*Call me what you want—who cares? (Literally, Call me a nutcracker!)*

## S

**S'art aykh?**
*What does it matter to you? Does it bother you?*

**Se brent nit!**
*Don't get excited! (Literally, It's not on fire!)*

**Se shtinkt!**
*It stinks!*

**Sha!**
*Be quiet!*

**Zol zayn sha!**
*Let there be quiet! Shut up!*

**A shande un a kharpe.**
*A shame and a disgrace.*

**Es iz a shande far di kinder!**
*It's a disgrace for the children!*

**Sheygets ayner!**
*Impudent fellow. (Sometimes used to berate an irreligious Jew.)*

**Sheyn vi di levone.**
*As pretty as the moon.*

**Sheyn vi di zibn veltn.**
*Beautiful as the seven worlds.*

**Sheyne meydl.**
*Pretty girl.*

**A sheynem dank.**
*Thank you very much.*

**A sheyner gelekhter.**
*A hearty laugh. Some laugh (sarcastically)!*

**Shihi-pihi.**
*Mere nothings; also, laziness.*

**A shlekht vayb.**
*A bad wife; shrew.*

**Zolst nit visn fun keyn shlekhts.**
*You shouldn't know from evil.*

**Sholem aleykhem.**
*Hello. (Literally, Peace be upon you.)*

**Aleykhem sholem.**
*Response to Sholem aleykhem.*

**Shlog zikh mit Got arum!**
*Go fight city hall! (Literally, Go fight with God!)*

**Shoyn eynmol a metsie!**
*A real bargain!*

**Shoyn fargesn?**
*You've forgotten already?*

**Shoyn genug!**
*Enough already!*

**Shoymer mitsves.**
*Pious person (literally, observer of commandments).*

**Zitsn af shpilkes.**
*To sit on pins and needles; to fidget.*

**A shreklekhe zakh.**
*A terrible thing.*

**Shtark gehert.**
*Smelled bad (only in reference to food; literally, strongly heard).*

**Shtark vi a ferd.**
*Strong as a horse.*

**Shtik drek** *(vulgar/taboo)*.
*Piece of shit; shithead.*

**A shtik nakhes.**
*A great joy.*

**Zol zayn shtil!**
*Silence! Let's have quiet!*

**Zolst es shtupn in tokhes!** *(taboo/insult)*
*Shove it up your ass!*

**Staytsh?**
*How is that? How is that possible? How come?*

**Strashe mikh nit!**
*Don't threaten me!*

**A shvarts yor.**
*Bad luck (literally, a bad year).*

**A shvartsn sof.**
*A bad end (literally, a black end).*

**A sof! A sof!**
*Let's end it! End it!*

## T

**Take a metsie.**
*A real bargain (sometimes used sarcastically).*

**Tam gan eyden.**
*Fabulous (literally, a taste of the Garden of Eden).*

**Tate, tatele, tatinke.**
*Endearments for father: papa, daddy, pop.*

**Tate-mame.**
*Parents (literally, papa-mama).*

**Tatenyu.**
*Father dear.*

*The Yiddish suffix* **-nyu** *adds endearing intimacy.* **Tatenyu-Foter** *means Dear God, our Father.*

**Er makht a tel fun dem.**
*He ruins it. (Literally, He makes a ruin of it.)*

**Tokhes afn tish!**
*Put up or shut up! Let's get it over! (Literally, Backside on the table!)*

**Tokhes-leker.**
*Brown-noser, ass-kisser.*

**A tokhes un a halb** *(slang/offensive)*.
*A voluptuous woman (literally, a backside and a half).*

**Es toyg af kapores!**
*It's good for nothing! Worthless!*

**Tsetumlt.**
*Confused, bewildered.*

**Tu mir a toyve.**
*Do me a favor.*

**Tu mir nit keyn toyves.**
*Don't do me any favors.*

**A treyfener kop** *(offensive).*
*A Jew who does not observe Jewish law (literally, a nonkosher head).*

**Treyfene bikher.**
*Forbidden literature (literally, nonkosher books).*

**Trog gezunterheyt!**
*Wear it in good health!*

**Tsatskele di mames.**
*Mother's favorite, mother's pet.*

**In di alte gute tsaytn.**
*In the good old days.*

**Tsegeyt zikh in moyl.**
*It melts in the mouth; delicious.*

**Tsebrokhener english.**
*Fractured English.*

**Af tsores.**
*In trouble.*

**Gehakte tsores.**
*Utter misery (literally, chopped troubles; troubles compounded).*

**Ikh zol azoy visn fun tsores.**
*I should know as little about troubles.*

**Kom mit tsores!**
*Barely made it! (Literally, With some troubles!)*

**Zol ikh azoy visn fun tsores!**
*I haven't got the faintest idea! (Literally, I should so know from troubles as I know about this!)*

**Tsu gezunt!**
*To your health! Bless you!*

**Tsufil!**
*Too much! Too costly!*

**Tsum glik, tsum shlimazl.**
*For better, for worse.*

**Es tut vey dos harts.**
*To be heartbroken.*

**Vos tut zikh?**
*How are things? What's doing?*

## U

**Umgelumpert.**
*Awkward, clumsy.*

**Di untershte shure.**
*The bottom line.*

**Untervelt mentsh.**
*Racketeer (literally, underworld person).*

## V

**Valgern zikh.**
*Wander around aimlessly.*

**Vayberishe shtiklekh.**
*Female tricks.*

**Vays vi kalkh.**
*Pale as quicklime.*

**Vemen narstu?**
*Whom are you fooling?*

**Ver farblondzhet!**
*Get lost! Go away!*

**Ver veyst?**
*Who knows?*

**Ver volt dos gegleybt?**
*Who would have believed it?*

**Vern a tel.**
*To be ruined.*

**Vern farheyrat** (*standard Yiddish,* **Hobn khasene**).
*To get married.*

**Vey is mir!**
*Woe is me!*

**Veys ikh vos!**
*Stuff and nonsense! Says you! (Literally, Know from what!)*

**Groys vi a barg.**
*Large as a mountain.*

**Vi azoy?**
*How?*

**Vi der Ruekh zogt gut morgn.**
*In an outlandish place or condition. (Literally, Where the Devil says good morning.)*

**Vi geyt dos gesheft?**
*How's business?*

**Vi geyt es?**
*How's it going?*

**Vi geyt es dir?**
*How goes it with you? How are you doing?*

**Vifil?**
*How much?*

**A vilder mentsh.**
*A wild person.*

**Vos art es (mikh)?**
*What does it matter (to me)? What do I care?*

**Vos hakst mir in kop?**
*What are you talking my head off for?*

**Vos hert zikh?**
*What do you hear around? What's up?*

**Vos hert zikh epes nayes?**
*What's new?*

**Vos hob ikh dos gedarft?**
*What did I need it for?*

**Vos iz der mer?**
*What's the matter?*

**Vos iz der khilek?**
*What's the difference?*

**Vos iz der takhles?**
*What is the outcome?*

**Vos iz di khokhme?**
*What's the trick?*

**Vos iz di untershte shure?**
*What's the point? What's the outcome? (Literally, What is the bottom line?)*

**Vos iz mit dir?**
*What's wrong with you?*

**Vos kokht zikh in tepl?**
*What's cooking? (Literally, What's cooking in the pot?)*

**Vos makht a yid?**
*How's it going? (Literally, What is a Jew doing?)*

**Vos makht dos oys?**
*What difference does it make?*

**Vos makht es mir oys?**
*What difference does it make to me?*

**Vos makht ir?** *(singular formal and plural)*
*How are you?*

**Vos makhstu?** *(singular informal)*
*How are you?*

**Vos meynt es?**
*What does it mean?*

**Vos nokh?**
*What else? What then?*

**Vos redt ir epes?**
*What are you talking about?*

**Vos vet zayn, vet zayn!**
*What will be, will be!*

**Vos zogt ir?** *(singular formal and plural)*
*What are you saying?*

**Vos zogstu?** *(singular informal)*
*What are you saying?*

**Vu den?**
*What else? Of course!*

**Vu tut dir vey?**
*Where does it hurt?*

**Vuhin geystu?**
*Where are you going?*

## Y

**(Ya)sher koyekh!**
*Congratulations! (Literally, May your strength continue!)*

**Ya-tebe-dam.**
*A threatening man; one who acts like a big shot.*

**Yene velt.**
*The other world; the world to come.*

**Yente telebende.**
*A gossipy woman. A Mrs. National Enquirer.*

**Yeshive bokher.**
*Student in a Talmudic academy; yeshiva student.*

**A yunge tsatske.**
*A beauty, a living doll.*

**A yung mit beyner.**
*Strongly built person; powerhouse (literally, a youth with bones).*

**Yung un alt.**
*Young and old.*

## Z

**A zaftige moyd.**
*A voluptuous girl.*

**Zay gezunt.**
*Stay well; good bye.*

**Zay mir freylekh!**
*Be happy!*

**Zay mir gezunt!**
*Be well!*

**Zay mir matriekh.**
*May I trouble you (for a favor).*

**Zay nit a nar!**
*Don't be a fool!*

**Zay nit kayn vayzoso!**
*Don't be an idiot! Don't be a damn fool!*
*Vayzoso was one of Haman's sons in the biblical* Book of Esther.

**Zayt azoy gut.**
*Please. (Literally, Be so good.)*

**Ze nor, ze nor!**
*Look here, look here!*

**Zeyer sheyn gezogt!**
*Well said! (Literally, Very beautifully said!)*

**Es zhumet in kop.**
*There's a buzzing in the head.*

**Zindik nit.**
*Don't complain. Don't tempt the gods. (Literally, Don't sin.)*

**A zise neshome.**
*A sweet soul.*

**Zise reyd.**
*Sweet talk.*

**Zog a por verter.**
*Say a few words.*

**Zogn a lign.**
*Tell a lie.*

**Zol es zayn!**
*Let it be! That's all!*

**Zol zayn azoy!**
*Let it be so! So be it!*

**Zol zayn mit mazl!**
*Good luck!*

**Zorg zikh nit!**
*Don't worry!*

# Yiddish Food and Cooking

## For Noshers and Fressers

*bobe mamele noodge delicious dishes geshmake maykholim babka bagel batamt bialy bialystoker kukhen blintze blintz schmear boykh challah shabes challeh hallah chaloshes chaloshesdik chazerai cholent [illegible] fleishig fleyshik forshpayz fress fresser gefilte fish gemish geshmak [illegible] kasha kasha varnishkes [illegible]shke kishka. derma stuffed derma knaidlach kneydlekh knish Yonah Schimmel knobl kreplach kreplekh. kreplech kugel latke lox laks mamaliga mandelbroyt maychel maykhl maykholim milchig milkhik nosh chazer nova retach rugelach rogelach schmear schmaltz schmaltzy shtikl shtik shtikele taam a tam gan eden tam tayglach tayve tref trayf tzibele tzimmes tsimmes chopped liver onion olive oil chicken fat chicken livers clove garlic hard-boiled eggs mayonnaise salt sauté food processor purée chill serve crackers chicken cracklings white fish carp pike spring water pepper eggs sugar matzo meal carrots dough ed bliss potatoes unbleached flour whole*

God, Jews, and a passion for food go way back. When Jews were finally freed from slavery in Egypt, they had to make a quick exit before the Pharaoh changed his mind. With no time to bake their bread in ovens, they baked unleavened bread in the sun. Known as **matzo**, Jews eat it to this day, during the holiday of Passover commemorating the end of Egyptian bondage. For the next forty years Jews wandered in the desert and, fortunately, God provided manna from heaven for their main meal. It wasn't until they reached the Promised Land that Moses showed them how to grow wheat in the land of "milk and honey." Wandering became part of thousands of years of Jewish history and along the way they developed a unique cuisine, taking a dish from here, an herb or spice from there. We may think of Jewish cuisine as unique, but many dishes came from Germany and Eastern Europe (not to mention the Middle East and Spain). Many have secret ingredients which have made them family treasures and part of fond family memories. Ashkenazic cooking incorporated lots of garlic, parsley, dill, and bay leaf; chicken fat and butter for frying or mixing; deeply browned onions for extra flavor; horseradish, smoked fish, sweet and sour dishes; and honey and cinnamon for sweetness. Dairy foods (**milkhik** in Yiddish) were also a favorite, with sour cream and soft cheeses (cottage, farmer's, cream) added to make toppings, sauces, and fillings.

From Germany dishes like **challah**, **gefilte fish**, **chopped liver**, and **cholent** were modified along with recipes for **blintzes** and

**knishes**. Poland provided a fondness for carp and salted herring, dark breads, rye bread, the famous bialy, and sweet and sour meals like stuffed cabbage. The Ukraine and Russia added roots and grains to get through the cold winters, including beet soups (**borscht**) and **kasha**, knishes, and **pirogen**. If you're lucky, your grandmother was from the old country or your mother used **bobe's** (grandma's) recipes. The house filled with aromas that set you salivating: briskets stewed with prunes; **knaidlach** (matzo balls) that floated like angels in chicken broth; **kreplach** filled with spicy stuffing; cold gefilte fish sitting on a bed of lettuce and fish jelly and garnished with tangy horse radish. And of course knishes, blintzes, cholent, **kasha varnishkes**, **kugel**, **holishkes—all** foods to die for.

You might even be lucky enough today to have a good Jewish delicatessen in the neighborhood where you can get a close semblance to one of **mamele's** great meals. But it could never have the love that came out of her kitchen. She was cooking with her soul so you would live such a long life and be healthy! Why do you think chicken soup is called Jewish penicillin? It's not just the garlic—all that care and love coming into your sickroom are very healing. That's why Jewish mothers are such **noodges** about food.

And for Jews to celebrate with a lovingly cooked meal is a way to honor God and partake in His bounty. So, you're not hungry? Impossible! Here are the Yiddish names for some of these celebrated delicacies for the next time you're ordering at a Jewish deli. And if you can't wait, a few of our favorite family recipes follow. **Es a bisl!** Eat a little something!

## Delicious Food Terms, Delicious Dishes
## *(Geshmake Maykholim)*

**babka** *noun*. A pastry shell dessert with different fillings, which originated in Poland. The dough is rolled into tight cylinders and filled with such favorites as chocolate or a mixture of cheese and raisins.

**bagel** *noun*. A hundred years after the **bagel** left the **shtetl** it finally hit a food bull's-eye. This quintessential Jewish food of Ashkenazic origin is now part of our breakfast. The dough is first boiled, then baked to give it a crispy brown exterior. When baked and served correctly, with a smear of butter or cream cheese and lox (don't forget a little red onion and lemon juice), this is one of God's other mannas. When done poorly, it can taste like stale or heavy white bread or used as a paperweight. Some say the water is the secret ingredient and most ex-New Yorkers would probably agree. The hole is for contemplation.

**batamt** *adjective.* A synonym for **geshmak**—delicious and tasty.

**bialy** *noun.* A baked white-flour roll, often sprinkled with onions; shape can be circular with an indented center (where the onions live), cylindrical, or even flattened into a sheet. A delicious bread that has never been quite as popular as a bagel. Originated in the town of Bialystok, Poland, where it was called **bialystoker kukhen** (Bialystok cakes).

### Bialy—the Other Kukhen

Reviewing Mimi Sheraton's book, *The Bialy Eaters: The Story of a Bread and a Lost World,* in his language column in the Sunday *New York Times Magazine,* William Safire drew an important distinction that every lover of baked goods must take to heart. "A *bialy* is to a bagel," wrote Safire, "what Bialystok is to Vladivostok—that is, a world apart. A *bialy* is a round, saucer-size *pletzl,* 'flat bread,' that has its center mushed in to form a depression made delectable with bits of onion."

Ms. Sheraton, the noted food critic and author of such books as *The Whole World Loves Chicken Soup* and *Is Salami and Eggs Better than Sex?* (with Alan King), defines the bialy in more loving detail: "...the small, round bialy is characterized by an indented center well that is ringed by a softer, higher rim, all generously flecked with toasted onions and, at its most authentic, with a showering of poppy seeds."

In her book on this flavorful bread, she writes that the bialy's full and official name was **Bialystoker kukhen** (Yiddish for Bialystok cake), and that it originated in Bialystok, a city in northeastern Poland. The Jews of Bialystok were such prodigious devourers of bialys that they were nicknamed **Bialystoker kukhen fressers** throughout Eastern Europe.

Whatever its origin, some of the bialy's rising popularity with movie- and theatergoers may be attributed to the word's association with the name of Max Bialystock, the unscrupulous producer played by Zero Mostel in Mel Brooks' film classic and, more recently, by Nathan Lane in the smash hit Broadway musical *The Producers*. But there is nothing phony or dishonest about the bialy; it is an honest-to-goodness Jewish **maykhl** and a worthy competitor with that other kukhen, the bagel.

**blintze** *noun*. The Jewish answer to French crêpes. A mixture of flour, cake meal, salt, and eggs creates a batter that, when poured onto a hot skillet, creates a blintze shell with a "blistered" top. Blintzes can be filled with any number of wonderful stuffings: apricots and cherries, blueberries, cottage cheese and chopped almonds, even vegetables or meat for a main meal. Sour cream is the preferred topping. A blintze is not to be confused with a blimp, which is how you feel if you eat too many. Also spelled **blintz**. See recipe below.

**borscht** *noun*. A beet soup adapted from Russia. It can be served hot or cold with a **schmear** of sour cream and a sprinkle of dill or slices of cucumber. An inexpensive **shtetl** meal, as beets were cheap and could last through the winter. See recipe below.

**boykh** *noun*. Belly, stomach.

**challah** <′khah-leh> *noun*. A white-flour bread made with eggs, glazed with egg white, and often sprinkled with poppy seeds. It has a unique, fragrant, almost sweet taste, and a pale- to deep-yellow color. Eaten on holidays to celebrate, and on Friday night and Saturday to honor the beginning of the Sabbath. **Challah** is often braided to represent the interconnected nature of the weekdays and the sanctified day of rest, called **shabes** in Yiddish (often also spelled **shabbos**). Also spelled **challeh** or **hallah**.

**chaloshes** <khah-′loh-shes> *noun*. Something that's revolting. On a mundane level refers to food and drink; on a higher level to ethical matters or conduct.

**chaloshesdik** <khah-′loh-shes-dik> *adjective*. The opposite of **geshmak**; unappetizing, disgusting.

**chazerai** <khah-zeh-′rye> *noun*. **Chazer** means pig and this is pig's food, or junk food. When referring to items, they're trashy, pure junk, or crap (like a pink flamingo or kitschy porcelain dolls).

**cholent** *noun*. An Ashkenazic Sabbath stew. **Cholent** is a mixture of potatoes, beans, onions, carrots that is traditionally cooked for 18–24 hours before eating. It's usually cooked the day before the Sabbath and left to simmer overnight so it's ready to eat the next day when cooking is prohibited. On weekdays, **cholent** can be made the same day, simmered for 3–4 hours. Every housewife has her special ingredient that makes it unique—and non-vegetarians add meat. It is believed to derive from the French, *chaud lent*, meaning to slow heat, and it's not unlike their pot-au-feu—the stew that can simmer for days and be eaten as leftovers.

**chreyn** <khreyn> *noun*. Horseradish. Essential for gefilte fish. Can be eaten from prepared bottles (red or white variety) or straight from the root if you want to clean out your nasal passages and tear-wash your eyes. Creates an effect similar to eating green wasabi mustard with sushi.

**esn** *verb*. To eat.

**farfel** *noun*. A matzo leftover made by breaking the matzos into pieces and mixing with egg and salt, then fried to golden brown crispness. Can be served with soup or as a side dish.

**flanken** <ˈflahng-ken> *noun*. Strip of beef, usually fatty, taken from the front end of the ribs, often boiled or stewed.

**fleishig** *adjective*. Pertaining to meat, poultry, or products prepared with animal fat. Under kosher dietary laws not to be eaten with dairy products. From Yiddish **fleyshik**.

**fligl** *noun*. A wing.

**forshpayz** *noun*. An appetizer.

**fress** *verb*. To consume large amounts of food and with great pleasure; eat with gusto, often quite quickly with a lot of noise. A **fresser** (noun) is an overeater who, God forbid, pigs out.

**gefilte fish** *noun*. Balls or cakes of chopped fish (usually whitefish, carp, or trout) mixed with eggs and **matzo** meal, served hot or cold with bracing **chreyn** (horseradish). See recipe below.

> Jews are encouraged to enjoy sex and procreate—after all, it pleases God. Fish is a symbol of fertility in many cultures, so what better food to eat on Friday night and have fun (not work hard!) before a day of rest on Saturday.

**gemish** *noun*. A mixture.

**geshmak** <geh-ˈshmock *or* ˈgeh-shmahck> *adjective*. Delicious and tasty; for example, a toasted bagel with cream cheese and lox.

**gribenes** *noun*. Chicken fat (schmaltz) used to be an all-purpose flavoring for Yiddish meals. And the biggest treat was to take those lush yellow gobs and deep-fry them with a little salt until they became golden dark brown and crunchy.

Oy, if we only did not have to think about cholesterol and hardening of the arteries with this dish, it would replace fries as a Jewish fast-food snack.

**gridzhe** *verb*. To gnaw or chew noisily. Also to nag or complain. From Yiddish **gridzhen**.

**holishkes** *noun*. Stuffed cabbage usually with ground meat, spices, and tomatoes. The cabbage leaves are boiled first. This is a classic stomach stuffer and an inexpensive meal. See recipe below.

**kasha** *noun*. A carbohydrate staple made from buckwheat groats boiled with egg and water. Also, figuratively, a big mess.

**kasha varnishkes** *noun*. A dish that sounds like the name of a lost shtetl or relative and is definitely harder to pronounce than prepare. It's a hardy and basic meal made from a mixture of buckwheat groats (the **kasha**) and egg noodles (purists use the bow-tie variety). The groats are toasted to make them crunchy and the soft noodles add textural contrast. Spices and herbs can be added to personalize the dish.

**kishke** *noun*. Intestine, gut. Also a sausage filled with meat and spices. When you overeat or are extremely nervous you can get a pain in your **kishkes**. Also spelled **kishka**. Also called **derma** or **stuffed derma**.

Originally this was a cow intestine casing stuffed with goodies. Sounds terrible, tastes great. Nowadays we pass on the cow part and use parchment paper or plastic, which we stuff with onions, carrots, celery, flour, and spices.

**knaidlach** <keh-'neyd-lekh> *noun plural*. Matzo balls (made from matzo flour). Usually found floating in chicken soup, especially on Passover. From Yiddish **kneydlekh**. See recipe below.

Usually two or three small-size balls (or one very large one) float in the clear broth along with a few slices of carrot or celery. A perfect matzo ball almost defies gravity and can barely stay in the bowl. A failed matzo ball is as heavy as lead and sits in your stomach with the same intensity. If it's not floating in the broth, beware! Matzo ball soup is a dish that most Jews associate with Passover (Pesach), though it can be eaten year-round

**knish** <keh-'nish> *noun*. Another culturally prevalent snack (**nosh**) of a baked dough pocket filled with delicious goodies. It's eaten with the fingers, often as a fast food, and it's hard to eat just one. The classic is a potato **knish** (with some small chopped onions baked in): a cheap meal that assuaged many hungers. Like the bagel, it has become bastardized with fillings from chocolate to strawberries. Relatives of the **knish** include the samosa from India and the taco from Mexico. Yonah Schimmel's has the best ones on New York City's Houston Street. See recipe below.

**knobl** <keh-ˈnoh-bel> *noun*. Garlic.

**kreplach** <ˈkrep-lekh> *noun plural*. Triangular dumplings stuffed with delightful edibles. Eat one, you gotta have two, or three. From Yiddish **kreplekh**. Also spelled **kreplech**.

It's a variant on the culturally ubiquitous dumpling, with relatives in the Chinese won ton, the Polish pirogi, and the Italian ravioli. Basically a boiled white-flour shell in the shape of a triangular pocket filled with good things including spicy meats and/or chopped vegetables, **kasha**, cottage cheese, potato.

**kugel** *noun*. A pudding that can be made from potatoes or noodles. Its many variations include adding cottage cheese, prunes, apples, nuts, and even meat. From Yiddish **kugl**.

**latke** *noun*. Potato pancake often made with chopped onion. The thin pancakes are cooked on a skillet until crispy brown. Can be served with sour cream and/or applesauce. See recipe below.

**lox** *noun*. Smoked salmon that's usually salty. Essential with a bagel. From Yiddish **laks**. See **nova** below.

**mamaliga** *noun*. A cornmeal porridge that has its origins in Romania. It's a hearty and inexpensive meal often made by adding the cornmeal to boiling water. Cottage cheese or sour cream can be added for flavor and protein. A distant relative of Italian polenta.

**mandelbroyt** *noun*. A cookie similar to Italian biscotti. It means "almond bread" but it is not a bread. It's cut into slices for toasting.

**maychel** <ˈmy-khel> *noun*. A little gift for the stomach; a treat. A bit more cheesecake at the end of dinner, a nosh—but not enough to make you plotz. From Yiddish **maykhl**; *plural*, **maykholim** <my-ˈkhoh-leem> (literally, food dish).

**milchig** <ˈmil-khik> *noun*. Dairy foods, such as cottage or cream cheese. In kosher homes, not to be mixed with meat dishes. From Yiddish **milkhik**.

**nosh** *noun*. A satisfying nibble, just enough to still your hunger between meals. —*verb*, **nosh**. Noshing certainly sounds better than raiding the fridge and eating like a **chazer**.

**nova** *noun*. The higher priced unsalted lox from Nova Scotia.

**rugelach** *noun plural*. A pastry desert shaped like small crescents and filled with a variety of ingredients, including chocolate, raspberry, apricots, and raisins. Also spelled **rogelach**.

**schmear** *noun*. A glop of food, as cream cheese on a bagel. Other meanings include a bribe; the whole package; a blow. —*verb*, **schmear**. From Yiddish **shmir**, **shmirn** (smear).

**schmaltz** *noun*. Fat drippings usually from chicken. A mainstay of Jewish cooking. **Schmear** it on bread and you've got a power food or death by cholesterol, depending on your point of view. Other meanings include corny or mawkishly sentimental things or behavior. —*adjective*, **schmaltzy**.

**shtikl** *noun*. Just a sliver or small piece and not quite enough to fill your mouth. What your mother gave you before a meal so as not to spoil your appetite. Diminutive of **shtik** but a bit more than **shtikele**.

**taam** *noun*. Taste, zest. Creamed chopped herring with **tzibeles** has **a tam gan eden** (it tastes heavenly). Also spelled **tam**.

**tayglach** *noun plural*. A pastry desert in which small balls of dough are shaped into nuggets and then boiled in a honey-lemon syrup. They are crisp on the outside, soft on the inside, stuck together with honey syrup and candied cherries, then sprinkled with nuts. It originated in Lithuania, and it's a favorite during Jewish holidays. See the recipe below.

**tayve** <ʹtie-veh> *noun*. A strong urge or desire for a **maychel**.

**tref** *adjective*. (Of food) unkosher; not eaten by observant Jews. Applies to foods that are banned in the Bible, such as pork or shellfish. Also spelled **trayf**.

**tzibele** *noun*. Onion. Cooked for flavoring; raw for bite.

**tzimmes** *noun*. Usually a sweet side dish that can be a mixture of fruit and vegetables, or just fruit (like stewed prunes or plums). Often meat is mixed in. Also means an involved procedure or big fuss. Also spelled **tsimmes**.

Here are a few of Payson's sister's recipes which have been handed down through the family for at least three generations.

# Favorite Family Recipes

By Ilya Sandra Perlingieri, Ph.D.

I am the keeper of my family's recipe cards, many of which are over 100 years old. They have stories to tell of delicious meals and happy memories of both my maternal grandmother, Bertha Miller Coval, and my maternal great aunt, Anne Miller. Reading recipes written in their own handwriting is an instantaneous connection to the warmth and love of kitchens past.

Grandma Bertha was married to my grandfather, Jacob Paul Miller, a noted dentist who came to America from Kiev, Ukraine, in 1890 when he was a small child. Grandma, too, came to America from Kiev. Aunt Anne was Grandpa Jacob's sister. She was a fabulous cook, and for a while was a chef and also owner of different restaurants. I spent many happy hours learning to cook from different family members including my mother, Naomi Miller Coval-Apel, who was a tornado in the kitchen, churning out delicious food, but a disaster to clean up after!

I have been using only organic ingredients in my cooking for more than twenty years. For the best flavors and health, I encourage their use. After all, in 1900, when Grandmother Bertha was using these recipes, all her ingredients were organic, and I'm sure that added to the special flavors!

## Chopped Liver

1 medium onion, diced

3 tablespoons olive oil or 3 tablespoons chicken fat

1 pound chicken livers (You can substitute calf's liver. Beef liver is too hard.)

1 medium clove garlic, mashed

2 large hard-boiled eggs, chopped

mayonnaise to taste

salt to taste

- Sauté onions in olive oil (or chicken fat) for 5 minutes. Add chicken livers and garlic. Cook about 7 minutes until the livers are no longer pink. Let cool.
- In food processor, purée liver and onions. Add hard-boiled eggs, mayonnaise, and salt to taste. Mix well. Chill until ready to serve. Serve with crackers.

## Grandma Bertha's Gefilte Fish

2 pounds whitefish fillet

2 pounds winter carp fillet

2 pounds pike fillet

4 large onions, chopped

2 quarts spring water

2–3 teaspoons salt

1 teaspoon pepper

3 large eggs

3/4 cup ice spring water

1/2 teaspoon sugar

3 tablespoons matzo meal

3 carrots, diced

- Ask fishmonger to fillet all the fish and give you the heads, skin, and bones. To make the fish stock: Place the fish trimmings, 3 of the chopped onions in 2 quarts of spring water with 2 teaspoons salt, and 3/4 teaspoon pepper. Bring to a slow boil, then simmer while preparing fish fillets.
- In a food processor, grind the fish fillets and remaining onion. In a glass bowl, add the eggs, 3/4 cup ice spring water, sugar, matzo meal, remaining pepper and salt. Make sure all the ingredients have been ground very fine.
- Moisten your hands and shape this mixture into balls. Drop these into the boiling fish stock. Add carrots. Cover and cook over low heat for 1 1/2 hours. Remove the cover for the remaining 1/2 hour.
- Let the pot and gefilte fish balls cool before removing them and the carrots to a serving dish. Strain some of the stock over carrots and gefilte fish balls.
- Chill. Serve with matzos and horseradish. Keeps refrigerated about 4 days. Makes about 35 balls.

## Knishes

Chicken fat imparts an Old-World Jewish flavor that butter or oil cannot match.

Pastry dough:

3 large red bliss potatoes, quartered

2 large eggs

salt to taste

Enough unbleached flour to make the dough workable, about 1 1/2 cups

- Boil potatoes in water, about 35 minutes. When cooked, remove and drain. Peel potatoes. Mash and let stand until cool. Add eggs and salt. Mix well adding enough unbleached flour to make a soft dough. Chill for about 20 minutes, so it is workable.
- Roll out dough and cut into 2–3 inch squares and add 1–2 tablespoons of filling to each.

Filling:

1 medium onion, minced

3/4 cup rendered chicken fat

4 cups mashed potatoes

½ cup potato flour

3 large eggs

½ teaspoon salt, or to taste

¼ teaspoon freshly ground white pepper

- Sauté onion in 4 tablespoons chicken fat. Cool.
- Knead together remaining chicken fat, mashed potatoes, potato flour, eggs, salt and pepper.
- Add a teaspoon of browned onions to each square. Fold over, pinching the edges together. You can use an egg-yolk/spring-water wash to seal them tightly. Placed on lightly buttered baking sheet. Bake at 350°F for about 25 minutes, until golden. Makes about 2 dozen.

## Chicken Soup

1 whole chicken, cut up

olive oil or chicken fat

whole garlic bulb, each clove peeled and cut into small pieces

1 medium onion, diced

2 medium carrots, sliced

8 cups spring water

fresh parsley, minced

salt to taste

- In a large pot, sauté the chicken lightly in the oil or fat. Add garlic, onion, and carrots. Stir for 2–3 minutes. Add water, bring to a boil. Simmer for 45 minutes. Skim off any froth that appears. Cool.
- The chicken fat floating on the surface can be skimmed off and saved for other recipes.
- Debone the chicken and cut into smaller serving pieces. Serve plain or add matzo balls. Makes 1 to 1½ quarts.

## Ilya's Knaidlach (Matzo Balls)

There are two views for making the right kind of knaidlach, Yiddish for matzo balls. One group says big, thick ones are best. My children call mine "angel's matzo balls." Light and fluffy, they do not sit heavily in your stomach. They certainly leave room for other parts of a meal.

2 large eggs

½ cup matzo meal, or enough matzos ground fine in a food processor to make ½ cup. (Do not use matzo ball mix!)

2 tablespoons chicken fat, skimmed from freshly made chicken broth, melted. Do not substitute vegetable oil. It does not have the same Old World flavor.

2 tablespoons homemade chicken broth

- Beat eggs in mixer until thick, about 7 minutes.
- Pour matzo meal into eggs. Stir well. Add chicken broth.
- Using a teaspoon dipped into water (to keep the matzos from sticking), shape into small balls. Place on large plate. Cover with wax paper. Refrigerate for at least 2 hours, or overnight.
- In a large stock pot, filled with boiling water, gently put in each cold matzo ball. When all the balls are in, bring water to boil again. Reduce heat and gently simmer for about 1 to 1½ hours, until a cake tester comes out of center of a ball clean. Balls should triple in size and be very light and fluffy.
- Remove from water. Add to freshly made chicken soup. This makes approximately 20 matzo balls.

## Grandma Bertha's Russian Borscht

Grandma Bertha sometimes made this borscht with brisket and water instead of chicken stock. It then has a much hardier, richer flavor. Catherine the Great of Russia's Imperial Palace Guards had a Jewish cook whose borscht recipe was said to taste biblically divine.

1 medium onion, diced

Olive oil

3–4 fresh beets, peeled and grated

4 medium cloves garlic, minced

6–8 cups of freshly made broth (vegetable if kosher, chicken if not)

sour cream

minced parsley and salt to taste

- Sauté onions in olive oil for 10 minutes. Add beets and garlic. Pour in broth. Bring to a boil and reduce immediately. Simmer for ½ hour, until vegetables are tender and broth has turned a rich red color.

- Serve with a dollop of cold sour cream and sprinkle with parsley. Makes 1½–2 quarts.
- Variation: Grandma also made borscht using a small head of red cabbage, finely sliced, and chopped stewed tomatoes. Just add these ingredients to the above recipe.

## Ilya's Blintzes

For the crêpes:

¾ cup, unbleached flour

2 large eggs, beaten

1 cup whole milk

1 tablespoon unsalted butter, melted

- Blend all ingredients in blender until smooth. Pour about ⅛ cup batter into a well-buttered hot crêpe pan (or a small heavy skillet). Immediately, swirl batter around pan, until there is only a thin layer. On medium heat, cook until lightly browned, about 4 minutes. Cook only one side and place each cooked crêpe on paper towels to drain.

For the filling:

½ pound cottage cheese

2 large egg yolks

¼ teaspoon cinnamon

2 tablespoons sugar

- Mix all ingredients together. Put 1–2 tablespoons of filling onto center of crêpe. Fold over edges and press firmly.
- Fry in butter until golden on all sides. Serve with sour cream and applesauce. Makes 6–8 servings.

## Holishkes (Stuffed Cabbage)

This has always been a great favorite.

1 large 2-pound head of cabbage

Filling:

1–2 cups cooked white rice

2 pounds raw ground sirloin

2 peeled and grated medium carrots, steamed until soft

½ cup cooked peas

2 small cans (about 6 ounces or 170 grams each) tomato paste

2 cans (about 28 ounces or 794 grams each) tomatoes

3 tablespoons apple cider vinegar

1 tablespoon brown sugar

2 bay leaves, minced fine

Sauce:

½ cup spring water

½ cup puréed tomatoes

- Separate the cabbage leaves, and set aside the largest ones for stuffing. Place the leaves in boiling spring water and blanch until the leaves are just pliable (about 1–2 minutes).
- Prepare the filling by mixing all ingredients until well combined. Fill the center of each leaf. Fold edges of leaves towards center and roll up.
- Place cabbage rolls in roasting pan filled with mixture of ½ cup water and ½ cup puréed tomatoes. Cover pan with foil. Bake in 350°F oven for 1 hour. Remove cover 10 minutes before baking is done to brown top. Makes enough to serve 6.

## Aunt Anne's Latkes (Potato Pancakes)

Latkes are traditionally eaten during the festival of Chanukah, because they are fried in oil, alluding to the miracle of the cruse of oil that lasted eight days.

4 medium red bliss potatoes, grated

2 medium onions, finely grated

½ cup flour

olive oil

sour cream or applesauce

- Squeeze out excess liquid from grated potatoes. Transfer potatoes to bowl. Add onions and flour. Shaped into 4-inch flat pancakes.
- Sauté each pancake in olive oil. When golden brown, turn over, and cook until brown and golden around edges.
- Serve either with dollops of sour cream or applesauce. Makes approximately 8–10 pancakes.

## Anne's Carrot Tzimmes

Tzimmes is traditionally made on Rosh Hashanah, because its sweetness augurs for a sweet new year. The Yiddish word means "a to-do or mix-up." And that is what this dish is: a mixture of fruits, vegetables. Some recipes add meat.

2 tablespoons butter or margarine

1 pound medium carrots, peeled and thinly sliced

1/2 cup apple cider or ginger ale

2 tablespoons brown sugar

1/4 teaspoon powdered cinnamon

1/8 teaspoon nutmeg, finely ground

1/2 pound prunes, pitted and coarsely chopped

- Place all ingredients, except prunes, in a glass pot and cover. Cook over medium heat for 15 minutes. Add prunes and simmer for another 5–10 minutes, until all liquid has evaporated and mixture has begun to slightly caramelize. Makes about 3–4 cups.

## Aunt Mamie's Tayglach

Aunt Mamie made her tayglach by mounding the balls into a pyramid and filling the cracks with pieces of chopped nuts and glazed fresh cherries.

4 cups unbleached flour

2 teaspoon baking powder

8 large eggs

1 pound light honey, such as lavender honey which adds an excellent flavor

1 cup vanilla sugar (recipe follows)

1/2 cup walnuts, chopped

1/2 cup fresh cherries, chopped—leave some whole

- Mix flour, baking powder, and eggs to form a stiff dough. Knead it until firm. (This also can be done in a food processor.) On a lightly floured board, roll pieces of dough out into 1/2-inch-wide strips. Slice into 1-inch lengths. Roll into balls.

Syrup:

- Put honey in a non-reactive pot. Add vanilla sugar. Bring to a boil.

Reduce heat to a simmer. Put the dough balls a few at a time in the honey syrup. Stir frequently. They are cooked when they rise to the top, and are lightly browned. Remove and mound on large platter. Decorate with walnuts and cherries.

## Vanilla sugar

Cut one large vanilla bean in half. Scrape out the inside seeds into 2 cups of sugar. Mix the seeds and bean into the sugar. Cover. Shake occasionally. Let sit at least two weeks. My grandmother made large batches of vanilla sugar (and kept it in a dark place in her large pantry), so it was always on hand for whatever recipe she needed.

## Bertha and Naomi's Passover Cake

My mother, Naomi, used her own mother's recipe. Aunt Anne told me that it had been brought from Russia and passed down for generations. The key is beating the eggs until they are light and fluffy and a ribbon forms; then, carefully folding in the matzo cake meal. Be gentle or the cake will be hard.

12 large egg yolks

2 cups vanilla sugar

minced rind and juice of 1 lemon

1 cup matzo cake meal, sifted (plus extra for dusting the loaf pan)

- In mixer, beat eggs until light and fluffy. Add sugar in stream.
- Add lemon rind and juice. Fold in matzo flour.
- Butter and lightly dust loaf pan. Shake off excess. Pour in batter.
- Bake at 350°F, 40–50 minutes, or until a cake tester comes out clean from center of loaf.

## *DON'T PLAY WITH YOUR FOOD*

—Typical Jewish holiday: They tried to kill us, we survived, let's eat!

***

—About a century or two ago, the Pope decided that all the Jews had to leave the Vatican City. Naturally there was a big uproar from the Jewish community. So the Pope made a deal. He would have a religious debate with a member of the Jewish community. If the Jew won, they could stay. If the Pope won, the Jews would leave.

The Jews realized that they had no choice. So they picked a middle-aged man named Moishe to represent them. Moishe asked for one condition to the debate. To make it more interesting, neither side would be allowed to talk. The Pope agreed.

The day of the great debate came. Moishe and the Pope sat opposite each other for a full minute before the Pope raised his hand and showed three fingers. Moishe looked back at him and raised one finger. The Pope waved his fingers in a circle around his head. Moishe pointed to the ground where he sat. The Pope pulled out a wafer and a glass of wine. Moishe pulled out an apple. The Pope stood up and said, "I give up. This man is too good. The Jews can stay."

An hour later, the cardinals were all around the Pope asking him what happened. The Pope said: "First I held up three fingers to represent the Trinity. He responded by holding up one finger to remind me that there was still one God common to both our religions. Then I waved my finger around me to show him that God was all around us. He responded by pointing to the ground and showing that God was also right here with us. I pulled out the wine and the wafer to show that God absolves us from our sins. He pulled out an apple to remind me of THE original sin. He had an answer for everything. What could I do?"

Meanwhile, the Jewish community had crowded around Moishe. "What happened?" they asked. "Well," said Moishe, "First he said to me that the Jews had three days to get out of here. I told him that not one of us was leaving. Then he told me that this whole city would be cleared of Jews. I let him know that we were staying right here." "And then?" asked a woman. "I don't know," said Moishe. "He took out his lunch and I took out mine."

***

—Max was sitting on a bench in Central Park eating his Passover lunch. As Jews do not eat baked bread during this eight-day holiday, Max was eating matzo, a flat crunchy unleavened bread that comes in individual flat sheets with dozens of perforations (for easy breaking).

A bit later a blind man came by and sat down next to Max. Feeling neighborly, Max passed a sheet of matzo to the blind man.

The blind man ran his fingers over the matzo for a few minutes, looked puzzled, and finally asked: "Who wrote this crap?"

***

—Towards the end of World War II, three partisans are captured and sentenced to death. Right before their execution, the Commandant asks what they'd like for their last meal.

The Italian responds, "Pizza with everything. Long Live Italy!" The pie comes, he eats it, and then is immediately executed.

The Frenchman requests Coq au Vin. His chicken dish is brought to him and after finishing it, he is shot before the firing squad.

Finally they ask the Jew from Poland what he wants, and he asks for a plate of fresh strawberries.

"Strawberries?" the Commandant asks.

"Nu? Yes, fresh strawberries."

"But it's winter, strawberries are out of season!" the Commandant retorts.

"Ekh, don't worry, I can wait!"

***

—A man goes into a Jewish deli and places his order in Yiddish with a Chinese waiter who understands him completely. The man calls over the manager and says:

"This is amazing, a man from China who speaks perfect Yiddish! How did he learn it?"

"Not so loud," replies the manager, "The waiter thinks I'm teaching him English."

***

—Milton closes a big business deal and decides to celebrate with his wife at a fancy restaurant. Though they keep a kosher home, he decides to order whatever is the most expensive dinner on the menu. After a long wait, the chef brings out a roasted suckling pig with all the trimmings, including its mouth stuffed with fruit. Just as Milton is about to eat this forbidden food, his rabbi walks in and comes over to greet them.

Milton jumps up to embrace the rabbi and nervously says:

"Would you believe such a restaurant, look how they serve a baked apple."

***

—A very pious rebbe dies and goes to heaven. The first day an angel brings him a bowl of plain cholent and a glass of tea. While eating, the rebbe sees down into Hell where people are dining on brisket of beef, with cherry strudel for dessert. On the second day the Angel again brings the same meal. Down in Hell, the rebbe notices they're feasting on kishka and kasha, apricot kugel, and chocolate rugelach.

Unable to contain himself, the rebbe demands of the angel:

"How come they're eating so well down there, while all I get is cholent and warm tea?"

"Nu? What can you expect?" replies the angel, "I should work to cook for only two people?"

# Yiddish Food Proverbs

**Alts ken der mentsh fargesn nor nit esn.**
*One can forget everything except eating.*

**Az men hot broyt, vil men koyletsh.**
*When one has bread, one wants challah.*

**Az s'iz nito keyn fish, iz hering oykh a fish.**
*Where there is no fish, herring will do.*

**Khreyn iz gut far di tseyn, yoykh is gut farn boykh.**
*Horseradish is good for the teeth, [but] soup is good for the stomach.*

**Ver s'hot farkokht a kashe, zol zi oyfesn.**
*He who cooked up a kasha should be the one to eat it.*

**Er meynt nit di hagode, nor di kneydlekh.**
*He doesn't mean the haggadah, but the matzo balls.*

**Vi di gendz, azoy di grivn.**
*The way the goose is, so are the cracklings.*

**Der raykher est ven er vil, der oremer ven er ken.**
*The rich eat when they want to, the poor when they can.*

**Der zater gleybt nit dem hungerikn.**
*The one who is full doesn't believe the one who's hungry.*

**Got iz gerekht: tsum raykher git er esn; tzum oremer git er an apetit.**
*God is just: the rich he gives to eat, the poor he gives an appetite.*

**Az di kishke is zat, freyt zikh der tokhes.**
*If the guts are full, the buttocks are happy.*

**Vos fuler der boykh alts leydiker der kop.**
*The fuller the stomach, the emptier the head.*

## Hebridish: Yiddish in Israel

Yiddish is considered an important subject of study and research in Israel. At least three universities, the Hebrew University in Jerusalem, Bar-Ilan University in Ramat Gan, and the University of Haifa, have Yiddish departments and publish papers and studies dealing with Yiddish.

The influence of Yiddish on *Ivrit*, or Modern Hebrew, has long been a popular topic of discussion in Israel, and is in a way comparable to the Yiddish influence on English. In both cases, Yiddish has infiltrated the common vocabulary. There is a certain irony in the Yiddish/Hebrew convergence: Yiddish borrowed heavily from Hebrew since its beginnings, and now Hebrew has returned the favor and absorbed a sizable number of words from Yiddish. It seems to be a case of what goes around comes around.

Below is a selection of Yiddish words that have found a comfortable home in Hebrew. They are a small part of the many Hebridish words heard on the streets of Jerusalem and Tel Aviv.

**abi**. As long as.

**aftselukhes**. On purpose; for spite (from Yiddish **af tsulokhes**).

**alte zakhn**. Old stuff; old hat.

**ayene**. Some (used ironically), as in **Ayene gibor!** (Some hero!)

**ayzen**. Very good (literally, iron).

**beheyme**. A fool (from Yiddish, literally, a cow, a beast; from Hebrew *behema*).

**bis**. A bite, a morsel.

**bobe-mayse**. Nonsense; not true; a lie (from Yiddish, old-wives' tale, tall tale).

**bok**. A blockhead, an idiot (from Yiddish, literally, a he-goat).

**epes**. Something, as in **epes lo keseder** (something isn't right).

**eysikhvos**! It never happened! (From Yiddish **Veys ikh vos?!**, literally, What do I know?!)

**oy-veyzmir**. Oh, woe's me.

## *Se Habla* Yiddish

The majority of Jews who emigrated to Latin American countries from the 1880s onward came from Eastern Europe and spoke Yiddish. This language is commonly used by the generation of post-World War II immigrants and often by their children.

The following usages, picked from studies of Argentine, Mexican, and Chilean Spanish, show how Yiddish-origin words are adapted and integrated into Latin-American Spanish:

**bojer.** A young person, youth (from Yiddish *bokher*; the Spanish *j* for Yiddish *kh*).

**golpear la pava.** To babble nonsense (Argentine Spanish slang; literally, to bang on the teakettle; translation of Yiddish *hakn a tshaynik*).

**guefilte fish.** Gefilte fish ("guefilte" reflects the Spanish spelling for "hard g" pronunciation).

**jajamim.** The (Talmudic) sages (from Yiddish *khakhomim*).

**Januca.** Chanukah.

**jasidico.** Hasidic.

**jupa.** A bridal canopy (from Yiddish *khupe*).

**lejayim!** To life! (a toast) (from Yiddish *lekhayim!*).

**levone.** The moon.

**Meshiaj.** The Messiah.

**sitra ajra.** The company of Satan (from Yiddish *sitre-akhre*, from Aramaic; literally, the other side).

**yidish.** Yiddish.

# The Story of Yiddish Theater

## From *Purimshpil* to *The Dybbuk*

*Purim-play Purimshpil book of Esther Haskalah Abraham Goldfaden Serkele Solomon Ettinger Berl Broder Shmendrik Der Fanatik oder di Tsvey Kuni Lemels [illegible]anatic o[illegible] Two Lambkins [illegible]ulamis Bar Kok[illegible] [illegible]andlen Ra[illegible] Almonds [illegible]uni [illegible]wicked witch Bobe Yak[illegible]ne [illegible]b Adler [illegible]tha Kalich Ida Kamin[illegible] Th[illegible]op on Main Street Molly Pic[illegible] Yente th[illegible] Matchmake[illegible] Fiddler on the Roof Di Kishefmakhern The Sorceress Boris Thomashefsky Hamlet Romeo and Juliet Richard the Third Sigmund (Zelig) Mogulesco Jacob Gordin Sibirya Siberia Abraham Cahan Der Yidisher Kenig Lir The Jewish King Lear Elisha ben Avuya dayt-shmerish Germanized Yiddish Got, Mentsh, un Tayvl God, Man, and Devil Peretz Hirschbein Af Yener Zayt Taykh On the Other Side of the River Di Erd The Earth Grine Felder Green Fields S. A. An-Ski Shloyme-Zanvl Rappoport The Dybbuk Tsvishn Tsvey Veltn Between Two Worlds Reb Azrielke Rav Shimshon, exorcised Maurice Schwartz Peretz*

The Yiddish theater came of age in the 19th century and reached its pinnacle in the 20th. At the height of its popularity, it brought to the Yiddish-speaking audience dramas and comedies created for the Yiddish stage, as well as plays adapted from Shakespeare, Goethe, Schiller, Ibsen, Chekhov, and other world-famous dramatists. Audiences flocked to both professional and amateur Yiddish productions in all the major cities of Europe and America. At its height, Yiddish theater reflected the language and voice of the Yiddish-speaking public more than any other art form. Its decline began precisely at the point where Yiddish ceased to be spoken by the masses. It would seem by all accounts that the last Yiddish theater should have closed its doors in the 1960s or thereabouts. It did not. The theater's hold on the Yiddish imagination has kept its force long past its heyday. Yiddish plays are still performed in the United States, Canada, Israel, Australia, Latin America, and Europe. Perhaps the Yiddish theater serves as a metaphor for the language that created it: it endures.

Historians trace the prehistory of the Yiddish theater to the traditional Purim-play (in Yiddish, *Purimshpil*) staged on Purim, the festival celebrating the victory of the Persian Jews over the evil Haman as told in the Biblical book of Esther. Purim-plays were celebrated among Yiddish-speaking Jews as far back as the 1500s. The first Purim-plays were simple monologues in which a performer recited and acted out a long narrative poem dealing with the story of Purim. Later, several performers joined together to perform skits and playlets, often comic parodies, as

Purim entertainment. The presentations often followed a formula which ended with the Yiddish verse, **Haynt iz purim, morgn iz oys, geb mir a groshn un varf mikh aroys!** (Today is Purim, tomorrow it's out, give me a groschen [penny] and throw me out!). This kind of entertainment was tolerated within the religious confines of Jewish communities because it was connected with a Jewish holiday; any other form of theater fell under the prohibition of "Do not follow their [other nations'] traditions" (Leviticus 18:3).

While the adherents of the **Haskalah** or Jewish Enlightenment movement of the 18th and 19th centuries had no compunctions about writing secular plays in Hebrew and Yiddish, they had no hopes of actually seeing them performed on stage. (See "Yiddish Enlightenment: Haskalah.") But almost by accident one man of genius, Abraham Goldfaden, found a way of parlaying the traditional *Purimshpil* into real theater with real plays and real actors. Goldfaden's achievement has earned him the epithet of "father of the Yiddish theater."

Purim players pose in costume at a Sholem Aleichem Folk School, New York, around 1920. (YIVO Institute for Jewish Research)

## *Abraham Goldfaden (1840–1908)*

Born in a small town in Ukraine, Abraham Goldfaden received a typical Jewish education, and at the age of seventeen entered the government-run rabbinical and teaching academy in Zhitomir, where he came under the influence of various teachers who were adherents of the Haskalah. Under their guidance, he began composing Hebrew and Yiddish songs and poems. When in 1862 the academy's principal decided to stage a Purim play based on a posthumously published drama, *Serkele*, by the Yiddish writer Solomon Ettinger (1803–1856), he cast the young Goldfaden in the role of Serkele, a woman bent on gaining wealth and power. Though he played the role of a woman (since female players were not even considered in a rabbinical school), Goldfaden's participation in the acting and staging of *Serkele* transformed a mere Purim play into a full-fledged theatrical piece. It also prepared him for what was to be years later the creation of the first Yiddish theater group.

After years of teaching and writing in Ukraine and Poland, in 1876 Goldfaden moved to Jassy, Romania, where he joined forces with the Broder singers, one of various troupes of Yiddish singers and performers who sang and acted in skits in small towns, inns, and taverns. Building on a friendship with Berl Broder, the singer and composer who headed the group, Goldfaden transformed the troupe's routine singing and monologues into a two-act play complete with dialogue and plot. The first performance of the play, in a Jassy wine cellar in October 1876, marks the beginning of Yiddish theater.

Afterwards Goldfaden's name became permanently linked with the Yiddish theater, providing players with a full repertoire of plays, many of them his own—and acting not only as playwright and musical composer, but also as producer, stage manager, and impresario. The companies he formed traveled throughout Eastern Europe. Among Goldfaden's most popular musical plays were the comic operettas *Shmendrik* (1877), whose hero's name entered the Yiddish language as a synonym for a simple-minded and ineffectual person, and *Der Fanatik oder di Tsvey Kuni Lemels* (The Fanatic or The Two Lambkins, 1880). A romantic operetta, *Shulamis* (1880), was the first of a group of Goldfaden's plays with serious themes, including the historical *Bar Kokhba* (1887) and the drama *Ben Ami* (1907), the latter loosely based on George Eliot's novel *Daniel Deronda*. Goldfaden wrote many plays of great popular appeal that have continued to be staged throughout the 20th century. He also left his imprint on Yiddish music: his classic lullaby *Rozhinkes mit Mandlen* (Raisins and Almonds) has been sung by generations of parents. And his picturesque characters, including Shmendrik, Kuni Lemel, and the wicked witch Bobe Yakhne, remain staples of Yiddish humorous vocabulary.

The year 1883 marked a turning point in the fortunes of the Yiddish theater. The Russian government, alarmed by the growing popularity of this form of entertainment, which it deemed overly nationalistic, issued an edict prohibiting the performance of Yiddish plays. The effect of the edict was to encourage actors, playwrights, and producers to emigrate to Western countries, where they established theaters in major cities such as London, Paris, and New York. The London and Paris enterprises enjoyed moderate success until World War II, but it was in New York that the Yiddish theater developed and matured into a world-class art form. The growth and worldwide fame of the American Yiddish theater are mainly associated with the work of such playwrights as Goldfaden, Jacob Gordin, Sholem Asch, and Peretz Hirschbein, and with such larger-than-life actors as Boris Thomashefsky, Jacob Adler, and Maurice Schwartz.

Among the actresses who dominated the Yiddish stage for much of the twentieth century were Sarah Adler, wife and associate of Jacob Adler (see below), and Jacob Adler's daughter Celia, who was born in 1889, made her debut at the age of nine, and in 1925 directed her own repertory company; Bertha Kalich (1875-1939), the first actress of the Yiddish stage who made a successful transition to the American theater; Ida Kaminska, born in Poland to an illustrious Yiddish theatrical family, who attained international fame for her role in the film *The Shop on Main Street* (1965); and Molly Picon (1898–1992), who joined a Yiddish repertory company when she was six and is still remembered for her role as Yente the Matchmaker in the film musical *Fiddler on the Roof*.

The first stage performance of a Yiddish play in the United States was held in New York's Turn Hall, on East Fourth Street, on August 12, 1882. The play was a Goldfaden operetta, *Di Kishefmakhern* (The Sorceress), and among the actors was a fourteen-year-old choir singer, Boris Thomashefsky, who went on to become a major figure of the American Yiddish theater for the next half-century.

## *Boris Thomashefsky (1868–1939)*

Born in Ukraine, like Goldfaden, Boris Thomashefsky was the son of a Yiddish actor and playwright, Pincus Thomashefsky, who emigrated to the United States in 1881, settling in New York City. Blessed with a fine singing voice, Boris soon joined a synagogue choir, where he befriended a wealthy synagogue trustee, Frank Wolf. He talked Wolf into backing the New York appearance of a Yiddish company from London. This was the company that staged the production of *Di Kishef-makhern* at Turn Hall, and through Wolf's influence Thomashefsky obtained a singing part in the operetta. Vociferous opposition from German and Orthodox Jews, who considered Yiddish theater vulgar and sacrilegious, forced the play to close. But within a few months, as another Yiddish company gained foothold in New York, performing regularly at the Bowery Garden, young Thomashefsky obtained frequent parts in female roles, since women singers and actresses were still scarce on the Yiddish stage.

Thomashefsky continued to act in musical plays, chiefly those of Goldfaden, whose popularity increased with the years. He also produced plays of his own in the sentimental and melodramatic genre created by Goldfaden. But it was as an actor of serious plays, mostly Yiddish translations or adaptations of plays by Shakespeare and Goethe, that he achieved his greatest success and fame. Among those plays were such classics as *Hamlet, Romeo and Juliet, Richard the Third,* all performed in the 1890s, and Goethe's *Faust* (1902). The heroic roles in these plays suited Thomashefsky's flamboyant personality and enhanced his popular following. In 1912 Thomashefsky created the National Theater in New York, where Yiddish plays and shows were staged until the 1950s. He also toured extensively and stimulated Yiddish theatrical activity in many parts of the United States and Europe.

## *Jacob Adler (1855–1926)*

The "golden epoch of Yiddish theater," as the 1890s have been called, came about largely through the work of two men: the playwright Jacob Gordin and the actor Jacob Adler. For thirty years, the handsome Adler's towering figure dominated the Yiddish stage as he performed masterfully in Gordin's dramatic plays. Adler also gained fame as the founder of a great theatrical family that included his wife Sarah (1858–1953), their children Julia, Stella, and Luther, and his daughter from an earlier marriage, Celia.

Born in Odessa, Russia, Jacob Adler acted as a leading man in many of Goldfaden's plays until the edict of 1883 caused him to emigrate, first to London, then to New York. His dynamic, though often histrionic performances in genre plays brought him success. But critics were clamoring for more serious Yiddish drama, one that could measure up to the great European plays of the period. Adler was not deaf to the criticism. The breakthrough came in 1891, when a fellow actor, Sigmund (Zelig) Mogulesco, arranged a meeting between Adler and Gordin. Adler, impressed with Gordin's ideas about the need to reform Yiddish theater, asked him to write a play. The result was the groundbreaking *Sibirya* (Siberia), Gordin's first play, produced in November 1891, with Adler in the leading role of a wealthy Russian Jew who is arrested for having escaped from Siberian exile as a youth.

The critical success of *Sibirya*, hailed by the influential Abraham Cahan, editor of the *Jewish Daily Forward*, as a revolution on the Yid-

Jacob Adler (1855–1926) and the Adler theatrical family, when they appeared in Jacob Gordin's play *Der Vilder Mentsh* (The Wild Man), New York, 1920s. (YIVO Institute for Jewish Research)

dish stage, led to a collaboration between Adler and Gordin in a series of plays that lifted Yiddish drama to new heights, replacing what was considered "trashy" romanticism and sentimentality with realistic characters and situations. Among them were *Der Yidisher Kenig Lir* (The Jewish King Lear), a Yiddish version of *The Merchant of Venice* in which Adler electrified the audience with his moving interpretation of Shylock, and the historical drama *Elisha ben Avuya*, produced in 1909.

In later years Adler managed several theaters in which he and members of his family performed together in numerous plays until he was felled by a stroke in 1920. He remained, however, a legendary figure in the theatrical world long after his death in 1926.

## *Jacob Gordin (1853–1909)*

A Russian journalist by profession, and politically a populist and Jewish sectarian (he founded a sect that rejected rabbinical Judaism), Jacob Gordin did not write in Yiddish until he was nearly forty years old.

Driven out of Russia in 1891 for his dissident activities, he came to the United States with his large family. After various unsuccessful attempts to make a living, he finally found the only work for which he was suited: as a Yiddish journalist. A fortuitous meeting with Jacob Adler led him to write his first play, *Sibirya*, which, thanks largely to Adler's promotional skills, proved to be a critical success and a catalyst of reform in the Yiddish theater.

What this and other Gordin plays achieved was to introduce a nitty-gritty realism as well as a typically Russian soulfulness to the stage. He replaced song-and-dance pageantry and spectacle with serious drama. Realism also meant naturalistic expression, in the kind of informal, everyday Yiddish spoken on the street, devoid of the affected "stage Yiddish" filled with *daytshmerish* (Germanized Yiddish) that was common in earlier plays. Gordin's plays were not without fault, though. He deliberately imbued his dramas with didactic and moralistic sentiments and consciously used the stage as a lecture platform. He felt that the purpose of theater was not just to amuse and entertain, but to educate the public and raise its social consciousness. But in his day the audience found his moralizing not merely palatable but uplifting. His plays clearly touched a sensitive chord among the immigrant workers of New

York's East Side who looked to the theater as a source of both entertainment and instruction.

Most of Gordin's many plays (there were some seventy) were popular successes and several became classics that are still performed in various parts of the world. There is a receptive audience in Israel, for example, for such Gordin standards as *Der Yidisher Kenig Lir* (1892), *Mirele Efros* (1898), and *Got, Mentsh, un Tayvl* (God, Man, and Devil, 1900). The latter, an adaptation of the Faust legend, is about a poor weaver in a Russian **shtetl** who strikes a deal with the Devil, becomes a wealthy but slave-driving manufacturer, and in the end, tormented by his conscience, kills himself. Gordon borrowed liberally from the classics of the world stage, starting with his successful adaptation of Shakespeare's *King Lear*. But he went further, and extended the theme of conflict between parents and children to the equally successful *Mirele Efros*, whose original subtitle was *Di Yidishe Kenign Lir* (The Jewish Queen Lear) and whose heroine is a Jewish mother of heroic stature. This play is probably Gordin's most popular creation. The part of Mirele has been played by countless actresses, and the play itself has been translated into nearly a dozen languages.

At the turn of the 20th century, the American Yiddish theater was enjoying its golden epoch. Besides New York's Second Avenue, theatergoers flocked to Yiddish plays in Philadelphia's Arch Street, National, and Standard theaters; and Yiddish theater flourished in cities like Chicago, Boston, Cleveland, and Detroit. But after Gordin's death in 1909, a gradual decline in the quality of Yiddish theater in the United States set in, mainly due to a diminishing audience of playgoers as the trend toward Americanization gained steam. The younger-generation immigrants were eager to become culturally assimilated in the great American melting pot, so that many of them chose to distance themselves from their native Yiddish-based culture. Those who still clung to Yiddish had to find solace in the old-fashioned school of pageant, melodrama, and romance popularized a generation earlier by Goldfaden and later by his many imitators.

But while the Yiddish theater was foundering in America, it enjoyed a miraculous revival in Eastern Europe when, in 1908, the Russian government repealed its edict against the performance of Yiddish plays. In the same year, a twenty eight-year-old playwright named Peretz

Hirschbein organized a group of actors in Odessa whose goal was to create a professional Yiddish theater of the highest quality.

## *Peretz Hirschbein (1880–1948)*

Peretz Hirschbein was born into an Orthodox family in eastern Poland, where he grew up as a typical yeshiva student of his day. As an adolescent, he started writing poetry and stories in Hebrew and Yiddish, and at the age of twenty four moved to Warsaw, where he joined a circle of writers that included contemporaries like Sholem Asch and iconic literary figures like Isaac Leib Peretz. Influenced by them, he began writing plays. His first two Yiddish plays, *Af Yener Zayt Taykh* (On the Other Side of the River, 1905) and *Di Erd* (The Earth, 1907) were, as their titles suggest, bucolic romances, foreshadowing his lifelong interest in rural and pastoral life that led to the creation of his 1923 masterpiece, *Grine Felder* (Green Fields).

The theatrical group Hirschbein organized in 1908 lasted only a few years, disbanding in 1910. But in that period the group produced only quality plays—those of Sholem Asch, Sholom Aleichem, Jacob Gordin, Peretz, and Hirschbein himself, thereby serving as a precursor to the famed Vilna Troupe of 1916.

This theatrical company, which moved to Warsaw in 1917 but retained its original name, presented a number of outstanding Yiddish plays. But it was in 1920, with the production of S.A. An-ski's *Der Dibek* (The Dybbuk), that the company became internationally famous. And through this production, the play's author also rocketed to fame.

## *S.A. An-Ski (1863–1920)*

Although S.A. An-ski (pen-name of Shloyme-Zanvl Rappoport) wrote only one Yiddish play, *Der Dibek* (The Dybbuk), his play has the distinction of being the most famous Yiddish drama ever written and a world-class masterpiece comparable to the best of Chekhov and Ibsen. Not only was this play, originally titled *Tsvishn Tsvey Veltn* (Between Two Worlds), translated and produced in all major languages, but it inspired a number of musical versions, including two operas, and two film versions (1937, 1968). Curiously, An-ski wrote the play twice. The original, unpublished manuscript was translated into Hebrew by the poet Chaim Nachman Bialik in 1918. Some time later An-ski lost the original and was forced to translate Bialik's Hebrew text back into Yiddish. This highly Hebraicized version was the one published in 1920 by An-ski and produced in the same year by the Vilna Troupe.

Born in the city of Vitebsk, Belorussia (Belarus), the young Shloyme-Zanvl was an outstanding yeshiva student until the age of seventeen. Having discovered and absorbed the writings of various adherents of the Haskalah (Jewish Enlightenment) movement, he turned away from Judaism and after some years of aimless travels he became a populist and went to live among the Russian peasantry, where he acquired the name Semyon Akimovitch. (This Russian name was the source of the initials S.A. As to the origin of the pseudonym An-ski, he made it up by combining his mother's name, Anna with the common Russian name-suffix, *-ski*.) At the age of twenty-eight, the restless, ever-searching An-ski threw off his peasant clothing and went to Paris as an émigré. There, he successively joined the Jewish Labor Bund, flirted with Jewish nationalism, and somewhere between political activities read I.L. Peretz's writings and discovered Yiddish. In 1905 he returned to Russia and earnestly embarked on a new career as a Yiddish writer and journalist. He wrote realistic stories about Jewish life in the Pale of Settlement, tales about Hasidim in the manner of Peretz, and various Jewish folktales. His interest in folklore led him, in turn, to join the Jewish historic, literary, and ethnographic societies that sprang up in St. Petersburg at that time. From 1912 to 1914 he led a Jewish ethnographic expedition to collect folkloric material, traveling through the great Jewish centers of Podolia and Volhynia. It was this firsthand experience that inspired An-ski to write *Der Dibek*.

The story of this play is easy to recapitulate, but no summary can do justice to the mystical, mysterious atmosphere in which it unfolds. Briefly, it is the story of Khonon and Leah, who were pledged in marriage to each other prenatally by their respective fathers. After Khonon's father dies, the pledge is forgotten, and Leah's father, Sender, betroths her to another young man, Menashe. When Khonon, who has immersed himself in the mysteries of kabbalah, hears the news from Sender's lips, he falls dead. Then, on the eve of Leah's marriage to Menashe, the wandering soul of the dead Khonon enters Leah's body as a **dybbuk**. Though a dybbuk is usually conceived of as an evil spirit (see "Dybbuks—Evil Spirits of the Shtetl"), in An-ski's tale it is the rest-

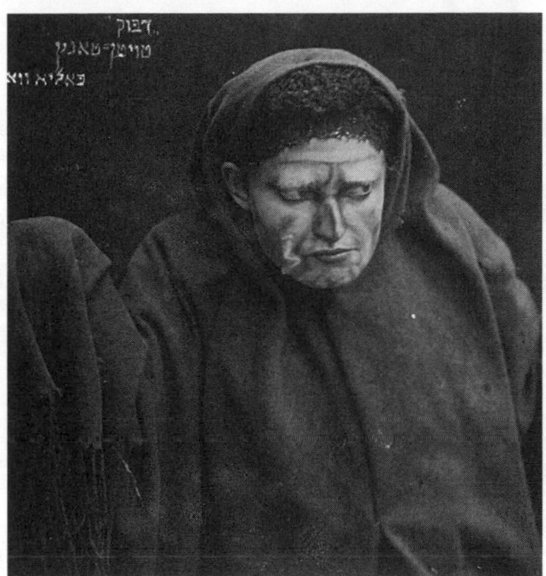


The toytn-tants (death dance), just before the spirit of the dybbuk is exorcised, performed by the actress Paula Walter, in S. A. An-ski's play *Der Dibek* (The Dybbuk), undated. (YIVO Institute for Jewish Research)

less, wandering soul of a deeply afflicted dead person. Through the combined efforts of the Hasidic sage Reb Azrielke and the town's rabbi, Rav Shimshon, the dybbuk is exorcised. But the souls of the young couple remain inseparable, and in the end Leah gives up her soul to join that of Khonon.

An-ski (sometimes Anglicized as Ansky) produced an impressive body of other work, most of it published in fifteen volumes after his death (1920–25). But his enduring fame rests upon his play.

The Yiddish theater's European revival, as embodied in the Vilna Troupe, pumped new blood into the flagging American theater. Following World War I, a new generation of playwrights and actors emerged on the Yiddish stage, and their enthusiasm and vitality extended the theater's life into the 1930s and 1940s. Undoubtedly the leading figure of this generation was Maurice Schwartz, actor extraordinary and founder of the Yiddish Art Theater.

## Dybbuks—Evil Spirits of the Shtetl

Ghosts and spirits have long been a tradition of the Jewish occult and folklore, and **dybbuks** hold a special place in the Yiddish imagination. Dybbuk comes from the Hebrew word meaning cleaving or clinging and that's what happens to an unlucky person possessed by one. A dybbuk is the spirit of a doomed soul that takes control of the living and controls his or her behavior. The dybbuk often has some claim on this person, such as being a scorned lover or a deceived partner. When a dybbuk took hold, unspeakable anguish resulted, with the dybbuk speaking through the tormented person's mouth. The possessed person could be driven to sinful acts, irrational behavior, madness, and even death. Tragically, the dybbuk itself often could not find peace because of its own unforgiven sins.

Possessions by dybbuks were particularly active during the 16th and 17th centuries in the **shtetls** of Eastern Europe. Simple folk believed that dybbuks were responsible for a wide range of problems: lost or hidden objects, thwarted plans, sickness, nervous and mental disorders, hysteria, and epilepsy. Unlike an **eyn-hore** or evil eye, a dybbuk was hard to fight off. There were ways to ward off the evil eye, as by using incantations, making protective hand gestures, and wearing amulets. Parents would refuse praise for a child, even going so far as to spit on him or her or to cover the child with soot and dirt so as not to attract the malignant stare of an evil person. But an evil spirit or dybbuk was hard to avoid.

Fortunately dybbuks could be exorcised by a rabbi or a holy man. Special prayers would be said ordering the dybbuk to depart. With characteristic compassion, the dybbuk would be also entreated to find peace and eternal rest in God's name. It was said that the sign of a successful exorcism was a bloody exit hole in the small toe.

In Yiddish folklore, one favorite form of exorcism of dybbuks was for a **rebbe** and **bal-moyfes** (miracle worker) to stretch out his right arm toward the possessed person and shout: "Listen, wicked one! My decree is that you shall leave this woman (or man, boy, etc.) through the little finger of her left hand and enter into someone as wicked as you are!"

*The Dybbuk* was a famous play written by S. An-ski in 1920 and performed in Yiddish theaters around the world. Leonard Bernstein used the play as the basis for his ballet, *The Dybbuk* (choreographed by Jerome Robbins of *West Side Story* fame). Isaac Bashevis Singer used dybbuks liberally in his stories and novels and dybbuks have been the subject of films and television.

## *Maurice Schwartz (1890–1960)*

A man of boundless energy and ambition, Maurice Schwartz single-handedly built and maintained a vibrant Yiddish repertory company for three decades. As a leading actor of stage and screen, often called "the John Barrymore of the Yiddish theater," his career spanned nearly forty years. As stage director and manager of his Yiddish Art Theater, he was a charismatic figure who gathered around him a gifted group of actors who helped him stage scores of memorable productions, some 150 altogether. His taste was eclectic: he delighted as much in staging Goldfaden's *Shmendrik* as he did Gordin's *Der Yidisher Kenig Lir* or An-ski's *Der Dibek*. But this very eclecticism enabled him to keep his company open even as most of the famed Second Avenue Yiddish theaters (more than twenty in the 1920s) were closing their doors for lack of audiences.

Born Avrom-Moishe Schwartz in the town of Sedikov, Ukraine, Schwartz arrived in New York with his parents in 1901. His acting talent was spotted as soon as he started performing in plays at the Lower East Side school he attended, and by the time he was fifteen he landed a part in a Yiddish stock company in Baltimore. In 1912 he joined the repertory company of the newly established David Kessler Theater on Second Avenue, which opened a year later. He built up his craft and reputation working with the actor-director David Kessler for the next six years, and in 1918 organized a group of performers, among them Jacob Ben Ami and Celia Adler, to form the Yiddish Art Theater. The company, housed at the Irving Place Theater in the Bowery district, staged its first performance on November 16, 1918. The play was a pastoral comedy by Peretz Hirschbein, *A Farvorfn Vinkl* (A Secluded Corner), and to many theatergoers it was a refreshing and welcome change from the weighty didactic plays of Gordin and his school. They hailed it as heralding the advent of a new, aesthetically pleasing Yiddish theater that evoked the simple, natural beauty of rural Jewish life. Above all, it was "art," versus heavy-handed urban "realism," and therefore a new lease on the life of Yiddish theater.

It did not last long. By 1922 Schwartz had shed "art" in favor of variety, mounting productions of every kind in order to please a fickle and diminishing audience. While the crowds kept dwindling in the "art" theaters, Schwartz's productions, ranging from Goldfaden standards to Hirschbein's pastorals, from translations of the Russian and German

## Ida Kaminska—Star of the Yiddish Theater

Ida Kaminska (1899–1980) descended from an illustrious family of Yiddish actors. The daughter of Abraham Isaac Kaminski and Esther Rachel Kaminska, pioneers of the Yiddish theater in Eastern Europe, Ida started her career as a child of seven in the theatrical company founded in Warsaw by her father. Following in the footsteps of her mother, who had acted in the first Yiddish films made in Warsaw and had been a founding member of the famous Vilna Troupe, Ida Kaminska co-founded the Warsaw Yiddish Art Theater before World War II and starred in many of its stage productions.

When Poland was invaded in 1939, she fled to the Soviet-occupied territories, where she performed at every opportunity before adoring Yiddish audiences. A versatile actress, she had mastered a large repertoire of roles in Yiddish plays as well as in Yiddish translations of plays by Ibsen, Dumas, Schiller, and other world-class dramatists. On returning to Poland after the war, she single-handedly took over the reconstruction of the Yiddish theater. Enlisting the Polish government's support, she established in Warsaw the Jewish State Theater, which she then led as director for the next two decades. Her company gained international fame as it toured Israel, North and South America, Australia, and Western Europe, presenting outstanding Yiddish plays before audiences who flocked to the theater to see Kaminska in one of her legendary performances.

The world came to know her in the mid-1960s, when she starred in a widely acclaimed Czech film, *The Shop on Main Street*, in a role for which she won an Academy Award nomination. In 1968, when a rise in anti-Semitism forced many Jews to emigrate, Ida Kaminska left Poland for the United States. A measure of her achievement was the continued activity of the Jewish State Theater in Poland even after she left.

Ida Kaminska (1899–1980) as Esmeralda in a Yiddish stage adaptation of Victor Hugo's *Hunchback of Notre Dame*, Vilna in 1925. (YIVO Institute for Jewish Research)

masters to adaptations of Sholom Aleichem's stories, continued to draw Yiddish-speaking audiences. His company was a breeding ground for many actors who wound up on Broadway or in Hollywood, such as Paul Muni, Sophie Tucker, and Molly Picon. But for most audiences, it was Schwartz's performances as an actor that attracted them to his theater. His dark, brooding presence dominated the stage, and his strong hypnotic baritone cast a spell over the audience. He could be soft-spoken and gentle as well as operatically grand. Some of his most popular performances included the title role in *Der Yidisher Kenig Lir* (The Jewish King Lear) and as Shylock in the Yiddish version of *The Merchant of Venice*. But he received his greatest acclaim for his role as Reb Melekh in *Yoshe Kalb* (Yoshe the Fool), a dramatization of I.J. Singer's novel of the same name.

The novel *Yoshe Kalb*, published in 1932, was well-received but had little impact until Maurice Schwartz dramatized it. After the play became a sensation, the novel gained a wide public and is today considered a Yiddish classic. Its plot centers on the predicament of Nokhem, a sensitive soul given to mystical visions, who unwittingly commits adultery with the shrewish third wife of his father-in-law, the aging Hasidic rabbi Reb Melekh. The remorseful youth runs away to another town, Bialegura, where his silence and simple ways earn him the nickname of Yoshe Kalb. After fifteen years of exile, Nokhem returns to his former home, where he is now regarded as a holy man who might someday inherit Reb Melekh's position. However, on the eve of Rosh Hashanah the visiting rabbi of Bialegura recognizes him as Yoshe Kalb and accuses him of being an adulterer. The two towns quarrel over Nokhem, and the resulting scandal leads to the convening of a rabbinical court to decide Nokhem's true identity. Nokhem appears before the court but maintains his silence, whereupon the saintly rebbe of Lizhane proclaims that Nokhem is a **gilgl**, the reincarnation of a dead man's wandering soul. At this, Reb Melekh collapses and dies, and Nokhem is driven out, even as a fight breaks out between Reb Melekh's heirs, and the townspeople clamor for Nokhem's return as the rightful heir to Reb Melekh's position.

Schwartz's Yiddish Art Theater remained an institution through World War II and quietly folded about 1950. But Schwartz, now a legendary figure, continued to stage plays outside New York, and as late as 1960 tried to revive Yiddish theater in Israel. Had he lived, he might have seen Yiddish theater flourish in Israel during the 1970s, with several companies performing new Yiddish plays in Tel Aviv and Jerusalem. Schwartz's legacy goes on, for as recently as in the year 2000, *The Rothschilds*, a spectacular Yiddish musical born on Broadway, was drawing record audiences in Jerusalem.

To say that Yiddish theater is dead is nearly as accurate as saying that the Yiddish language is dead. The bond between the two will not easily break, and one breathes life into the other. Yiddish plays are still being performed in Europe, Israel, Latin America, and North America. For example, the Yiddish Theatre in Montreal, founded by Dora Wasserman forty years ago, produces several plays each year and regularly tours Europe, Israel, and North America. In New York, the Folksbiene Yiddish Theater, which is the longest-lived, continuously performing Yiddish theatrical institution in the world, goes on producing Yiddish plays year after year. The competing Yiddish Public Theater has challenged its supremacy with such classics as Hirschbein's *Grine Felder*. And enthusiasts are promoting the development of a Yiddish National Theater. None of this compares, of course, to the glory days of the Yiddish theater in the 1920s and 1930s. But just because a person or institution is old and somewhat creaky, it does not make either one dead.

Over a hundred years ago, the distinguished historian Leo Wiener, in his *History of Yiddish Literature in the Nineteenth Century* (1899), concluded the book with the observation that Yiddish in America "is certainly doomed to extinction. Its lease on life is commensurate with the large immigration to the New World." He would most certainly have said the same thing about Yiddish theater.

Notwithstanding his and others' prophecies of doom, both the Yiddish language and its offspring, the Yiddish theater, continue to survive.

## A Yiddish Bestiary

Yiddish is graced with a rich trove of real and fabled animal names, many of which are applied to people. Here is a sampling for all animal lovers:

**beheyme.** A word of wide application. It can mean a head of cattle, a cow, a beast, or any dumb animal. When applied to people (which is most often), it is an insulting term meaning a lamebrain, blockhead, idiot, and the like.

**feygele,** *plural* **feygelekh.** A little bird. Figuratively, a homosexual.

**ferd** (*singular and plural*). A horse. Figuratively, a stubborn mule.

**kelev,** *plural* **kelovim.** A vicious dog; cur. When referring to a person, it denotes a mean or ruthless beast.

**khamer,** *plural* **khamoyrim.** A donkey, an ass. Figuratively, a stupid person, a dunce.

**khaye.** A beast, often used in the phrase **a vilde khaye** (a wild beast), when describing a vicious human being, a brute.

**khazer,** *plural* **khazeyrim.** A pig. A favorite when referring to an insatiable fresser or glutton, or to a filthy slob, and sometimes to a penny-pinching skinflint.

**lemele,** *plural* **lemelekh.** A little lamb. Figuratively, a simple-minded, naïve, or innocent person.

Many Yiddish family names derive from animal names. For example:

**Einhorn.** From Yiddish **eynhorn,** a unicorn.

**Klepfish.** From Yiddish **klepfish,** cod.

**Laks** or **Lachs.** From Yiddish **laks,** salmon or lox.

**Shvalb.** From Yiddish **shvalb,** a swallow (bird).

**Sokol.** From Yiddish **sokol,** a falcon.

**Soloveitchik.** From Yiddish **soloveitshik,** little nightingale.

# Yiddish Music

## Klezmer and Beyond

*cantorial klezmorim kley-zemer musical instruments dancing freylekhs merrymaking sher scissor dance violin viola cello lute harpsichord clarinet trumpet Slavic Gypsy Balkan krekhts groan dreydlekh trills [illegible] bulgar Doyne goldene medine golden land broygez tants angry dance flash tants bottle dance Az der Rebe Tantst When the Rebbe Dances Rumenye Rumenye Romania Romania landsmanshaftn [illegible] wedding entertainer 78 rpm "Klezmer Revival" Klezmorim Kapelye The Klezmer Conservatory Band Neo-Klez New Klez Klezmania, Klezmaniacs Klezmerica KlezMishpoche Klezmiracles Kleztets Chernobyl Berlin Brave New World klezmer supergroup The Klezmatics jazz rock funk reggae hip-hop World Beat Itzhak Perlman, In the Fiddler's House Andy Statman Klezmer Orchestra all-women KlezMs Mikveh Pharoah's Daughter Hasidic Middle Eastern folk-rock Jewish liturgy Slavic Polish Ukrainian Balkan Bulgarian Romanian Greek Gypsy Romance Hebrew Aramaic Slavic Germanic*

Music has played an integral part in Jewish life since Biblical times. The Bible tells us that Jubal was the first to play the harp and flute (Genesis 4:21) and tradition has it that he was the originator of the art of music. King David was an accomplished player of the lyre as well as a dancer, and the singing of the Psalms was a part of the services in Solomon's Temple. Musical instruments frequently mentioned in the Bible include flutes, trumpets, ten-stringed harps, lyres, tambourines, cymbals, and bells. After the destruction of the Second Temple in 70 C.E., instrumental music was prohibited in synagogue services and replaced by unaccompanied singing. Chanting of sacred songs by cantors and choirs became the main form of music, beside the cantillations used in reading the Hebrew Bible and Prophets.

While the cantorial tradition remained dominant through most of the Diaspora, a parallel development was the advent in 17th-century Europe of wandering Jewish folk musicians who came to be known as **klezmorim** for the *kley-zemer* (Hebrew for musical instruments) they used. They were especially prevalent in Eastern Europe, where they performed at weddings and other social functions. In large cities, such as Prague, they participated in public processions honoring the monarch. All through the 18th and 19th centuries, these professional musicians played a major role in the East European Jewish shtetls, bringing joy and hope into the squalid lives of their inhabitants.

# Traditional Klezmer Music

The original **klezmer** bands played music for dancing—group dancing and square dancing, like the lively **freylekhs** (merrymaking) and the **sher** (literally, scissor, a wedding square dance). The instruments the klezmer used were usually a violin or two, a viola or cello, a lute, a harpsichord, a clarinet, and an occasional trumpet. The music they played was a blend of Slavic, Gypsy, and Balkan tunes, and the style was an ornamental, improvisational baroque. Its most conspicuous feature, however, was the Jewish **krekhts** (groan), a sobbing, heart-tugging sound that probably reflected centuries of Jewish suffering. Another feature were the **dreydlekh** or trills emulating the coloratura of cantorial singing. But the music was secular, with no religious associations.

In the Jewish communities of the shtetls and ghettos, **klezmorim** belonged among the lower strata of society. They were wanderers, outsiders, a sort of Jewish gypsies. They were welcomed at **simkhes** (joyous occasions) because they made the occasion merry; but they were not otherwise admired or honored the way musicians and other performers are today. Consequently, many klezmorim formed their own guilds or maintained family circles in which the musical mantle was passed on from fathers to sons across the generations. Their relative isolation brought them in close contact with other ethnic groups, especially Ukrainians, Russians, Romanians, and Hungarians, and they adopted many musical modes, especially dances, from these groups. The most popular dances at the turn of the 19th century were Romanian, like the *Bulgar* and the *Doyne*, and these were the first to be transplanted to America.

The mass immigration of Jews from Eastern Europe between the 1880s and the 1920s brought to the United States millions seeking a better life in **di goldene medine** (the golden land). Among them were many klezmorim, who performed here the same function as they did in Europe: they played dance music at weddings, bar and bas mitzvahs, and other celebrations. Many of the tunes they played are still heard at traditional functions: dances like the **broygez tants** (literally, angry dance between a groom, his father, and his father-in-law) and the **flash tants** (literally, bottle dance, in which men dance while balancing bottles on their heads), and popular songs like *Az der Rebe Tantst* (When the Rebbe Dances) and *Rumenye Rumenye* (Romania Romania), whose nostalgic refrain (when sung) brought tears to many an immigrant's eyes: *Oy, Rumenye Rumenye / Geveyn amol a land a ziser a fayner!* (O Romania Romania, that was once a sweet and fine land!).

In the United States, a new and exciting venue opened up to klezmer with the introduction of the Yiddish theater on the American scene. (See "The Story of Yiddish Theater: From *Purimshpil* to *The Dybbuk*.") Abraham Goldfaden's musical plays provided jobs for Yiddish musicians, who often went on to develop careers in the theatrical world. In the 1910s and 1920s, when commercial recording firms tapped into the ethnic market with records of various kinds of ethnic music, a number of klezmorim recorded their dance music on 78 rpm phonograph records issued by such firms as RCA Victor and Columbia. For less talented or ambitious Yiddish musicians, there was work in vaudeville, in the functions of **landsmanshaftn** (societies of Jews from the same town or region in Europe), and in the Catskill bungalow colonies and resorts that came to be called the Borscht Belt. Though they were no longer a guild or united by hereditary bonds, klezmorim stuck together and even unionized, becoming part of the United Hebrew Trades Union.

Klezmorim, most of them members of the Faust family, Rohatyn, Ukraine, 1912. (YIVO Institute for Jewish Research)

Like most Jewish immigrants in the early 20th century, klezmer musicians were eager to become "Americanized." The Yiddish press glorified the American experience and encouraged its readers to learn English and adopt American cultural mores. Yiddish musicians, falling in step with the trend, began adding American popular music to their repertoire and adapting Yiddish music to American styles, especially jazz in its various forms. By the 1930s, as the Great Depression set in, ethnicity was on its way out and traditional klezmer music seemed to be destined for oblivion, along with other Yiddish cultural artifacts, most notably the Yiddish language itself.

In Eastern Europe, meanwhile, traditional klezmer prevailed until the Holocaust. This is substantiated in the many Yizkor memorial books written by Holocaust survivors about their shtetls, since the end of World War II. The following, for example, is an excerpt from a description of a typical wedding in prewar Kitaigorod, a shtetl in the province of Podolia, Ukraine, as recorded on the Jewish Genealogy Web site (www.jewishgen.org):

> The musicians played.... We had begun to dance quadrilles, the scissors dance, waltzes and Bulgar dances. The musicians were paid for each dance. The musicians left the wedding place and went to the groom's house to play for the family and then they returned to play at the groom's table.... Both mothers, of the bride and of the groom, were joyful, dancing ladies. They took each other by the hand, the other hand on each other's dress and they danced.... Then they removed the benches and the **badchan** (wedding entertainer) invited people to dance with the bride. He would call on each father and each would take a piece of cloth and the bride would take the other end while the musicians played lively dances.

## The Klezmer Revival

The Americanization process, the Depression, and finally World War II and the Holocaust brought about the decline and virtual disappearance of klezmer music in the United States—until the 1970s. At that time, a general interest in ethnicity and genealogy, in the "roots" of immigrant and racial groups, took hold of the American public, and young Jews began to reach back in time to recapture their past. Among them were a number of young musicians who, reexamining the large collections of 78 rpm recordings of traditional klezmer music of the

1910s and 1920s, discovered in klezmer a challenging new way of expressing their American Jewish identity.

The "Klezmer Revival," as it has come to be known, was started by second- and third-generation American Jews of East European descent who had grown up on a diet of pop, rock, country, jazz, and classical music, but who were now eager to blend into this mix the musical legacy of their ancestors. The challenge they faced was to develop an idiom that would speak to other members of their generation.

The most noteworthy aspect of the Revival was that the musicians performed in concerts rather than at weddings and other traditional functions. This alone set them apart from the original klezmorim, who had been working musicians, not performing artists. Another important difference was in the content of the performances: whereas the traditional klezmer played almost exclusively dance music, or music to be danced to, the Revivalists took on the role of performers and entertainers, including vocalists and even humorous monologues or repartee in their performances. Still, the reintroduction of klezmer on the musical scene was a novelty and it gained immediate popularity. Such early Revival groups as the Klezmorim, Kapelye, and The Klezmer Conservatory Band, drew their material not just from the 78 rpm records but from other Yiddish sources, including folk songs, theater musicals, and even liturgical or cantorial pieces. Their broad appeal attracted a wide Jewish audience, not only in the United States, but in Europe, Israel, and other countries. Kapelye, for example, attracted an audience of teenage and college fans of alternative rock and folk music with its fusion of traditional and contemporary music.

The Klezmer Revival, also called "Neo-Klez" and "New Klez," created music that was original and different from traditional klezmer, resembling jazz in the use of improvisation and interplay between soloists and instrumental chorus. The lilting, raucously joyous melodies—a vaudevillian medley of notes and rhythms—had a contagious, intoxicating effect on players and audience alike. It was not unusual for the audience to clap, sing, and dance along with the performers, who were often charismatic and cultivated a following much as rock groups have today. A host of new klezmer bands sprang forth between the 1970s and the 1990s, with names like Klezmania, Klezmaniacs, Klezmerica, KlezMishpoche, Klezmiracles, Kleztets, many of them originating in countries like Germany, the Netherlands, Australia,

Canada, Great Britain, and even China. Contemporary klezmer music had become an international phenomenon.

A new direction in the Revival movement came about in the late 1980s, when several klezmer musicians began to experiment with novel and more sophisticated musical modes. They envisioned a new form of klezmer for the concert stage, one that combined the artistry of classical music with the freedom of jazz and the soul and passion of traditional East European music. The group at the forefront of these so-called experimentalists was Brave Old World, organized in 1989 by four pioneers of the contemporary klezmer scene. The group not only fulfilled its mission of bringing a "classical," elegant klezmer to the concert stage, but updated the klezmer tradition by creating new Yiddish compositions dealing with contemporary issues, such as "Chernobyl," about the nuclear disaster that occurred there, and "Berlin 1990," about the fall of the Berlin Wall. Brave New World was the first klezmer supergroup, internationally acclaimed for bringing art music to the klezmer scene.

Another enormously successful experimentalist group, The Klezmatics, fused traditional klezmer with jazz, rock, funk, reggae, hip-hop, and World Beat music to create what has been called "Jewish roots music for the 21st century." A prominent figure connected with the Klezmer Revival has been the world-renowned violinist Itzhak Perlman, whose concert tours in the 1990s, titled "In the Fiddler's House" and "Live in the Fiddler's House" and recorded on CDs, included performances by Brave New World, The Klezmatics, The Klezmer Conservatory Band, and the Andy Statman Klezmer Orchestra, which introduced Hasidic themes into a mix of traditional klezmer and improvisational jazz.

One of the strikingly new aspects of the Klezmer Revival is that for the first time in the history of klezmer, Jewish women became an integral part of the movement. There had been no women musicians in traditional East European klezmer bands. In America, in the early decades of the 20th century, as women began to appear in the Yiddish theater and movies, women musicians figured in a few klezmer bands. The Klezmer Revival changed that, and a number of women not only joined male bands (Kapelye, Klezmatics), but became band leaders of predominantly male bands like the Wholesale Klezmer Band (Massachusetts), the Maxwell Street Klezmer Band (Chicago), and Metropolitan Klezmer (New York).

In the late 1990s, all-women bands broke into the klezmer field with considerable success. Among the best-known ones were KlezMs, Mikveh, and Pharoah's Daughter. KlezMs combined traditional Jewish folk music with Middle Eastern rhythms spiced with jazz. Mikveh, a quintet of highly accomplished musicians and singers, attracted a huge female Jewish and non-Jewish audience and earned the title of "first women's supergroup of New Klez." Pharoah's Daughter played a mix of Hasidic, Middle Eastern, and folk-rock music, and was noted for its seamless blending of secular musical styles with traditional Jewish liturgy.

## Yiddish Radio in America

The last large immigration of Eastern European Jews who came to America in the 1920s quickly embraced the relatively new medium of radio. From the mid-1920s to the 1950s, Yiddish radio shows flourished in America, with over one hundred stations around the country serving over two million Yiddish speakers.

Programming was varied and included radio dramas (such as Nahum Stutchkoff's "Round the Family Table"), news, editorials, advice, game shows, commercials, and even man-in-the-street interviews. A well-known New York radio station was WEVD, created in 1927 by the Socialist Party. It was taken over by the *Jewish Daily Forward*, which introduced the "Forward Hour," a very popular variety program. Another program, "Reunion," brought together families separated by the Holocaust. Music programs were also very popular and provided **klezmer** and other musicians with a broadcast venue. Over 5,000 records were produced during this period.

Many of the fragile recording disks from this period were collected and archived by author and klezmer musician Henry Sapoznik. They offered an aural journey into the life of immigrants struggling in America and became the basis for the Yiddish Radio Project which aired on National Public Radio's "All Things Considered" in the Spring 2002.

Source: National Public Radio,
www.npr.org/programs/atc/yiddish/index.html

# Beyond Klezmer

Klezmer music started off as the most secular of all forms of Jewish music, since its players had no association with traditional Jewish music, which was liturgical, and borrowed liberally from the music of Slavic (Polish, Ukrainian), Balkan (Bulgarian, Romanian, Greek), Gypsy, and other ethnic groups. It was thus genetically programmed to blend in smoothly with almost any other kind of music, be it American jazz or rock, Spanish flamenco, or Middle Eastern oriental. Nevertheless, from its beginnings to the present, klezmer has kept its identity as *Yiddish* music, since its roots belong to the Yiddish-speaking shtetl culture of Eastern Europe. Its parallel to the Yiddish language is inescapable. Just as Yiddish is a classic example of a fusion language, absorbing and assimilating Romance, Hebrew, Aramaic, Slavic, and other elements within its Germanic core, so klezmer can be called a "fusion music," one that can and does reach out to all kinds of music and embraces it as its own.

Klezmer is, of course, Jewish music, since most of its practitioners are Jews, just as most Yiddish speakers are Jews. But its appeal, as the appeal of Yiddish, crosses many boundaries and has no links to a particular territory. "You don't have to be Jewish to love Yiddish," as the saying goes, and the same has been said of klezmer. Within the Jewish world, klezmer is most closely associated with the secular Yiddishist movement, which is devoted to the maintenance and perpetuation of Yiddish culture, the culture in which klezmer is firmly rooted. Yet there are critics who argue that to limit klezmer to Yiddishism is to cut off its feet, to curb its natural development. There are, after all, elements in the Klezmer Revival that have strong Jewish religious roots, such as Hasidism, Kabbalism, Zionism, and Jewish liturgy.

However one defines present-day klezmer, it is the general consensus that klezmer, like jazz, is not one thing but many things. Modern jazz is many-faceted and hard to classify, and so is klezmer. Both are open-ended. And if that is so, klezmer in the future may expand its horizons and transcend its Yiddishist connection. In a 1998 interview on radio station WNET, the writer and authority on klezmer, Henry Sapoznik, put it this way:

> The term [Klezmer] has become so amorphous that you now have stratification in Klezmer. You can get people together who say, "Oh,

I play Klezmer," and someone else says they play Klezmer, but they don't share a common repertoire; they don't share a common ability to produce the sound, ornament, phrasing, or rhythmic structure. But it's all Jewish, Jewish as opposed to Yiddish, as Jewish really refers to a much broader worldview.... "Yiddish" is a subheading. Yiddish talks about a specific civilization, Eastern European, with its own language, its own literature, and its own particular history. "Jewish" is a more flexible term. You can use it as a way to express an inclusive attitude that allows different ways to identify yourself.

Source: www.klezmershack.com

## Klezmography

### Video

Henry Sapoznik, *Klezmer—Fiddler on the Hoof*, featuring Kapelye, Klezmatics, Klezcamp Festival, 1990 (Rhythm of the World series).

### Recordings

These are listings of some classic recordings. There are many more recent ones listed on Klezmershack.com

Kapelye, *Levine and his Flying Machine*, Shanachie 21006, 1985.

Klezmer Conservatory Band, *Yiddishe Renaissance*, Vanguard VSD 79450, 1984.

*Klezmer Music: Early Yiddish Instrumental Music—The First Recordings*, 1910–1927 (editor, Martin Schwartz), Folklyric 9034, 1982.

*Klezmer Music*, 1910–1942, Recordings from the YIVO Archives (editor, Henry Sapoznik), Folkways FSS 34021, 1981.

Klezmorim, *Notes from Underground*, Flying Fish FF 322, 1984.

### Books

Henry Sapoznik, *Klezmer! Jewish Music From Old World to Our World*, Schirmer Books, New York: 2000.

Seth Rogovoy, *The Essential Klezmer: A Music Lover's Guide to Jewish Roots and Soul Music, from the Old World to the Jazz Age to the Downtown Avant Garde*, Algonquin Books of Chapel Hill/Workman Publishing, New York: 2000.

## Yiddish-Theme Painters: Chagall and Soutine

Biblical law forbade representative images, and it wasn't until the 20th century that Jews joined the ranks of important artists, becoming some of its great figures: Marc Chagall, Chaim Soutine, Amadeo Modigliani, Alfred Steiglitz, Jacques Lipchitz, Leon Baskt, Tristan Tzara, Chaim Gross, Mark Rothko, Man Ray, Ben Shahn, Arthur Szyk, Diane Arbus, Frank Gehry, Frida Khalo, Jim Dine, Larry Rivers, Lee Krasner, Judy Chicago, and Roy Lichtenstein. Though some came from the poor villages of Eastern Europe, only a few achieved world renown drawing on **shtetl** life themes.

The most famous was **Marc Chagall** (1887–1985), whose lyrical work combined folklore and fantasy to create a unique vision of

Painting by Marc Chagall (1887–1985),
"The Violinist, 1911–1914."
(© 2002 Artists Rights Society [ARS],
New York/ADAGP, Paris.
© Copyright Giraudon/Art Resource,
New York)

the world. He was born in Vitebsk, Russia, into a poor family named Segal. His mother recognized his drawing talent and Chagall studied art in St. Petersburg and later Paris. He returned to Russia in 1914 and participated in the post-revolution activities as an artist and director of the Moscow Jewish State Theater. Increasing pressure and opposition to his non-political art forced him to emigrate to Paris. Chagall became a French citizen and spent the rest of his life there. During World War II the Nazis considered him a "degenerate Jewish artist" and he took refuge in United States until after the war.

Though Chagall's vision draws on Russian expressionism and aspects of French cubism, he developed a unique style using brilliant, strong color. Chagall's work spoke to the individual's artistic expression and he resisted political or art movement pressures throughout his life. Central to Chagall's vision was his Jewish heritage, biblical themes, and shtetl life. Humor, fantasy, surreal exploits, and unconscious imagery created a world of fiddlers on thatched roofs, flying blue cows, hovering betrotheds kissing under marriage **chupahs**, and scenes from the Old Testament. Chagall's brightly colored canvases, lithographs, and stained glass are derived from childhood memories where Jewish proverbs mixed with Russian folktales and sometimes the humor of Yiddish jokes.

Chagall's output was extensive and included paintings (for example, "I and the Village," "The Praying Jew"); theater set and costume design (Mozart's "The Magic Flute"); print making and book illustration ("The Bible" and Gogol's "Dead Souls"); large murals (New York Metropolitan Opera at Lincoln Center); and stained glass commissions (Hadassah-Hebrew University, Jerusalem). Chagall tapped the core of his shtetl origins, to become one of the most important artists of the 20th century.

Another artist with roots in the shtetls of czarist Russia, **Chaim Soutine** (1893–1943) came from a very poor, large family from the village of Smilovichi (near Minsk), where his father was a tailor. Soutine studied art in Vilna, Lithuania, and like Chagall went to Paris to escape shtetl life. Unlike Chagall, Soutine's work was filled with a powerful and painful emotional quality using a vivid and clashing color palette. Even though he had the help of his friend and fellow artist Amadeo Modigliani, Soutine remained an outsider, though he had patrons. Soutine's imagery did not directly draw on the shtetl, but the suffering he endured there and later in life was expressed in portraits of poor and common people and numerous still lifes of animals butchered for the meal. Soutine's reputation continues to grow as a wider audience discovers the intense quality of his work.

## Yiddish Movies

### The Golden Age

Yiddish films were being produced in Poland long before the "talkies" were introduced in 1927 by *The Jazz Singer* (see "Modern Yiddish-Theme Movies" below). The 1910s saw the first film version of Jacob Gordin's *Mirele Efros* (see "The Story of Yiddish Theater: From *Purimshpil* to *The Dybbuk*") and several of his other plays. In the 1920s, films based on Yiddish folktales were especially popular, and included such classic silents as *Tkies-kaf* (The Vow; literally The Handshake), which was later reproduced in a talking version.

The absence of Yiddish speech in these early films limited their appeal. It was after the debut of talking pictures in the 1930s that Yiddish movies became popular and something of an industry. The following are some of the classics of this period, all with English subtitles.

***Mir Kumen On*** (Here We Come) (1935): Produced under the auspices of the Polish Jewish Labor Bund, this is an early documentary depicting the squalid life of Jews in Poland before World War II.

***Yidl Mitn Fidl*** (Yidl with His Fiddle, 1936): This has been one of the most popular and widely exhibited Yiddish movies. Starring Molly Picon, it is a nostalgic musical look at Jewish life in rural Poland. Picon plays a young girl who pretends to be a boy in order to join a **klezmer** band and in so doing, becomes involved in some comic and picaresque adventures.

***Tkies-kaf*** (The Vow, 1937): A tale strongly reminiscent of An-ski's play *The Dybbuk*, in which two yeshiva students who are close friends solemnly promise to each other that if one should have a son and the other a daughter, the two will be married. Once the years pass and the vow is forgotten, tragedy ensues.

***The Dybbuk*** (1937): Film version of An-ski's great play, directed by Michal Vashiasky.

***Mamele*** (Little Mother, 1938): Starring Molly Picon, the film is set in Picon's own Polish hometown, Lodz. It is a melodrama centering on the optimistic heroine's tireless efforts to keep her family together after her mother's death.

***Mirele Efros*** (1939): The talking film version of Jacob Gordin's play about a wealthy and pious matriarch and her King Lear-ish problems with her children. Produced and directed by Joseph Berne.

Superstar of Yiddish stage and screen, Molly Picon (left) (1898–1992), in the Yiddish film *Jolly Orphan*, 1929. She also starred in the famous 1971 English-language film version of *Fiddler on the Roof*. (American Jewish Historical Society, Waltham, Massachusetts, and New York, New York.)

***A Brivele der Mamen*** (A Letter to Mother, 1939): A moving story of a family torn apart by poverty and separation is set in two worlds, Ukraine and America, and is one of the last Yiddish films made before the Nazi invasion of Poland.

***Der Vilner Shtot Khazn*** (The Vilna Town Cantor, 1939): A sentimental story of a cantor who, having decided to leave his town to become a big-city opera singer, is burdened by his conscience and returns home on Yom Kippur to beg for atonement. The film's main character was played by the famous cantor Moyshe Oysher (1907–1958).

## Modern Yiddish-Theme Movies

Apart from the golden age of Yiddish-language movies of the 1920s and 1930s, a number of contemporary American and foreign films have delighted audiences with Yiddish themes. Many deal with **shtetl** life, traditional versus modern values, the Holocaust, Hasidism, and the conflict with and transition into American culture. It's impossible to list all of these titles, but here are a few favorites, including two oldies from the 1920s and 1930s, and two documentaries.

***The Chosen*** (1981): A story of the friendship and conflicts of two Jewish teenage boys in the 1940s. One is a Hasidic Jew, the other is from a modern Zionist family. Rod Steiger gives a great performance as a Hasidic **rebbe**, who is the father of one of the boys. Based on the novel by Chaim Potok.

***Crossing Delancey*** (1988): Taking place in the Lower East Side of Manhattan, this charming film deals with clashing values that a young Jewish woman faces as she approaches marriage.

***Fiddler on the Roof*** (1971): Based on the Tevye the Milkman stories of Sholom Aleichem, this film embodies shtetl life in 19th-century Russia. It's a classic musical whose songs reinforce the conflicts of tradition facing the modern world.

***Heart of New York*** (1932): Even though much of Hollywood was run by Jews in its early years, not many films produced then focused on Jewish themes. This one deals with a poor Lower East Side family and its struggles to stay afloat.

***Hester Street*** (1975): The story of a Jewish woman who comes to America to join her husband. He's already adapted, she wants to hold on to her values. Lots of spoken Yiddish and real footage interspersed with the story.

***The Jazz Singer*** (1927): The first talking motion picture. Al Jolson stars as the son of a rabbi who wants to be a jazz singer and must deal with all the conflicts. There were remakes—in 1953 with Danny Thomas, and in 1980 with Neil Diamond.

***The Pawnbroker*** (1965): A painful film about a Holocaust survivor's bitter and agonizing life in America. Rod Steiger gives a brilliant performance as a pawnbroker with a shop in Spanish Harlem.

***The Shop on Main Street*** (Obchad Na Korze) (1965): A Czech film dealing with the relationship between an old Jewish woman and the non-Jew who takes over her shop as her Aryan Controller. The film explores the Holocaust, its victims, and its agents. Starring Ida Kaminska.

***Yentl*** (1983): A musical about a young Jewish shtetl woman who decides to study the Talmud, which was forbidden for women. Barbra Streisand disguises herself as a boy with all the attendant comical problems. Based on a story by Isaac Bashevis Singer.

***

***Hollywoodism: Jews, Movies, and the American Dream*** (1998): A documentary on the Jewish immigrants from Eastern Europe who created Hollywood and became moguls. An important look at film history and Jewish assimilation.

***A Life Apart: Hasidim in America*** (1997): A documentary on contemporary American Hasidism seen through many points of view. Narrated by Leonard Nimoy and Sarah Jessica Parker.

For a more comprehensive listing of Yiddish-theme films and videos go to www.jewishfilm.com.

# Reference Section

## Yiddish Basics

**1. The alphabet.** Yiddish is written in the Hebrew alphabet, which consists of the following 22 letters:

*reading from right to left*

א ב ג ד ה ו ז ח ט י כ ל מ נ ס ע פ צ ק ר ש ת

א (alef)
ב (beys)
ג (giml)
ד (daled)
ה (hey)
ו (vov)
ז (zayen)
ח (khes)

ט (tes)
י (yud)
כ (khof)
ל (lamed)
מ (mem)
נ (nun)
ס (samekh)

ע (ayen)
פ (pey)
צ (tsadek)
ק (kuf)
ר (reysh)
ש (shin)
ת (sof)

Yiddish has combined some of these letters, and added some diacritics, to better represent the speech sounds of the language. Some of these letters are:

אַ (=a) אָ (=o) בֿ (=v) פֿ (=f) וי (=oy) טש (=tsh)

Yiddish is read from right to left (as is Hebrew). In words of more than one syllable, the accent usually falls on the next-to-the-last syllable, as in <ah-ˈlee-yeh>, <pahs-ˈkood-neh>.

**2. Grammar.** The following is a greatly simplified description of some of the basic rules of Yiddish grammar. For serious study, we recommend Uriel Weinreich's classic text, *College Yiddish*, published by the YIVO Institute for Jewish Research.

**Articles.** The Yiddish indefinite article, *a, an*, is used the same way as the English article *a, an*. But unlike in English, the Yiddish definite article is distinguished by gender in the singular: **der yingl** (the boy, masculine); **di mame** (the mother, feminine); **dos kind** (the child, neuter). The plural has only one definite article, *di:* **di kinder** (the children).

**Adjectives.** Gender is important also in forming adjectives. When modifying a masculine noun, the adjective ending is *–er* (masculine): **a guter fraynd** (a good friend); with a feminine noun, the ending is *–e:* **a gute neshome** (a good soul); with a neuter noun, the adjective ending is also *–e* when it is preceded by a definite article; and regardless of gender, the plural ending of an adjective is also *–e:* **di sheyne hayzer** (the beautiful houses).

**Nouns.** Yiddish nouns take chiefly the following plural endings:

*-n, -en,* as in **shuln** (schools), **nodlen** (needles)

*-er,* as in **kinder** (children), **hayzer** (houses)

*-s, -es,* as in **fishers** (fishermen), **zaydes** (grandfathers)

*-ekh,* as in **shtetlekh** (towns)

*-im,* as in **khaveyrim** (friends)

**Verbs.** The infinitive of Yiddish verbs has the ending *–n* or *–en,* as in **esn** (to eat), **zingen** (to sing). The past participle of Yiddish verbs is formed by adding the prefix *ge-* and the ending *–(e)n* or *–t* to the base of the verb. For example, the past participle of **kumen** (to come), is **gekumen**, and of **nitsn** (to use), is **genitst**. The past tense of verbs is formed by adding the past participle to the auxiliary verbs **hobn** (to have) or **zayn** (to be)—for example, **ikh hob gezen** (I saw, I have seen); **zey zaynen** (or **zenen**) **gekumen** (they came, they have come).

# Yiddish vs. Hebrew

Contrary to what people might think, Yiddish and Hebrew are very different languages. The reason why the two are often linked in people's minds is that Yiddish speakers have usually learned how to read Hebrew in childhood, since the Bible and Jewish prayers are written in classical Hebrew. But this form of Hebrew is very different from the modern Hebrew spoken and written in Israel, which few Yiddish speakers speak or understand. The fact is that linguistically Yiddish and Hebrew are as different from one another as Japanese is from Chinese.

The Japanese-Chinese example is actually a close parallel to Yiddish-Hebrew, for this reason: just as Japanese borrowed from Chinese its system of writing along with many Chinese words, so Yiddish borrowed its system of writing from Hebrew as well as many Hebrew words. And just as Japanese and Chinese are two totally different and unrelated languages, so too are Yiddish and Hebrew.

The few similarities between Yiddish and Hebrew can be summed up as follows:

- Both Yiddish and Hebrew are spoken and written primarily by Jews, and are the most widely spoken Jewish languages in the world.
- The two languages share the same alphabet.
- Both languages are read from right to left.
- Neither language uses capital letters.
- Words shared by both languages (Yiddish having borrowed them from Hebrew) are spelled identically—though their Romanized transcriptions may differ slightly to account for differences in pronunciation. Examples of such words are Hebrew *shalom*, Yiddish **sholem**, both meaning peace; Hebrew *yom tov*, Yiddish **yontev** (holiday); Hebrew and Yiddish **emes** (true); **sheker** (falsehood). Yiddish has acquired hundreds of such common words from Hebrew.

The most important differences between Yiddish and Hebrew are these:

- Yiddish is a Germanic language, belonging to the Indo-European family of languages; while Hebrew is a Semitic language, belonging to the Afroasiatic family of languages.
- Yiddish is what linguists call a "fusion language," meaning that it has integrated within its Germanic structure elements from such diverse languages as Hebrew, Aramaic, Old Italian, Old French, Czech, Polish, Ukrainian, and Russian. By contrast, Hebrew consists almost entirely of pure Semitic stock.
- Yiddish is spoken chiefly by Jews of East European origin or descent. Hebrew is spoken chiefly by Israeli Jews or Jews of Middle Eastern origin or descent.
- In Yiddish, words of more than one syllable are generally stressed on the penultimate or next-to-the-last syllable. In Hebrew, words of more than one syllable are generally stressed on the last syllable. For example, Yiddish <′shoh-lem>, Hebrew <shah-′lohm>.

# The YIVO Transcription Scheme

In order to transcribe Yiddish words into Roman or Latin letters, a standard system of romanization, known commonly as the YIVO system (after the YIVO Institute for Jewish Research), was devised over fifty years ago. In this system, the Yiddish consonants generally correspond to the English ones, with the following exceptions:

*kh* (representing the sound of ח and כ) is pronounced as in English *loch*

*sh* (representing the sound of ש) is pronounced as in English *shy, tissue*

*tsh* (representing the sound of טש) is pronounced as in English *chain*

*ts* (representing the sound of צ) is pronounced as in English *sits, Ritz*

*zh* (representing the sound of זש) is pronounced as in English *treasure*

The sounds of the Yiddish vowels and diphthongs are pronounced as follows:

| Romanization | Pronounced As | Yiddish Examples |
|---|---|---|
| *a* | in English *car, balm* | **mame**, **latke** |
| *ay* | in *my, pie* | **dayge**, **nasheray** |
| *e* | in *bed, set* | **ganef**, **gelt** |
| *ey* | in *hey, day* | **meydl**, **peyes** |
| *i* | in *hit, bin* | **kishke**, **bris** |
| *o* | in *ford, ball* | **bobe**, **lokshn** |
| *oy* | in *boy, toil* | **goylem**, **oy** |
| *u* | in *full, rule* | **frum**, **pupik** |

Like Hebrew, Yiddish does not have capital letters. But when Yiddish is romanized, the convention is to capitalize proper names and the first word in a sentence or a title.

The following is a simplified version of the transcription (romanization) scheme of the YIVO system. The first column lists the Yiddish letters and letter-combinations; the second column gives the names of the letters and letter-combinations; the third column provides the approximate English sound equivalents of the Yiddish letters; and the fourth column gives an example of the sound in a transcribed (romanized) Yiddish word.

Note also that the five letters צ, פ, נ, מ, כ have variant forms when they appear at the end of a word. The word-final letters are respectively ץ, ף, ן, ם, ך.

| Letter | Name | Sound | Example |
|---|---|---|---|
| א | shtumer alef | (silent alef) | |
| אַ (=a) | pasekh alef | a, as in *car, balm* | **mame** (mother) |
| אָ (=o) | komets alef | o, as in *ford, ball* | **bobe** (grandmother) |
| ב (=b) | beys | b, as in *bag* | **boym** (tree) |
| בֿ (=v) | veys | v, as in *van* | **rov** (rabbi) |
| ג (=g) | giml | g, as in *gum* | **regn** (rain) |
| ד (=d) | daled | d, as in *dog* | **dire** (apartment) |
| ה (=h) | hey | h, as in *hat* | **hunt** (dog) |
| ו (=u) | vov | u, as in *put, rule* | **gut** (good), **ru** (rest) |
| וו (=v) | tsvey vovn (2 vovs) | v, as in *oven* | **vort** (word) |
| וי (=oy) | vov-yud | oy, as in *toy* | **oylem** (audience) |
| ז (=z) | zayen | z, as in *maze* | **azoy** (thus, so) |
| זש (=zh) | zayen-shin | as the s in *measure* | **rozhinke** (raisin) |
| ח (=kh) | khes | as the ch in *loch* | **khazn** (cantor) |
| ט (=t) | tes | t, as in *tea* | **tate** (father) |
| טש (=tsh) | tes-shin | as the ch in *rich* | **tshepn** (bother) |
| י (=i) | yud | i, as in *hit, feet* | **nit** (not), **mid** (tired) |
| י (=y) | yud | y, as in *yes* | **yor** (year) |
| יי (=ey) | tsvey yudn (2 yuds) | ey, as in *hey* | **meydl** (girl) |
| ײַ (=ay) | pasekh tsvey yudn | as the *ie* in *pie* | **dayge** (worry) |
| ך, כ (=kh) | khof | as the ch in *loch* | **brokhe** (blessing) |
| כּ (=k) | kof | k, as in *kin* | **koved** (honor) |
| ל (=l) | lamed | l, as in *love* | **lets** (buffoon) |
| ם, מ (=m) | mem | m, as in *map* | **mame** (mother) |
| ן, נ (=n) | nun | n, as in *nine* | **nomen** (name) |
| ס (=s) | samekh | s, as in *sun* | **simen** (sign) |

| Letter | Name | Sound | Example |
|---|---|---|---|
| ע (=e) | ayen | e, as in *men* | **esn** (eat) |
| פּ (=p) | pey | p, as in *pan* | **epes** (something) |
| ף, פֿ (=f) | fey | f, as in *fun* | **efsher** (maybe) |
| ץ, צ (=ts) | tsadek | ts, as in *hats* | **tsatske** (trinket, toy) |
| ק (=k) | kuf | k, as in *kin* | **kop** (head) |
| ר (=r) | reysh | r, as in *error* | **rirn** (touch, move) |
| ש (=sh) | shin | sh, as in *rush* | **tish** (table) |
| שׂ (=s) | sin | s, as in *sun* | **simkhe** (joy, party) |
| תּ (=t) | tof | t, as in *tea* | **talmed** (student) |
| ת (=s) | sof | s, as in *sun* | **takhles** (result) |

# Virtual Yiddishdom on the Web

Inclusion in the following listings does not indicate support of any organization by the authors or publisher, nor endorsement of the accuracy of information provided. Listings are not represented as being complete. Listing and Web site information are as described by organization and/or search engines. Check Internet search engines for additional listings and information. And remember, Web site addresses (URLs) tend to change over time.

## *Institutes, Archives, Organizations*

### American Jewish Historical Society (AJHS)

www.ajhs.org/

Founded in 1892 as a membership organization, research library, archives, and museum, AJHS is the oldest ethnic historical organization in the United States.

### Center for Jewish History

www.cjh.org/

A repository for the cultural and historical legacy of the Jewish people that includes five major institutions of Jewish scholarship, history, and art: American Jewish Historical Society, American Sephardic Federation, Leo Baeck Institute, Yeshiva University Museum, and the YIVO Institute for Jewish Research.

**The National Yiddish Book Center**

www.yiddishbookcenter.org/

A non-profit organization working to rescue Yiddish and other modern Jewish books and celebrate the culture they contain. (See "The National Yiddish Book Center.")

**YIVO Institute for Jewish Research**

www.yivoinstitute.org/

The pre-eminent archive of East European photographs and Yiddish language books. (See "YIVO Institute for Jewish Research.")

**The Workmen's Circle (Arbeter Ring)**

www.circle.org/

Active since 1900 supporting Yiddish life and culture, including Jewish Book Center, summer camp, and geriatric centers.

## *General*

**All Things Yiddish**

jewish.virtualave.net/Yiddish

Yiddish Web page of a gateway to hundreds of Internet resources on Judaism, with links to Yiddish language, literature, and resources.

**Der Bay**

www.derbay.org/

California-based "Golden Gate" to the worldwide Yiddish community. Fosters the preservation and continued propagation of the Yiddish language, culture, music, theater, literature, and poetry via the International Association of Yiddish Clubs.

**Hot Yiddish Sites**

www.jr.co.il/hotsites/j-yidish.htm

Personal site of Jacob Richman, with links to his hot picks of Yiddish sites.

**Jewish Web site**

www.zipple.com/

All things Jewish Web site (dubbed a "Jewish Yahoo") with a Yiddish section.

**Lower East Side Association**

www.lowereastsideny.com/

This pluralistic and ecumenical site is testimony to the changes that have occurred on New York's Lower East Side in recent years. "Visitor's Services" gives information on weekly free walking tours during spring and summer, starting in front of Katz's Delicatessen.

**Maven**

www.maven.co.il/

Israeli-based portal to the Jewish world, with news, singles, shopping—and Yiddish links (reached via the alphabetical index to All Subjects).

**Virtual Shtetl**

www.ibiblio.org/yiddish/

Yiddish language and culture, featuring a bookstore and numerous international links, including to synagogues worldwide.

**Yiddish Homepage**

www.bergen.org/AAST/Projects/Yiddish/English/

Yiddish language and culture project, hosted by the Bergen County (New Jersey) Technical Schools.

**Yiddish Voice**

www.yv.org/

A Yiddish-language radio show serving Boston.

## *Yiddish Publications Online*

***Der Bavebter Yid***

www.cs.engr.uky.edu/~raphael/bavebter/index.html

Electronic magazine in Yiddish, hosted by the University of Kentucky College of Engineering.

***Forverts* (The Yiddish Forward)**

yiddish.forward.com/

Official Web site of the ***Forverts*** (The Yiddish Forward). It contains articles, news, and editorials that appear in the weekly newspaper. (See "*Jewish Daily Forward*: The Voice of Yiddish in America.") The English version is found at www.forward.com.

## Language

### About.com on Yiddish

hebrew.about.com/homework/hebrew/cs/yiddish/
Consult the Yiddish experts on the popular site About.com.

### The History of the Yiddish Atlas Project at Columbia University

www.columbia.edu/cu/cria/Current-projects/Yiddish/yiddish.html
An effort to bring Yiddish information and digitized samples to the Web based on data collected by the Language and Culture Atlas of Ashkenazic Jewry.

### Mendele

shakti.trincoll.edu/~mendele/
Mendele is a moderated mailing list dedicated to the lively exchange of views, information, news, and just about anything else related to the Yiddish language and Yiddish literature. It is open to all and subscriptions are free. Links to over thirty five interesting Yiddish sites.

### Yiddish Alphabet List

ccat.sas.upenn.edu/german/yiddish/project/letters/
Hosted by the University of Pennsylvania's Department of Germanic Languages and Literatures.

### Free English-Yiddish On-Line Dictionary

www.ectaco.com/online/diction.php3?lang=15
Hosted by company specializing in handheld electronic dictionaries and language software.

### Yiddish Language Links

languages-on-the-web.com/links/link-yiddish.htm
Not-for-profit site aggregating links on all major languages of the world.

### Yiddish Typewriter

www.cs.uky.edu/~raphael/yiddish/makeyiddish.html
Interconverts among various Yiddish representations, such as YIVO transcriptions and Hebrew. Hosted by University of Kentucky, Computer Science Department.

## *History*

### International Institute of Social History (IISH), Yiddish Collection.

www.iisg.nl/collections/yiddish/

The IISH has a unique collection of Yiddish material consisting of books, brochures, periodicals, and pamphlets of the early Jewish socialist and anarchist movement in Eastern and Western Europe.

### Tamiment Library, New York University

www.nyu.edu/library/bobst/research/tam/yiddish/Index/

Guide to Yiddish-speaking labor and radical movements.

### Yiddish Anarchist Bibliography (The Kate Sharpley Library)

dwardmac.pitzer.edu/Anarchist_Archives/yiddishbiblio.html

Extensive list of hundreds of books and periodicals.

### Yiddish Research Network

www.igc.apc.org/ddickerson/yiddish-research-network.html

Seeks the participation of researchers from all fields who are interested in topics dealing with Yiddish language, linguistics, literature, and culture. Joint project of American and German universities.

## *Studying Yiddish*

### Oxford Institute for Yiddish Studies (OIYS)

www.ljcc.org.uk/

London Jewish Cultural Center, incorporating the OIYS. Annual residential summer courses, and a one-year Yiddish diploma course for graduates.

### Yiddish Studies at Columbia University

www.columbia.edu/cu/cijs/yidd/

Includes undergraduate and graduate studies, plus the Yiddish Summer Program.

## *Buying Books, Music, Videos*

### America's Jewish Bookstore

www.judaism.com/

Books, music, and videos on Yiddish subjects.

**Worldlanguage.com**

www.worldlanguage.com/Languages/Yiddish.htm
Yiddish books, music, videos, software.

**The Yiddish Language Study Bookstore**

www.smokefreekids.com/yiddish.htm
Yiddish-language books in association with Amazon.com.

**The Yiddish Voice Store**

store.yv.org/
Books, music, and videos on Yiddish subjects.

## *Music and the Performing Arts*

**Browse Yiddish Music**

www.haruth.com/YiddishMusic.html
Virginia-based Web site with eclectic mix of American, Jewish, and Yiddish resources.

**The Folksbiene Yiddish Theater, New York City**

www.folksbiene.org/
Preserving and revitalizing Yiddish theater for current and future generations.

**Klezmer Shack**

www.klezmershack.com/
Eclectic, entertaining site dedicated to Klezmer music.

**Yiddish Songs**

yiddish.danieln.com/
Recorded sound clips on this eclectic Israeli-based site on "My Grandmother's Yiddish."

**Yiddish Song Database**

www.cs.uky.edu/raphael-cgi-bin/yidsong.cgi
Catalogues of the Robert and Molly Freedman Archive of Jewish Music at the University of Pennsylvania Library, containing 1720 recordings, with 24,886 selections.

**Zemerl: Jewish and Yiddish Song Database**

www.princeton.edu/zemerl/
Interactive database, hosted by Princeton University, of songs in Yiddish, Hebrew, and Judeo-Spanish.

## Yiddish Movies

**Internet Movie Database**

us.imdb.com/Sections/Languages/Yiddish/
Guide to Yiddish-language movies, currently with descriptions of more than 100 titles, including Yiddish dialogue. (An Amazon.com company.)

**Jewish Film Archive**

www.jewishfilm.com
Extensive links to various Jewish/Yiddish film resources. AOL keyword=Jewish.

**Yiddish Films in Distribution**

www.brandeis.edu/jewishfilm/yiddish.html
The Ruttenberg and Everett Yiddish Film Library of The National Center for Jewish Film at Brandeis University. Yiddish films available for purchase.

## Yiddish Literature

**Columbia University Jewish Studies**

www.columbia.edu/cu/lweb/indiv/mideast/cuvlj/yiddish_lit.html
Links to bibliographies and essays on the Yiddish greats.

**The National Yiddish Book Center**

www.yiddishbookcenter.org/
See above under "Institutes, Archives, and Organizations"

**Sholom Aleichem Network**

www.sholom-aleichem.org/
Not-for-profit membership organization for fans of this famous author.

**Sholom Aleichem Network on the Web**

tevye.net/links/

Links to everything related to the author, including a "ushop" to buy translated editions.

**Virtual Shtetl**

www.ibiblio.org/yiddish/shtetl.html

Includes library of resource and De Moykher Sforim Bookstore.

## *Food*

**The Food Maven**

www.thefoodmaven.com/

The Web site of Arthur Schwartz, host of a nationally syndicated talk radio program based in New York City. Provides recipes.

**Jewish Community Online**

www.jewish.com/search/Food/Recipes/more2.shtml

Links to recipe sources.

**Kosher FAQs**

www.cyber-kitchen.com/rfcj/kosherfaq.htm

Answers to common questions about Kosher food.

**Zipple.com**

www.zipple.com/food/recipes.shtml

Jewish recipes section on the site dubbed "the Jewish Yahoo."

# Bibliography

The following are some of the key titles that underpin the research for this book. Many other delightful and edifying books are also cited throughout the text, and are recommended for additional research into the world of Yiddish.

American Jewish Historical Society, *American Jewish Desk Reference*, New York: Random House, 1999.

*American Yiddish Poetry: A Bilingual Anthology* (edited by Benjamin and Barbara Harshav. Translations by B. and B. Harshav, Kathryn Hellerstein, and Anita Norich), Berkeley: University of California Press, 1986.

Ayalti, Hanan, J., *Yiddish Proverbs*, New York: Schocken Books, 1964.

Blech, Benjamin, *The Complete Idiot's Guide to Learning Yiddish*, Indianapolis: Alpha Books, 2000.

Comay, Joan, *The Diaspora Story*, New York: Random House, 1981.

*Encyclopædia Judaica*, 16 volumes, Jerusalem, Israel: Keter Publishing House, 1971.

Harkavy, Alexander, *Yiddish-English-Hebrew Dictionary* [Yidish-english-hebreisher verterbukh], New York: Schocken Books and YIVO Institute for Jewish Research, 1988 (reprint of 1928 edition).

Hoobler, Dorothy, and Thomas Hoobler, *The Jewish American Family Album*, New York: Oxford University Press, 1995.

Howe, Irving, *World of Our Fathers*, New York: Harcourt, Brace, Jovanovich, 1976. Schocken Books edition, 1989.

Howe, Irving, and Eliezer Greenberg, editors, *A Treasury of Yiddish Stories*, New York: Schocken Books, 1973. Penguin Books edition 1990.

*Jewish Language Review*, 7 volumes (edited by David L. Gold), Haifa, Israel: Association for the Study of Jewish Languages, University of Haifa, 1981–1987.

Joffe, Judah A., and Yudel Mark, *Great Dictionary of the Yiddish Language* [Groyser verterbukh fun der yidisher shprakh], 3 volumes, New York: Yiddish Dictionary Committee, Inc., 1961–1971.

Liptzin, Sol, *A History of Yiddish Literature*, Middle Village, New York: Jonathan David Publishers, 1985.

Liptzin, Sol, *The Maturing of Yiddish Literature*, Middle Village, New York: Jonathan David Publishers, 1970.

Liptzin, Sol, *The Flowering of Yiddish Literature*, New York: Thomas Yoseloff Publishers, 1963.

Nathan, Joan, *Jewish Cooking in America*, New York: Alfred A. Knopf, 1994.

*Never Say Die! A Thousand Years of Yiddish in Jewish Life and Letters* (edited by Joshua A. Fishman), The Hague: Mouton, 1981.

Peretz, I. L., *The I. L. Peretz Reader* (edited by Ruth R. Wisse), New York: Schocken Books, 1990.

*Penguin Book of Modern Yiddish Verse*, bilingual edition (edited by Irving Howe, Ruth R. Wisse, and Khone Shmeruk), New York: Viking Penguin, 1987.

Rosenbaum, Samuel, *A Yiddish Word Book for English-Speaking People*, New York: Van Nostrand Reinhold, 1978.

Rosten, Leo, *The New Joys of Yiddish*, New York: Crown Books, 2001.

Rosten, Leo, *Leo Rosten's Treasury of Jewish Quotations*, New York: Bantam Books, 1980.

Rosten, Leo, *The Joys of Yiddish*, New York: Pocket Books, 1968.

Sholom Aleichem, *Stories and Satires* (translated by Curt Leviant), New York: Thomas Yoseloff Publishers, 1959.

Silvain, Gérard, and Henri Minczeles, *Yiddishland*, Corte Madera, California: Gingko Press, 1999.

Singer, Isaac Bashevis, *An Isaac Bashevis Singer Reader*, New York: Farrar, Straus and Giroux, 1979.

Steinmetz, Sol, *Yiddish and English: The Story of Yiddish in America*, 2nd edition, Tuscaloosa: The University of Alabama Press, 2001.

Stutchkoff, Nahum, *The Thesaurus of the Yiddish Language* [Der oytser fun der yidisher shrakh], New York: YIVO Institute for Jewish Research, 1950.

Unterman, Alan, *The Wisdom of Jewish Mystics*, New York: New Directions, 1976.

Weinreich, Beatrice Silverman, *Yiddish Folktales* (translated by Leonard Wolf), New York: Pantheon Books and YIVO Institute for Jewish Research, 1988.

Weinreich, Max, *History of the Yiddish Language* (translated by Shlomo Noble), Chicago: The University of Chicago Press, 1980.

Weinreich, Uriel, *Modern English-Yiddish, Yiddish-English Dictionary*, New York: Schocken Books, 1977.

Weinreich, Uriel, *College Yiddish*, New York: YIVO Institute for Jewish Research, 1949 (5th edition, 1971).

Weiser, Chaim M., *Frumspeak: The First Dictionary of Yeshivish*, Northvale, New Jersey: Jason Aronson, 1995.

Weissler, Chava, *Voices of the Matriarchs: Listening to the Prayers of Early Modern Jewish Women*, Boston: Beacon Press, 1998.

*Yiddish Language and Culture: Then and Now* (edited by Leonard Jay Greenspoon), Omaha, Nebraska: Creighton University Press, 1998.

# Index

Page references set in **boldface** indicate a chapter, a sidebar, a section, or an extract devoted to the subject. Page numbers set in *italics* denote an illustration.